UNIVERSITY OF CALIFORNIA
PUBLICATIONS IN HISTORY

VOLUME LV

1958

EDITORS

JOHN GALBRAITH
ANDREW LOSSKY
THEODORE SALOUTOS
TRYGVE THOLFSEN

TIMAEUS OF TAUROMENIUM

BY

TRUESDELL S. BROWN

UNIVERSITY OF CALIFORNIA PRESS

BERKELEY AND LOS ANGELES

1958

University of California Publications in History

Editors (Los Angeles): John Galbraith, Andrew Lossky, Theodore Saloutos, Trygve Tholfsen

Volume 55

Submitted by editors November 23, 1956
Issued January 21, 1958
Price, $3.50

University of California Press
Berkeley and Los Angeles
California

◇

Cambridge University Press
London, England

IN MEMORY OF MY FATHER
CARLETON BROWN

PREFACE

THE THIRD CENTURY is the very heart of the Hellenistic period. When it began, the military supremacy of the Macedonians was still unchallenged, though the Battle of Ipsus (301 B.C.) had made it apparent that the unity of Alexander's empire would not be restored. A century later the picture changed greatly. Not only did Parthia emerge as an aggressive power threatening all Seleucid holdings in the east, but regionalism reasserted itself in Asia Minor with the arrival of the Gauls. In this vital area and on the islands off the coast, political allegiances continually shifted under the varied pressures of contending dynasties—Seleucid, Antigonid, Ptolemaic, and Attalid. In Greece itself the never-ending struggle of league, city-state, and monarchy was intensified by intervals of great economic distress and internal revolution, of which Sparta is merely the most conspicuous example. Only Egypt could still look forward to more than a century and a half of independence. Macedonia engaged in the war that was to reduce her within three years to the rank of a Roman client kingdom; only nine years after that Rome dictated peace to Antiochus III and became the arbiter for the whole eastern Mediterranean seaboard. The third century despite, or perhaps in part because of, the stirring of these political events was also a period of great intellectual activity. "Culture" was fashionable, and the rivalry between states aroused friendly competition attracting the ablest artists, poets, philosophers, and men of science. Historians also flourished, and the once rich historical literature from the third century now survives only in a pitifully inadequate residue of quotations, paraphrases, or bare references scattered through the works of later writers who still had access to the originals. However, this residue has been augmented somewhat in recent years from papyri and inscriptions, and its usefulness has been greatly enhanced by more than a century of careful study of the fragments by a host of scholars. How much has been accomplished in this direction can be appreciated readily by anyone who troubles to compare the mid-nineteenth-century edition of these fragments by Carolus Müller with the volumes that have already appeared in the new edition of Felix Jacoby. Such comparison also shows that the additional space allotted to individual historians in the current edition depends less on new material than on the expansion of the commentary. Since there is no reason to believe that the next century will add more to our meager store of fragments from the Hellenistic historians than the last has, we must come to grips with them by using the material we now possess. This effort is particularly needed for the third century because for the earlier period, from Alexander's death almost to the Battle of Ipsus (323–301 B.C.), we have the continuous narrative of Diodorus Siculus, summarizing Hieronymus of Cardia with reasonable accuracy; and in the second century what is left of Polybius inspires even more confidence.

The selection of Timaeus as the subject of the present study might be justified by pointing out that he is the most important third-century historian whose fragments survive in sufficient bulk to promise positive results. But it would be less than candid not to admit that my original plan, formulated some seven years ago, was much more ambitious, calling for the treatment of some six leading Hellenistic historians. This plan was abandoned, one author at a time, primarily because Timaeus proved more puzzling and also more interesting than anticipated. To indicate briefly a few notable things about him, he wrote the longest and what was for antiquity the definitive account of Sicilian history. Although a warm-hearted Sicilian patriot, he lived most of his life as an exile in Athens. He set new high standards of accuracy in chronology and in the use of documents, yet his judgment on individuals was apt to be exculpatory or vindictive. In an age of feverish political activity he remained a spectator, independent, bookish, and "impractical." Despite his antiquarian predilections he was a shrewd observer of contemporary events, perhaps the first Greek to sense the real importance of Rome. More than 100 years after his death, Timaeus' reputation was still so high that Polybius began his own account of events in the west where his Sicilian predecessor left off. Polybius also made one of the most detailed and worst-tempered criticisms of the man and his work ever made by one historian against another. These known facts raise interesting queries about Timaeus' personality and about his competence as a historian. The following suggested answers to some of these questions lie within the limits necessarily imposed by the state of our information.

ACKNOWLEDGMENTS

It is a pleasure to acknowledge my gratitude for having been allowed to spend most of 1950 in Athens on a Fulbright research grant, and also for having been fortunate enough later, in August of 1954, to be a year in England as a Guggenheim Fellow.

In Athens I was treated with great courtesy by everyone connected with the American School and was, under their auspices, able to visit the places I particularly wanted to see as well as to make use of the excellent library facilities of the School. In England my obligations are too great and too recent to be acknowledged properly here. I resided at Cambridge, where I was most kindly elected a Member of the Combination Room of Gonville and Caius College; at Oxford I was made to feel very much at home and permitted to read a paper on Timaeus; at the University of London, also, every kindness was shown me. I have avoided mentioning by name persons to whom I feel particularly indebted, because such a list would be out of all proportion to the size of this slender volume in which it would appear.

T.S.B.

CONTENTS

Chapter I

TIMAEUS' LIFE AND WRITINGS

WITH TIMAEUS we avoid the atmosphere of the Diadochi and their courts to breathe the freer air of the Greek city-state. No royal sponsor looked over Timaeus' shoulder while he wrote, nor were his books, when published, calculated to attract patronage of any kind. We may appropriately begin our discussion of his life where Timaeus himself would have begun, with the question of chronology. Unfortunately, there is only one date fixed in terms of that Olympic era adopted by Timaeus as the standard for historical reference. For that one date we are indebted to Polybius, who says (I, 5, 1 = Timaeus 566 T 6a):

We shall make our work begin when the Romans first crossed over from Italy, for this continues where Timaeus left off, and it falls in the 129th Olympiad [i.e., 264/3 B.C.].

From this we obtain a *terminus post quem* for his death of about 260. He can hardly be supposed to have concluded his history with a few last vigorous lines on first learning of the Roman invasion and to have expired immediately thereafter. Some time must be allowed for the significance of that event to impress itself sufficiently on his mind. It is not unlikely that the unexpected defeat of Pyrrhus in Italy may have attracted Timaeus' attention to Rome, and that much of his information about the Romans was obtained in the interval between Pyrrhus' departure from Italy and the outbreak of the First Punic War. One modern scholar, Richard Laqueur, who has made a detailed study of Timaeus, refuses to accept Polybius' statement at face value, on the ground that the First Punic War makes a good beginning but a bad ending for a history.[1] He seems to prefer the death of Pyrrhus (272 B.C.) as the terminal point.[2] To this it may be replied that Polybius was not the man to take lightly a discrepancy of eight years: Timaeus is known to have interested himself in Roman history; and to the historian of Sicily the arrival of Roman armies would probably seem more significant than the death of a thoroughly discredited ruler in a street fight in Argos. For Hieronymus, however, Pyrrhus' death marked an epoch, removing as it did the bitterest of the enemies of his patron, Antigonus Gonatas, and he may well have ended his own history at this point.[3] Polybius, however, who centers his history on Rome, chose to link his two introductory books with Timaeus' work, which then dominated the field of western

[1] For notes to chap. i, see pp. 109–117.

history. But when he had sketched in this background, he began his detailed narrative where Aratus of Sicyon left off.[4]

Leaving the solid ground of Olympiads, we find a statement in the Lucianic *Macrobioi* (*Macrob.* 22) to the effect that Timaeus lived ninety-six years, which, if accepted, gives us 356 B.C. as the earliest possible date for his birth. Timaeus, fond of synchronisms, would have enjoyed this particular one—to have been born in the same year as the great Macedonian, or perhaps at the very moment when the hated Philistus, historian and tyrant-lover, was torn by the mob in Syracuse![5] Poetic justice, perhaps, but can we trust Pseudo-Lucian? He is the same author who, on the doubtful authority of Agatharchides, vouches for Hieronymus' ripe old age of 104, despite wounds and fevers.[6] Furthermore, citing the authority of Demochares and Timaeus, he assures us that Agathocles lived for ninety-five years (*Macrob.* 10); yet Diodorus says that Timaeus, Callias, and Antander agree that he lived for only seventy-five years (XXI, 16, 5 = Tim. F 123a). We should have the courage to disregard Pseudo-Lucian's statements unless otherwise supported, rather than give him credit by the usual appeal to an error in the text. Failure to doubt him can have ludicrous results. Pietro Rizzo, for example, apparently bases his curious theory that Timaeus never returned from exile in Athens on Pseudo-Lucian alone when he says: "A sea voyage for an old man of ninety is no easy thing."[7]

But the best authenticated piece of information on Timaeus' whereabouts is the statement made by the historian himself as reported by Polybius (XII, 25h, 1 = Tim. F 34): "As Timaeus says in the 34th book, 'living for fifty years on end as a foreigner in Athens.' " To this we may add the statement of Diodorus that he was banished from Sicily by Agathocles (XXI, 17, 1 = Tim. T 4a), and Plutarch asserted that he wrote his history in Athens (*De exilio* 14 = Tim. T 4e).

Timaeus, then, belongs to that distinguished company of historians in exile,[8] but we would like very much to know when he spent those fifty years in Athens. Laqueur suggests four possibilities for the year in which he was driven out by Agathocles—317, 314, 312, and 310 respectively—each supported by a passage in Diodorus.[9] Müller, in the old *FHG*, preferred 310,[10] and Rizzo, who likes to fill in all the gaps, selects 314, at which time he says Timaeus was forty-five years old.[11] But are these the only possibilities? If they are, then Timaeus cannot have returned to Sicily before 267 B.C., perhaps not until 260, allowing for the fifty years in Athens.[12] Is it not strange that this fervent Sicilian patriot should have waited so long to return to his native land when the man who banished him had died in 289? But Diodorus, who is our only source here, may be translated as follows (XXI, 17):

> . . . banished from Sicily by Agathocles, so long as that ruler lived he was unable to resist him, but when he died, he damned him to eternity through his history.

Nothing in this passage proves that Timaeus was not in Athens at the time his banishment was proclaimed, or had not been living there for a number of years. The 317–310 period delimited by Laqueur, therefore, concerns only the date of official banishment and has little bearing on our understanding of Timaeus. We need to know when he left Sicily, not when his absence became compulsory.

Timaeus is usually referred to as a Tauromenian, but he is also called a Syracusan.[13] The Greek city of Tauromenium was a late foundation dating only from 358 B.C.[14] But the strategic importance of Mt. Taurus and its spurs must have been recognized by the early Greek colonists of Sicily, who perhaps named the mountain from the famous Cilician range.[15] Diodorus gives two versions of how Tauromenium was named, first by the Sicels, whom he mentions in connection with the military operations of Carthage and Dionysius in 396 (XIV, 59, 2), and then by Andromachus, the father of Timaeus, who founded the Greek city in 358.[16] Freeman believed that the discrepancy arose from Diodorus' use of different sources, Philistus for the Sicel foundation and Timaeus for the account involving his own father.[17] Pietro Rizzo has a most interesting and ingenious discussion of this matter, assembling the different bits of evidence, both literary and archaeological, and supporting his conclusions with an account of the topography based on his own visit to the area.[18] But our immediate concern is with the activities of Andromachus, described by Diodorus as follows (XVI, 7, 1 = Tim. T 3a):

> While these things were going on [i.e., Dion's expedition], Andromachus of Tauromenium, the father of the Timaeus who wrote the histories, and a man noted for his high-mindedness as well as his wealth, gathered together the survivors of Naxos, which had been completely destroyed by Dionysius. Colonizing the hill above Naxos, known as Tauris, and remaining there a long time he called the settlement *Tauromenium* from *remaining on Taurus*. [ἀπὸ τῆς ἐπὶ τοῦ Ταύρου μονῆς ὠνόμασε Ταυρομένιον.]

Rizzo suggests, plausibly enough, that the *remaining on Taurus* was reassertion of the prior rights of the Naxians, who had dominated the region for centuries.[19] Diodorus has probably muddled the sense by carelessly abridging his source, and that source was surely Timaeus.

The one passage where Diodorus refers to Timaeus as a Syracusan (XXI, 16, 5) contradicts all the reliable evidence we have, including

Diodorus elsewhere.[20] The discordant statement comes from the excerpts of the lost books of Diodorus and should not be given too much weight. Laqueur, however, is unwilling to dismiss it entirely. He suggests, on the analogy of Herodotus, that Timaeus inherited Syracusan citizenship from his father.[21] This is a rather poor analogy. When Herodotus was born, his adoptive city, Thurii, had not yet been founded, but Tauromenium was founded before Timaeus' birth and by his own father. True, Andromachus must have had a different citizenship at one time, but the fact that Diodorus once refers to Timaeus as a Syracusan should not be used as evidence for the father. Possibly Andromachus was one of the many Greeks forced into exile by his opposition to the policies of Dionysius I. He may, however, have come from any part of the Greek world, attracted by the possibilities for gain or adventure in troubled Sicily.[22] His name, Andromachus or "Fighting Man," was at least appropriate. Such a person, call him *condottiere* or patriot, might well have liked the idea of establishing a new city of which he would be the leader, and one whose location would commend itself to a military man. This is reminiscent of Xenophon and his hopes of founding a colony somewhere along the Black Sea coast after successfully escaping from Persia (*Anab.* V, 6, 15). Whatever his antecedents, Andromachus must have been very active in the interval between Dionysius' death in 367 and the founding of Tauromenium nine years later, when we are told he was well known "for his highmindedness as well as his wealth."[23] He seems to have played a part in bringing Timoleon to Sicily only four years afterward in 354;[24] certainly he received him with open arms in Tauromenium, giving him the *point d'appui* he so desperately needed.[25] Something about the meeting between these two "highminded" men piques our curiosity. Rizzo attempts to gratify it by an imaginative description. He pictures Timaeus, then eleven years of age, accompanied by his father, and suggests that Timoleon made an impression on the future Sicilian historian that lasted the rest of his life.[26] Andromachus and Timoleon are treated as two Garibaldis in a Risorgimento uncompromised by the worldliness of a Cavour. However, one dark shadow lies across this attractive picture. Diodorus tells us that Timoleon was responsible for the assassination of his own brother, who had seized control of Corinth, because Timoleon was "most antagonistic to one-man rule."[27] Marcellinus delineates the shadow when he says (*Vit. Thucyd.* 27 = Tim. T 13):

Timaeus of Tauromenium praised Timoleon immoderately, inasmuch as he had not overthrown the *one-man rule* of Andromachus, his father.

Evidently a bargain of some sort was struck between the two men, and that is our last detailed information about Andromachus.[28]

Another statement about Timaeus goes back to the problem of dating. He is said in the *Suda* article (*s.v.* Τίμαιος = Tim. T 1) to have studied under Philiscus of Miletus. Philiscus is difficult to fix chronologically. The former fluteplayer[29] was said to have been the pupil of Isocrates and the teacher of Neanthes of Cyzicus.[30] But it is known, through Athenaeus (XV, 57, p. 699 D), that a Neanthes of Cyzicus wrote a history of Attalus.[31] Since Attalus I died in 197 B.C., this puts quite a strain on Philiscus. Recognizing this, Müller tried to meet the difficulty by having Neanthes, as a very young man, study under Philiscus, as a very old man, in approximately 280 B.C.[32]—presumably because 280 is about the lower limit for a man whose teacher, Isocrates, had died in 338. But even this rather heroic measure is insufficient. Philiscus *might* have been teaching fifty-eight years after his master's death, but Neanthes cannot be supposed to have begun writing his history of Attalus *eighty-three* years after studying under Philiscus. Müller felt that he might have written on only the first part of Attalus' reign.[33] Although possible, this is unlikely; the time to write about Attalus was after his death when Pergamum was reaching the height of her power following the Second Macedonian War. The prevailing view is that an elder Neanthes studied under Philiscus and a younger Neanthes wrote about Attalus.[34] Something clearly had to be done, and the newly constructed Neanthes family offers as good a solution as any. There remains, of course, the possibility of an elder and a younger Philiscus. The chief interest in reference to Timaeus is that we need not date his arrival in Athens from the supposed period of Philiscus' activity; Philiscus is flexible enough to accommodate himself to any scheme that suits Timaeus.

Since Timaeus cannot be dated through Philiscus, is there any other evidence to help determine when he went to Athens? Precision is out of the question, but one or two indications lead me to believe Timaeus went to Athens much earlier than has usually been held. The last five books of his *History* were concerned with the career of Agathocles.[35] Bitter and sarcastic as he was when he wrote about Philiscus, Dionysius, and no doubt many others, Timaeus actually foams at the mouth when he comes to deal with Agathocles. He writes personally here, without taste, without wit, and apparently without judgment. Polybius notes this (VIII, 12, 12; XII, 15), and Diodorus is so disturbed that he writes (XXI, 17, 3):

... in all fairness one ought not to believe the last five books of this historian, in which he describes the deeds of Agathocles.

The last five books would be Books XXXIV to XXXVIII.[36] In Book XXXIV Polybius found Timaeus' statement that he had spent fifty years living in Athens as a foreigner (Polyb. XII, 25h, 1 = Tim. F 34). My own feeling is that the break in style and tone which Polybius and Diodorus notice in these books coincides with Timaeus' return to Sicily, a return that is implicit in his allusion to his fifty years abroad. Timaeus will have had to alter the habits of a lifetime in going back to Sicily, and he would have become aware at first hand of the shocking changes that had taken place during his absence. He must, naturally, have been reflecting about the misdeeds of Agathocles for a long time, but had he written about him from a distance, his diatribe would probably have been less hysterical, more professional. If this inference is sound, his return may be placed within the years immediately following Agathocles' death, the sooner the better, because the arrival of Pyrrhus soon changed the focus of Sicilian concern. The decade 289–278 may roughly serve our purpose, which yields 339–329 as the period within which Timaeus began living in Athens; this is twelve years before the earliest date suggested by Laqueur[37] and nineteen years before Müller's date.[38] Some support may be found in Polybius, who deplores Timaeus' lack of a practical understanding of military and political matters (XII, 25g, 3; 25h, 1; 28, 6); Cicero, too, infers that he had had no experience in speaking in public.[39] Is it likely that the son of the chief man—lest we call him the tyrant—of Tauromenium would have failed to acquire this experience unless he left home at a tender age? When we consider both his impracticality—in a Polybian sense—and his vast erudition, it becomes likely that he began his studies when very young, continuing them as it became increasingly clear that the political arena, for which he had been intended by birth, was forever closed to him. The mathematical reader will no doubt have already observed that these dates presuppose a considerable longevity for Timaeus, perhaps even a life span not too different from that suggested by the *Macrobioi*. But this should be thought of only as a happy coincidence!

The chief virtue of the foregoing analysis is to concentrate attention on Timaeus' Athenian period, which, lying between 339 and 279 B.C., must have included the forty years between 329 and 289. Since this means that Timaeus came to Athens as a very young person, it is evident that the background for his historical works must be sought in Athens rather than in Sicily. Presumably, like many another young man of means, he came to complete his education; but he must have found the environment so much to his liking that he had already stayed on a considerable time before Agathocles' actions made a return to Sicily impossible. Had his work survived, we would undoubtedly find many useful indications of his stay in Athens and of the impressions made upon him by world events, for those were exciting days. Fortunately, however, three fragments give us a glimpse of Timaeus and of Athens at three different times during his exile; characteristically, each is an attack on someone.

The first, for which we must thank Polybius, is directed against Aristotle (Polyb. XII, 8, 1–4 = Tim. F 156):

... hostility and vindictiveness toward others, such as Timaeus displayed toward Aristotle. (2) He says he was rash, licentious, hasty, and that in addition he had written recklessly about the Locrian state, saying that it was a colony of runaway slaves, menials, adulterers and slave dealers. (3) And that he says these things with such conviction that one might actually think him one of the generals who had *defeated the Persians in battle at the Cilician Gates* by his own cleverness, (4) instead of being a late learner, a detestable sophist who had only recently locked up his glorious surgery! In addition, that he was a man who leaped into every court and every dwelling; also, that glutton and cook were always at the tip of his tongue.

Timaeus' primary purpose is to make a historical point about Locri and, as we shall see later, he brought documentary evidence to bear; but not content with the positive proof, he also seeks to discredit the writer who holds a contrary opinion. Considering contemporary practice and Timaeus' own efforts on other occasions, his treatment of Aristotle is almost gentle. What interests us here is the time suggested by the "battle at the Cilician Gates." Once more Polybius comes to the rescue, this time by preserving a useful fragment of Callisthenes' account of the events leading up to the Battle of Issus, which may be translated as follows (Polyb. XII, 17, 2–3 = Callisth. 124 F 35):

I am speaking about the (*sc.* engagement) between Alexander and Darius in Cilicia, where he [Callisthenes] says that Alexander had already gone through the Narrows and the so-called Cilician Gates, and that Darius had entered Cilicia with his army by way of the so-called Amanian Gates. And that when he heard from the inhabitants that Alexander was advancing toward Syria, he followed, and made camp near the Narrows, alongside the Pinarus river. ...

The importance of the Cilician Gates emerges even in this abstract of Callisthenes. Faulty reconnaissance permitted the two armies unknowingly to pass one another during the night. Alexander was unpleasantly surprised when he learned later that the Persian army lay between him and Macedonia.[40] Since Alexander could not count on the sea, he was in a nasty position, from which he extricated himself by winning the Battle of Issus.[41] The battle was a near thing, decided only when Darius abandoned the field, taking the heart out of his soldiers.[42]

The very inexactness of Timaeus' reference to this as a "battle at the Cilician Gates" reflects the confusion that would naturally prevail in Athens in the period not long after the battle and before the facts were properly known. The Athenians were not sympathetic with Alexander and they must have disliked having his former teacher in their midst, presumably rejoicing over the latest bulletins from the front. Nor would their discontent have been alleviated when they reflected that it was Aristotle's kinsman, Callisthenes, who kept sending back vainglorious accounts of the war, accounts intended, through Athens, to persuade the world of Alexander's irresistible might. Alexander's policy toward Athens was two-sided: On the one hand he persisted in wooing Athens to obtain her good will, while on the other he left her as little freedom of action as possible. Both sides were in evidence after the Granicus engagement. He wooed her openly by a gift of 300 Persian panoplies taken from the spoils of battle, but at the same time the 2,000 Greek prisoners, including the Athenians, were fettered and transported to Macedonia to do forced labor.[43] When the Athenian envoys finally reached him at Gordium and begged that their fellow-citizens be released, Alexander refused.[44] He evidently regarded them as hostages. Nor did he release them after Issus. But when Egypt had fallen and the whole littoral was under his control, Alexander condescended to let them go at the request of the Athenian envoys sent out in the sacred Paralian galley to intercept him on his return to Tyre.[45] The timing most appropriate for Timaeus' jibe at Aristotle is before the return of the Athenian prisoners, because they would have been better informed about Issus and the Cilician Gates than Timaeus seems to have been in the fragment we are discussing. Also, his remark would lose its point as the Cilician Gates episode was eclipsed by later Macedonian exploits. Gaugamela, in 331 B.C., would have stopped people talking about Issus. Timaeus must have heard this *bon mot* about Aristotle while it was still on people's lips. Later, having occasion to attack the philosopher, he included it in his bill of particulars. By Polybius' time there had been a change of sentiment; Aristotle had become a classic and Polybius was, or professed to be, shocked.

Our second fragment is an attack on Callisthenes (Tim. F 155 = Polyb. XII, 12b, 2):

For he says that Callisthenes was a flatterer to write such things, and to have been far removed from philosophy, paying attention to ravens and women in Corybantic frenzy; and that he was rightly punished by Alexander for corrupting his soul to the extent of his ability. He praises Demosthenes and the other orators who flourished at that time, and says that they were worthy of Greece in that they opposed divine honors for Alexander, but that the philosopher who bestowed the aegis and the thunderbolt on one who was mortal by nature, justly received from that divinity what he did receive.

This fragment, too, bears an Athenian imprint and suggests the early years following Alexander's death. Why? Because Callisthenes is not depicted in the way the monarchical tradition of Ptolemy and Aristobulus depicted him, as justly punished for insubordination toward his lord and master,[46] nor yet as the sage confronting the tyrant, so popular in later times.[47] In point of fact, Callisthenes is condemned for writing poor history, and incidentally for having had a bad influence on Alexander by what he wrote. The fragments of Callisthenes illustrate Timaeus' remarks. The ravens were the birds that appeared so providentially to save Alexander and his train by showing them the way through the desert to Siwah after a storm had wiped out the road markers.[48] The oracle of Apollo at Branchidae is said to have resumed its prophetic role by proclaiming Alexander the Son of Zeus (Callisth. 124 F 14a). Also, the Pamphylian sea is supposed to have withdrawn itself before Alexander, acknowledging his rule (Callisth. F 31). The Athenians of Timaeus' day were still capable of scorn for such palpable exaggerations in Callisthenes' courtly history of Alexander.

Historically, this fragment is more than a little misleading. Divine honors for Alexander had not shocked the orators as much as the request that all the exiles be restored. This was a matter of property and therefore taken much more seriously than any honors granted to Alexander.[49] Also, it remains unlikely that Callisthenes ever advocated divine honors for a living king. He seems to have been preparing the way for posthumous deification, for which there were precedents.[50] Further, Timaeus chooses not to mention that Callisthenes incurred Alexander's wrath by effectively opposing the introduction of the *proskynesis* into the Macedonian court.[51] The truth has been distorted for rhetorical effect. This fragment, like the one just discussed, shows something of Timaeus' political sympathies. Both Aristotle and Callisthenes represented the Macedonian and therefore the antidemocratic influences in Athens.[52]

The third passage contains an attack on Demochares, whom Timaeus accuses of being the only Athenian whose behavior was so indecent that he was not allowed to kindle the sacred fire (Tim. FF 35a and 35b). This statement was made in the 38th book of his history, when Timaeus had probably returned to Sicily.[53] Presumably, the attack was motivated by something Demochares wrote in his history rather than by his public acts. We know he wrote about Agathocles from a reference in the Lu-

cianic *Macrobioi* (Demochares 75 F 5), where he is cited along with
Timaeus for the statement that Agathocles died at the age of ninety-
five; and it may be that Demochares was responsible for this figure, since
Timaeus probably has a different one.[54] The venom of Timaeus' attack
suggests that Demochares may have made some favorable remarks
about Agathocles. If he did so, Timaeus would no doubt seize on any
weapon that lay ready at hand. The particular one he chose may reflect
his enjoyment of antiquarian lore and the obscurities of religious law.
Polybius is particularly savage in denouncing Timaeus for his remarks
about Demochares, saying that "no educated man could possibly use
such abusive language, not even a brothel employee" (Polyb. XII, 13, 2
= Tim. F 35b). Yet when he says Timaeus goes even farther than the
obscene writers, Polybius betrays an acquaintance with their works, and
ironically he has preserved more of the kind of language to which he
objects than any other source on Timaeus.

But to appreciate the influence of Athens on Timaeus, we must go
beyond these three scolding fragments and consider his historical writing
in general. Three separate works are attributed to him: the *History*, a
work about Pyrrhus, and a treatise on the Olympic victors.[55] The *Olympionicae*, which was written first, paved the way for the *History* just as
Callisthenes' researches on the Pythian victors prepared the way for his
history of the Phocian War.[56] Callisthenes' investigations are known to
us through a Delphic inscription, partially preserved, recording the
honors of a crown and public thanks conferred on Aristotle and Callisthenes for their efforts in establishing the list of victors in the Pythian
games (SIG[3] 275 = Callisth. 124 T 23). We find a one-book *Scrutiny of
the Pythian Victors* assigned to Aristotle by Diogenes Laertius (D.L. V, 1,
26),[57] but no literary source mentions Callisthenes' connection with it.
Evidently this task was undertaken at the request of the Amphictyonic
Council and the field work was delegated by Aristotle to Callisthenes.
Unhappily, no Elean decree has survived to demonstrate an official
interest in the list of Olympic victors. It is easy to see that Delphi,
always quick to recognize changes in the political scene, would after the
Phocian War welcome the services of a scholar with Macedonian affilia-
tions. We do not, however, know whether Timaeus' work was or was not
officially sponsored; but it is worth keeping in mind that he was the son
of a man who evidently had wide political connections and influence. The
task of drawing up the list of Olympic victors was frequently undertaken.
The famous sophist, Hippias of Elis, perhaps influenced by feelings of
local pride, had drawn up a list of Olympic victors at the end of the fifth

century;[58] Aristotle wrote an *Olympionicae* from which some fragments have been saved;[59] Philochorus, Timaeus' contemporary, wrote an *Olympiades*, about which we would gladly know more;[60] and in the next century Eratosthenes found it necessary to construct an *Olympionicae* of his own.[61]

The importance of Timaeus' work on the Olympic victors is generally recognized. We need to ask how he approached his task. Did he go to Olympia to examine the documentary evidence, or did he remain in Athens, relying on the information available to him in libraries? Polybius is the fullest source on Timaeus, yet Polybius writes with acrimony, and often contradicts himself. After asserting that Timaeus always preferred report (ἀκοή) to observation (ὄρασις), he goes on to say (XII, 27, 4–6):[62]

(4) It is easy to see why he made such a choice in order to pry into books without risk or unpleasantness, if only someone provided this one prerequisite—that he might find a city containing a quantity of histories (ὑπομνήματα), or a library near at hand. (5) It remained to search the material for what he sought, and then to separate out the mistakes of the earlier historians, without any unpleasantness. (6) But the pursuit of knowledge (πολυπραγμοσύνη) requires great exertions and expense, involves comparisons on a large scale, and constitutes the most important part of a history.

Yet Timaeus claimed to have made great efforts in gathering material,[63] as Polybius well knew; and this same Polybius can also write (XII, 10, 4):[64]

(4) But there is one department in which Timaeus surpassed other historians . . . I mean his display of accuracy in chronology and in public records, and the pains he takes in such matters, for we are all aware of this.

Later, in the course of his attack on Timaeus for disagreeing with Aristotle about the antecedents of the Greek city of Locri in Italy, Polybius says Timaeus would have been the last man in the world to neglect to mention a document if he knew about it (XII, 11, 1–3):

For this is the man who made a tabulation from the beginning of the ephors and the kings in Lacedaemon, of the archons in Athens and the priestesses in Argos, setting them against the Olympic victors, and refuting the errors in the city records which amounted to more than three months. And Timaeus is also the one who discovered the stelae in the back of the building as well as the proxeny inscriptions on the door jambs of the temple. It cannot be believed that if anything of this kind existed he would not know about it, or that if he discovered it he would leave it out. . . .

All this yields a confusing picture of Timaeus, whom we find at one moment too lazy to leave the library, at another prowling around inside public buildings on the trail of new documentary evidence, even making a special journey to the Locrians of Greece to get at the facts (Polyb.

XII, 9, 2). Which Timaeus was it who wrote the *Olympionicae?* It is tempting, but quite fanciful, to surmise that the "stelae in the back of the building" were found at Olympia or Elis in the course of his investigation. It does remain likely, however, that Timaeus visited Olympia and interested himself in the inscriptions there. The use of inscriptions as historical evidence is one of the hallmarks of the Hellenistic period. Timaeus' learned contemporary, Philochorus, wrote a work on Attic inscriptions ('Επιγράμματα 'Αττικά), of which, unhappily, nothing remains;[65] and soon Craterus was to compile his famous collection of Athenian decrees.[66] Callisthenes had quoted an inscription in his account of the Messenian War (Callisth. 124 F 23 = Polyb. IV, 33), and Aristotle makes use of an inscribed discus to prove a point about Lycurgus and the Olympic games.[67] In fact, even a popular writer like Euhemerus, anxious to make his startling explanation of the origin of the Olympian gods as plausible as possible, supports his statements by an appeal to manufactured epigraphical evidence.[68] Therefore, it is not unreasonable to suppose that Timaeus, who based his whole chronology on the Olympiads, learned what could be learned from studying inscriptions on the spot.[69]

In using the first Olympiad (776 B.C.) as the basis for computing dates, Timaeus adopted what proved to be the most serviceable standard of reference for ancient scholars, though it never came into everyday use.[70] Timaeus was not the first to concern himself with the problem of chronolgy. In a sense this was a historical problem that demanded solution before there were historians, and some semblance of order had been brought to the events of mythology before the historic period had been properly worked out.[71] The Hesiodic *Theogony* provided a useful starting point in classifying the ages of man and bringing formerly disparate information within the compass of a single time sequence. After the heyday of epic poetry had ended, the task was undertaken of fitting the enormous numbers of heroes, many of whom were honored locally in widely separated parts of the Greek world, into a temporal and genealogical relationship with one another. And this in itself was not new; Babylonians, Egyptians, and Hebrews had had a similar problem that they solved in a similar way.[72] Certain events in the prehistoric past came to be convenient fixed points for general reference—events such as Deucalion's flood, the Calydonian Boar hunt, the Voyage of the Argo, the Trojan War, and the Return of the Heraclidae. Mythographers faced two major tasks simultaneously, the necessity to include all significant stories of heroes in a master plan and also to "explain" the historic distribution of the Greeks in the various parts of the Mediterranean world. The data at their disposal must have been considerable and the discrepancies great. The ingenuity with which they handled the traditional material developed critical faculties that later stood the historian in good stead and also provided him with a useful yardstick for reckoning by generations, three to each one hundred years.[73] But this was not history. Herodotus it was who, with some hesitation, perhaps, but unmistakably, set up a no man's land between mythological and historic times.[74] And for the historical period the rough chronology of interglacial or interpluvial epochs was inadequate; something more exact was needed. Herodotus failed to find a satisfactory solution.[75] Thucydides, writing the history of a war, was far too precise to adopt the Athenian archon list as his standard.[76] As far as his own account is concerned, he attained great internal accuracy, but offered no scheme applicable to history in general.[77] Hellanicus, whom Thucydides mentions, had made use of the list of Argive priestesses and also used the archons;[78] Ephorus, whom Jacoby classifies as the first writer of general history, had no new solution, but continued to reckon by generations.[79] In Timaeus' day there existed many local lists of kings or magistrates carried back to a remote antiquity. Unfortunately, they appear to have had no solid foundation beyond the seventh century B.C. and, also, they had been constructed more or less independently of one another. The great success of Timaeus, in Jacoby's words, came about because he "was the first to furnish parallel lists, in which Spartan kings, ephors, archons, priestesses of Hera, and Olympiads were arranged alongside in order to create a basis for chronological determinations."[80] To the convenience of his scheme was added the great weight of Eratosthenes' reputation when he too adopted the Olympic era.[81]

The *Olympionicae* was a brilliant scholarly monograph, but it remained to be seen how successfully the author would be able to put his theories into practice. Timaeus' choice of a subject was no accident. Archaeology, or rather antiquarianism, was fashionable, and in his contemporary, Philochorus, it reached a high level of attainment. Preoccupation with the remote past, particularly in Athens, was a good antidote for the realities of a present in which the old city-states played a less and less attractive role. Philochorus was to demonstrate in his *Atthis* the very combination of erudition with strong local feeling that is so characteristic of Timaeus.[82] But Timaeus evidently reacted against the tendency to orient Greek history around Athens, much as F. J. Turner objected to centering United States history on the Atlantic seaboard. Like many another exile, Timaeus may have found himself becoming more and more of a patriot the longer he stayed abroad; the more the Athenian environment made him feel he was a foreigner, the more he must have appreciated that he was a Sicilian. He decided to write a history of the west. But where did he expect to find his readers? It seems probable that he wrote primarily with the Athenian public in mind. Was it not their misconceptions about the west that he was especially anxious to correct?

Although read in Athens, Timaeus was also read in Alexandria. Istrus the Callimachean, a well-known historian, wrote a separate work attacking Timaeus and was responsible for giving him the unforgettable nickname of "Epitimaeus" or "fault-finder."[83] This mild, punning epithet was not intended to remind one of Timaeus' scurrilous remarks about Philistus or Demochares, but rather to ridicule his habit of petty historical criticism. Istrus was particularly interested in Athens, as his writings show by their titles, and there is little doubt that the name "Epitimaeus" would have appealed to the Athenians, if only because of Timaeus' criticism of the vapid but ever popular Ephorus[84] who had written a general history in which he had included the west.[85] Timaeus wrote a western history, partly to correct the previous eastern emphasis, but also, as Laqueur suggests, to emphasize the true Hellenism of the west.[86] The stories of the foundation of the various Greek colonies must be rehandled from this viewpoint, and the interest of Greek gods and heroes in the west from the earliest possible times must be made evident.[87] A favorite preoccupation of Greek historians was with the εὑρήματα, the "discoveries" or inventions that had made civilization possible or agreeable.[88] Timaeus is eager to press western claims in this field, however humble the invention. Even the chamber pot is not overlooked (Tim. F 50 = Athen. XII, 17, p. 519 E). He may have been influenced by Hellanicus in abandoning the no man's land left by Herodotus between history and myth.[89] He does seem to have tried to give some sort of a narrative from earliest times on down, but his emphasis on the Olympic era would suggest a carefully thought-out attitude to the two periods. But later in the book when the fragments are discussed individually, something of his point of view will emerge.

To turn now to the testimony of the ancients on the subject matter of Timaeus *History*, we will begin with the very broad statement made by Agatharchides (*De m. Rubr.* 64 = Tim. T 14):

The whole oecumene embracing four parts . . . both Lycus[90] and Timaeus have dealt with the West; Hecataeus and Basilis with the East; Diophantus and Demetrius with the North . . . we with the South.

Polybius confirms this when he remarks that Timaeus' *History* was concerned only with events "in Italy, Sicily and Libya" (Polyb. XXXIX, 8, 4 = Tim. T 6b). He also refers to Timaeus' special attention to "Colonies, Foundations and Peoples" (XII, 26d, 4 = Tim. T 7). Dionysius of Halicarnassus has this to say (*A.R.* I, 6, 1 = Tim. T 9b):

So far as I know Hieronymus was the first to touch on the subject of Roman antiquity ... and then Timaeus the Sicilian, including the early Roman history in his general work, described the wars against Pyrrhus in a separate treatise.

Here, quite unconsciously, Timaeus made his strongest bid for posthumous fame. He cannot possibly have realized in full the coming predominance of Rome, but he did take her achievements seriously and he did interest himself in her early history. Later, Polybius went much further in centering his own history around the Roman conquests; but Polybius lived when the might of Rome had become clear to everyone, whereas Timaeus divined the significance of Rome's crossing over into Sicily right after the event.[91] He adopted, if he did not invent, the persuasive idea that Rome and Carthage were founded at the same time.[92] Later, when the Romans became self-conscious about their new role, the works of Timaeus must have been much consulted. For Rome, too, sought ties with Hellenism and the Trojan War, and Timaeus had helped to suggest the way in which this could be managed.[93]

Although Timaeus eclipsed all rivals, he was not the first nor yet the last to write with a Sicilian emphasis. A word is called for on the earlier literature in the field. In Jacoby's fine edition the writers on Sicily and Magna Graecia are included in volume III B, which is devoted to writers on the separate cities and countries. These are arranged alphabetically, beginning with *Achaea* and ending with *Troezen*, and there are seventy-eight sections all told, *Sicily and Magna Graecia* comprising Section LXIX. The Individual authors, including some anonymous entries, make up Jacoby's Numbers 297–607. Of these, Numbers 554–577 are Sicilian writers, and their fragments extend over pages 540–688. What is lost may be dimly apprehended by noting that for Timaeus, the most voluminous writer on Sicily, just seventy-seven pages remain, and seventy-one pages remain for the other twenty-three entries. Further, in Number 577 Jacoby has lumped together selected passages proving the existence, at one time, of a rich Sicilian tradition that has all but disappeared.[94] That some new material has turned up on papyrus offers hopes, though not exuberant ones, for the future.[95]

Most of these names tell us little. A Hippys of Rhegium, born "at the time of the Persian War," wrote a work on Sicily, later abbreviated by the equally elusive Myes.[96] Less of a wraith is Antiochus of Syracuse, whom Dionysius refers to as a "very ancient historian" (*A.R.* I, 12, 3 = Antioch. 555 T 2a). Diodorus tells us he wrote a Sicilian history in nine books, beginning with Cocalus the King of the Sicans and continuing down to 424/3 (D.S. XII, 71, 2 = Antioch. T 3). Strabo, in his superior way, says that Antiochus was naive and wrote in an old-fashioned manner, not even distinguishing between the Lucanians and the Bruttians (VI, 1, 4 = Antioch. T 4). But Strabo made good use of him, as did Dionysius.[97] Josephus includes Antiochus in his list of the authors with whom Timaeus disagreed,[98] and there is little doubt as to his high reputation. Probably much of Antiochus still lies embedded in the *Historical Library* of Diodorus Sicilus.[99]

Of the special writers on Sicily, it was Philistus of Syracuse about whom Timaeus felt most strongly. Information about him in the *Suda* is dubious in a number of respects: the name of the author, given as Philistus or Philiscus; his place of origin, given as Naucratis or Syracuse; and the list of his writings, which includes rhetorical treatises and an *Aegyptiaca* in addition to the Sicilian history.[100] These ambiguities, however, can be accounted for. Philistus and Philiscus could easily become confused with one another. Once you have a Philiscus, it is easy to attribute to him rhetorical works belonging to someone else, for instance to the well-known rhetorician from Miletus.[101] Somewhere along the line an *Aegyptiaca* was introduced, perhaps because still another Philiscus had written one, and then it was natural for Naucratis to appear as the suggested birthplace.[102] There being no reliable tradition about the education of Philistus, a distinguished teacher had to be provided for him, on the usual doxographical principles. Philistus was therefore said to have studied under the elegiac poet, Evenus, a chronological impossibility.[103] But the main facts about the historian are fairly well established, ultimately no doubt from his writings. He was an onlooker in Syracuse when Gylippus defended that city against the Athenians (Philistus 556 F 56 = Plut. *Nic.* 19, 6). As a wealthy man, some eight years later (405/5 B.C.), he paid Dionysius' fine for him when the future tyrant made his sensational charges against the generals before the Syracusan assembly (Phil. 556 T 3 = D.S. XIII, 91, 4). Philistus was a staunch supporter of the tyranny until Dionysius exiled him (about 386/5 B.C.).[104] It was during this period that he composed most of his history.[105] Eventually Dionysius restored him to favor, and he soon became a leader of the faction opposed to Dion. He lost his life as the result of a naval battle in 356/5 in which he led the fleet of Dionysius II against the Syracusans. According to Diodorus he committed suicide to avoid being captured by his enemies (XVI, 16, 3). His *Sicilian History* consisted of thirteen books, seven on the period down to Dionysius I, four on the rule of that tyrant, and two on the first five years of Dionysius II.[106]

Such a man was bound to be a controversial figure, and such he remained until the lengthening shadow of Rome fell over all Greeks, eastern and western alike. Toward the end of the Republic and in the Augustan period, writers like Cicero and Dionysius could express themselves dispassionately about Philistus as a stylist and as a historian,[107] but detachment was impossible in the earlier period. Philistus must have been thought of as rather a Machiavelli, an advocate of dictatorship and the strong national state. That it was a Sicilian Greek who represented this view is not surprising. The western Greeks were subject to more and more pressure from aggressive neighbors, whether the Carthaginians in Sicily itself, or the Lucanians and Bruttians on the Italian mainland. The Athenian expedition, though a failure, had served to call attention to the dangers for the Greek cities in Sicily, faced by a determined adversary capable of playing on their mutual antagonisms. The same weaknesses existed farther east, but in a less acute form. In the philosophic schools of the fourth century tyranny continued to be denounced, at least on the surface, and the ideal of Plato and Aristotle was still a small, self-sufficient city-state. But the controversy continued for all that. Isocrates, superficial though he may have been, had great influence, and his method of resolving the tragic dilemma by employing a *deus ex machina*, be he a Dionysius, a Jason, or a Philip, who would save the situation by force and then return peacefully to Olympus, must have had a wide appeal.[108] It is interesting that the most popular historian of the fourth century, Ephorus, came to the defense of Philistus (Ephorus 70 F 220 = Plut. *Dion* 36). It is also significant that Aristotle himself writes brilliantly on how to be a successful tyrant.[109] Later, when the dust of conflict had settled and the *pax Romana* came to be taken for granted, the luxury of sentimentality could be indulged in, and the gentle Plutarch grieved, both that Ephorus should have defended Philistus and Timaeus should have attacked him so rudely (*Dion* 36). For Plutarch it is all a matter of taste; the issues are dead.

Considering Philistus' reputation the fragments are disappointing. Of the seventy-six attested fragments, forty-one come through Stephanus of Byzantium and are concerned with technical matters about place names and their spelling.[110] They do indicate a certain antiquarian in-

terest in Philistus, and certainly Timaeus made extensive use of him.
The Pindar scholiast cites Philistus three times on the exploits of Gelon
and Hieron, twice in conjunction with Timaeus.[111] Pliny also betrays
Philistus' preoccupation with Gelon, whose dog Pyrrhus he is said to
have mentioned.[112] On the Athenian expedition against Syracuse, Philistus seems to have followed Thucydides at all points, and for this Timaeus
criticized him.[113] He seems also to have tried to improve on Thucydides'
account by paraphrasing, an exasperating trait (Philistus 556 F 67, for
example). His own language occasionally struck later purists as bizarre
and "completely abominable" (see, for example, Pollux II, 154). He also
offended by stretches of bald narrative, of which Dionysius has preserved
an example for us (*Ad Pomp.* 5, 4 = Phil. 556 F 5). These deficiencies in
style may have militated against the survival of his work. Cicero couples
him with Cato and Thucydides in lacking admirers because of extreme
condensation.[114] But he attempted to be lively in writing about Dionysius, heralding his future greatness with supernatural manifestations
(Phil. 556 FF 57a and 58). Here we are fortunate in having a fragment
from Timaeus showing how he introduced Dionysius, evidently ridiculing
Philistus' account (Tim. 566 F 29).[115] Philistus' history must have made
better reading than can be guessed by what is left and by the strictures
on his style. Otherwise how can it be explained that Alexander, when he
sent back to Harpalus for something to read, asked for only one historian,
Philistus?[116]

The next four writers in Jacoby's collection merit only brief mention.
Of the first, Dionysius the Sicilian tyrant, we know only that he wrote
historical as well as dramatic works.[117] No fragment remains. Second
comes Hermias of Methymna, a fourth-century writer who brought his
Sicelica in ten or twelve books down to 376/5 B.C.[118] The one fragment
preserved by Athenaeus is valueless. Polycritus of Mende, whose activity
is placed by Jacoby circa 370/40, wrote at least two works Timaeus may
have found useful, one on the younger Dionysius, the other a *Sicelica* in
verse. The three fragments contain, respectively: information about
Dionysius' literary entourage; the description of a small lake capable of
expanding and contracting in surprising fashion; and an account of the
munificence of Gellias of Acragas.[119] Timaeus' own remarks about Gellias
probably owe something to Polycritus.[120] The fourth of these obscure
writers is Alcimus the Sicilian, who probably wrote his *Sicelica* in the mid-
fourth century. Little is left, but that little suggests a range of interests
paralleled only in Timaeus. These include a Heracles anecdote, explaining
the alleged sobriety of Italian women; the genealogy of Rhomus; and

how Aetna got its name.[121] Another work, *To Amyntas* (Πρὸς ’Αμύνταν),
while hardly a history, might have attracted Timaeus in that it accuses
Plato of borrowing heavily from Epicharmus.[122]

Timonides of Leucas cannot be overlooked, but it is difficult to assign
him his place among the historians of Sicily. Diogenes Laertius tells us
that Timonides wrote a history for Speusippus in which he related the
deeds of Dion (D.L. IV, 5 = Timonides 561 T 3b). Everything else
known about him comes from Plutarch's *Dion*. Not only the two fragments, but also the statements about Timonides' activities as a military
leader who took charge after Dion was wounded, probably derive from
Timonides (Plut. *Dion* 30, 10 = Timon. 561 T 2). But was it a *history*
or simply a long letter to Speusippus, describing the Dion adventure for
the benefit of the Academy? Regardless of the form his writing took, no
evidence appears for a wider subject than Dion's expedition.[123] But
Dion's expedition was only an episode in the prolonged struggle that
began with the death of Dionysius I and culminated with the restoration
of the constitutional governments by Timoleon. Timaeus was keenly
interested in this period, and may have found Timonides' eye-witness
account extremely helpful in supplementing his own information. But
Timaeus was so successful that Timonides ceased to be read, so his influence on our tradition can no longer be separated from that of his sup-
planter. There is no litmus paper test for distinguishing the two writers
in the fullest account, that of Diodorus. Both were hostile to Dionysius II
and to Philistus; both were probably favorable to Dion. In one instance
only can we separate the two. Ephorus said that Philistus committed
suicide after losing the last naval battle. Timonides, however, stresses
that he was captured alive by the Syracusans. Timaeus accepts this
version, but adds ghoulish details on the treatment of Philistus' body.[124]
There is another slight difference in detail pointed out by Plutarch.
Timaeus referred to Dion's son as Aretaeus, Timonides as Leptines.[125] So
far as we can see, then, Diodorus never read Timonides. What about
Plutarch? Could the differences he notes have been mentioned in
Timaeus' own account? This is unlikely, since to have reproduced the
more austere narrative of Timonides would have tended to throw doubt
on his own. Either, then, Plutarch read both authors or, as has been
suggested for his *Timoleon*, he also had a now vanished Peripatetic biography of Dion which made use of Timonides as well as Timaeus.[126]

Athanis of Syracuse wrote a *Sicelica* in thirteen books that probably
carried the story down to Timoleon's death. The first book served as an
introduction, summarizing events for the seven years after Philistus

broke off his account.[127] Athanis apparently was a prominent Syracusan popular leader, associated with Heraclides and opposed to Dion. His work would have been very useful to anyone interested, as Timaeus was, in the details of Syracusan internal politics. But the admiration of Timaeus was probably fatal to him, as it had been to Timonides. Only three fragments remain, a curious notice about Dionysius the Elder in Athenaeus and two references in Plutarch's *Timoleon*.[128]

To conclude this survey of the writers on Sicily before Timaeus, three historians are each credited with a work about Agathocles: Duris of Samos, Callias of Syracuse, and Antander of Syracuse. Duris, who had written many other books as well, is one of the sources, direct or indirect, of the account of Agathocles in Diodorus' *Historical Library*.[129] But we have no way of knowing whether Duris and Timaeus wrote independently of one another or, if there was a relationship, which derives from the other. Duris' objections to the Athenian bias that had colored accounts of Pericles would no doubt have appealed to Timaeus (Duris 76 F 67 = Plut. *Per.* 28). But it seems futile to discuss their resemblances in the present state of knowledge. The fragments of Duris' work on Agathocles do not give a glimpse of his point of view, unless Athenaeus' remark that he was once tyrant of Samos verifies the assumption that he approved of tyranny on principle.[130] Yet he may have disliked tyrants in the abstract as much as Dion did—who also became one. Callias and Antander may or may not have been used by Timaeus; but at least there is little doubt that they painted a favorable portrait of Agathocles. Diodorus tells us Callias' account was voluminous, consisting of twenty-two books, and he castigates the author for betraying "history the prophet of truth" in return for Agathocles' benefactions.[131] So Callias must have been an official court historian, and we would dearly like to recover more than the six fragments now extant. He seems to have written up the Libyan campaign in a lively, if not altogether reliable, fashion, if we are to judge by his remarks on the local methods of dealing with snake bites (Callias 564 F 3 = Aelian *N.A.* XVI, 28). Perhaps Timaeus obtained from him some of the details about Libya for which Polybius berates him (Polyb. XII, 3 = Tim. 566 F 81).[132] Antander was the brother and assistant of Agathocles. Unfortunately nothing is left. We are not told how extensive his work was, nor even its subject. We merely assume he wrote about his famous brother.[133]

CHAPTER II

GEOGRAPHY, MYTH, AND PREHISTORY

As ALREADY NOTED, three works can with some assurance be attributed to Timaeus: an *Olympionicae*, a *History*, and a work about Pyrrhus.[1] In the following chapters further effort will be made to see what can still be learned about them from the fragments. Richard Laqueur in a detailed study attempted to do a good deal more by attributing large amounts of additional material to Timaeus, notably from Diodorus Siculus, on the basis of language peculiarities and other criteria.[2] Students in the field owe him a debt of gratitude, and the obligation is not lessened by the fact that Laqueur's results are often unacceptable. Until he wrote, the possibility always existed that a way might be found to enlarge the passages at our disposal, but after his most ingenious and elaborate efforts, it is unlikely that anyone else will try this approach. But we have learned more about Diodorus and the whole complex problem of historical sources as a result of his investigations than was known before. Schwartz's success in establishing the pattern of the history written by Hieronymus of Cardia, from Diodorus and other sources,[3] not unnaturally led scholars to hope that the same methods applied elsewhere might be equally profitable. Timaeus seemed particularly promising because so many attested fragments served as a basis for interrogating Diodorus. But now we realize that although Timaeus' *History* was easily the most important work on Sicily in the ancient world, it did not furnish the only frame of reference available to later writers.[4] Then, too, Diodorus was himself a Sicilian, and as such more than usually familiar with a variety of sources when he came to write about his native land. Consequently, and partly as a result of Laqueur's study, it becomes clear that the only safe procedure is to adhere closely to the known fragments.

The standard edition of Timaeus' fragments for generations to come will probably be that of Felix Jacoby. His arrangement of them can be seen in the following table:[5]

FRAGMENTS	LOCATION
1–35	1. *Sicilian History*, Books I–XXXVIII
1–6	I–V (Introduction?)
7–33	VI–XXXIII (Before Agathocles)
34–35	XXXIV–XXXVIII (Agathocles)
36	2. *About Pyrrhus*
None	3. *Olympionicae*

[1] For notes to chap ii, see pp. 117–124.

The great advantage in this scheme lies in the clarity with which it reflects the various levels of our information about Timaeus. The first thirty-five fragments represent passages that Jacoby feels confident in attributing to a particular book in a particular work—the *Sicilian History*. Fragment 36 has its place in a particular work, but cannot be related to the structure of that work. Then we have a title, the *Olympionicae*, whose authorship is certain, but to which no fragment can be assigned with confidence. The fourth main heading includes the bulk of our material, passages that derive from Timaeus but which cannot be pinned down to a particular book or work. Here Jacoby has chosen to group the fragments in accordance with their subject matter, without attempting to integrate them into any imaginary restoration of Timaeus' original plan. Not that such possibilities are ignored. The predilections of the editor can be inferred from marginal notations—and doubtless will be developed in the commentary—but he has avoided Müller's earlier deceptive arrangement (*FHG* I, pp. 193–233). Under the fifth heading he has put those fragments that, for one reason or another, may not be genuine. In the last section he has printed a long passage from Diodorus that, despite the fact that Timaeus is cited only once, evidently includes a substantial amount of Timaean material.

Before turning to the fragments it may be helpful first to see where they come from. The total number of citations is much larger than the 163 numbers in the collection because Jacoby has grouped together separate statements obviously based on the same Timaeus passage under the same number, and also because he avoids reprinting identical statements from the *Suda*, Photius, and so on. Bearing this in mind, it is rather surprising to find only seventeen citations of Timaeus distributed among seven Latin authors, Cicero and Pliny accounting for most of them[6] and none at all from Livy. Of the Greek authors, Polybius and Athenaeus lead the list with twenty-five fragments each;[7] next come Diodorus and Plutarch with seventeen and fifteen respectively,[8] followed by Diogenes Laertius with nine[9] and Strabo with seven.[10] As a group, the scholiasts furnish thirty-six fragments,[11] and it is understandable that the Pindar scholiast leads with sixteen. The lexicographers, as one would expect, found Timaeus a useful source.[12] The earliest fragments date from writers in the third century B.C.,[13] and the very latest come from Tzetzes in the twelfth century A.D. (FF 95 and 146b). References tend to decrease after the second century A.D., with Diogenes Laertius and Stephanus of Byzantium notable exceptions; and to judge by the material at hand, Timaeus must have been more popular during the century before and the century after the birth of Christ than at any other time. One fact, at least, emerges. The systematic attacks on Timaeus by Istrus and Polemon and finally by Polybius seem not to have hurt him.[14]

Reading over the fragments, however arranged, the first impression is that of a strange hodge-podge of anecdote, rhetorical exaggeration, cantankerousness, and aridity, relieved by occasional bits of good historical writing. For this, no doubt, the sources are largely to blame. What if, instead of the full text of Herodotus, all we had to go by were the references in Plutarch's *De malignitate Herodoti* and the like? But if we can no longer recover the full sweep of Timaeus' work, we can, by careful reading, select and consider some of the subjects treated and recover something of the spirit in which Timaeus treated them. This seems more fruitful than attempting to discuss the fragments in terms of their original order in the *History*. The divisions adopted in this book ("Geography, Myth, and Prehistory"; "The Good Old Days"; "Modern Times") are roughly chronological, though the line between the first and second parts is necessarily arbitrary. "Modern Times" is treated as beginning with the Carthaginian attacks of 409/8 B.C.

Whether Timaeus attempted a general account of world geography is uncertain, but the fact that Timoleon is made to refer in a speech to the three parts of the oecumene as Asia, Libya, and Europe (Timaeus 566 F 31) shows that Timaeus accepted this conventional terminology. Polybius rebukes him roundly for his description of Libya (Polyb. XII, 3 = Tim. F 81):

... one would say not only that Timaeus was ignorant of conditions in Libya, but that he was childish and entirely illogical, still in the grip of the old reports handed down from antiquity, that all Libya is a barren sandy waste. And his account of animal life is of the same sort.

Polybius continues, asking if there is any writer who has failed to mention the teeming herds of Libya, the antelopes, the lions and elephants and wild cats that abound there: "None of which is mentioned by Timaeus, who describes conditions the opposite of those that actually prevail, as though he does it on purpose." Yet this same Polybius, a few chapters later, quotes from the speech attributed by Timaeus to Timoleon (Polyb. XII, 26a = Tim. F 31b):

For all of Libya is inhabited throughout and teeming with peoples, despite the fact that proverbially, when we wish to emphasize a solitude, we say, "more desert than Libya," not referring to a physical desert but to the lack of manliness in those who live there.

One must remember that Polybius is engaged in a prolonged attack on Timaeus, for which his abuse of Phylarchus offers the only true parallel.[15] But his attack on Phylarchus is much more consistent and better thought out. In his anxiety to show up Timaeus in every possible way, he has crossed his own trail. In ridiculing him for including the long-winded and inappropriate speeches in his *History*, Polybius demonstrates that Timaeus was well aware of the incorrectness of the "old reports handed down from antiquity, that all Libya is a barren sandy waste." More than that, he has given us a useful insight into Timaeus' point of view. Unlike Polybius, Timaeus has a respect for tradition as such, and he is trying, however clumsily, to explain that tradition. Like Tacitus, Polybius is an *honnête homme*. He may misinterpret, but he does not lie. This makes it probable that Timaeus attempted no over-all account of Libya, but contented himself with describing the areas closely connected with Sicilian history. The importance of the desert there is of course obvious. Polybius has conveniently confused the part with the whole—unfair, but not literally mendacious.

To judge by what is left, Timaeus was particularly interested in islands, and it is sad indeed that so little remains of what must once have been a detailed account of Sicilian geography. There is one statement by the scholiast on Apollonius Rhodius (IV, 965 = Tim. F 37):

Timaeus says Sicily was called *Thrinacia* because it has three promontories. But the historians say *Thrinacus* ruled over Sicily. . . . Mylos is the Sicilian peninsula where the cattle of Helios pastured.

This readily suggests the passage in the *Historical Library* where Diodorus writes (D.S. V, 2, 2): "Because of its shape, the island was called *Trinacria* [*i.e.* Three-Promontoried] in ancient times." This resemblance suggests that Timaeus' lost description of Sicily lies behind the surviving account of Diodorus, and this is a distinct possibility. Yet the fragment proper has *Thrinacia*, the name of a mysterious island in the *Odyssey*

(XI 107), obviously associated with the *thrinax* or "trident" of Poseidon. It is tempting to believe that Timaeus, in his desire to link Sicily with the older Greek tradition has consciously associated the three prongs of the trident with the three main promontories of the island. Since Diodorus fails to do this, he *may* be following a different source,[16] for it is unlikely that the scholiast has made a mistake. Elsewhere we find him referring to Corcyra as having once been called *Drepane* (that is, a sickle) because of its shape. And Timaeus is one of his authorities for this statement (Schol. Ap. Rh. IV, 982/92g = F 79). Moreover, Pliny tells us that Timaeus gave *Sandaliotis* as a name for Sardinia (*N.H.* III, 85 = F 63) because that island is shaped like a sandal.[17] Strabo seems to have missed the point entirely, his admiration for Homer notwithstanding. He writes (VI, 2, 1): "Sicily is triangular in shape and therefore used to be called *Trinacria*, which was later changed to *Thrinacis, for the sake of euphony.*" Therefore we remain in doubt as to the extent to which Timaeus' description of Sicilian geography may survive in Strabo or in Diodorus.

To turn to a very different part of the world, the outer ocean, particularly that portion lying to the west and north of Europe, three passages from Pliny's *Natural History*[18] refer to Timaeus' observances:

Timaeus the historian says that there is an island on the inside (*introrsus*), six days' sail from Britain, called *Ictis*, in which tin is produced. The Britons sail there in wickerwork boats stitched over with leather.

. . . crossing the Ripaean mountains, the shore of the northern ocean is to be found on the left, until Gades is reached. A number of unnamed islands are mentioned in that area, and there is one of them opposite Scythia and distant by one day's passage, which is called *Baunonia* (?), where Timaeus says amber is deposited by the waves in the spring.

Pytheas says the Guiones, a German tribe, inhabit an estuary of the ocean, called *Metuonis*, for a distance of six miles, and that the island of *Abalus* is a day's sail away; and that amber is the offscouring of the thickened sea. The natives use it as fuel for their fires, and sell it to the nearest Teutones. Timaeus accepts this, but he calls the island *Basilia*.

These passages furnish our only direct evidence for Timaeus' approval of the famous work of the Massiliote navigator, Pytheas. Mette has recently edited the fragments of Pytheas, along with a very useful discussion of the problems raised by them.[19] Scholars in the ancient world were sharply divided in their estimates of this work. Dicaearchus, in the fourth century, had thrown his weight in the scales against believing Pytheas,[20] before Timaeus had a chance to give his support.

Eratosthenes, probably the most distinguished ancient geographer, did not always agree with Pytheas, but took him seriously and did accept his views on the northern ocean.[21] Then Polybius poured his scorn on Pytheas and also on Eratosthenes for believing him, saying that "the Messenian (Euhemerus) was more trustworthy" (Strabo II, 4, 2). There is a barb in this comparison because Eratosthenes had referred to Euhemerus as "the Bergaean,"[22] that is, he had classed him with the romance writer, Antiphanes of Berge. Polybius supports his own sceptical view by arguing that no private person, and a poor man at that, could possibly have made such long voyages (Strabo II, 4, 2 = Polyb. XXXIV, 5, 7)—not an impressive deduction. Later, Posidonius not only supported Pytheas, but regarded him as the first man to put the interrelation of ocean and land in its proper perspective.[23] Posidonius was supposedly influenced by Crates of Pergamum, who had made good use of Pytheas.[24] Hipparchus, the celebrated astronomer, was another believer in Pytheas.[25] But Artemidorus followed Polybius.[26] Strabo, who is our chief referee on the views of his predecessors, also decided unfavorably (II, 4, 2). Honigmann feels that Strabo failed to appreciate Pytheas because he could not understand the mathematics involved.[27]

According to Mette, Pytheas' account was characterized by two kinds of data, distances in terms of so many days' sail (though land measurements were given as usual in stades), and estimates of the longest day at various observed points (reaching a maximum of twenty-four hours in Thule).[28] His more famous voyage took him up the coasts of Spain and France, over to Britain, and finally to Thule, some six days' sail north of Britain and near the "Solid Sea" ($\pi\epsilon\pi\eta\gamma\upsilon\iota\alpha\ \theta\acute{a}\lambda\alpha\tau\tau\alpha$) (Strabo I, 4, 2 = Pytheas F 6a). He observed the tides and connected their activity with the moon.[29] He also claimed to have made another voyage from Gades all the way to the Tanais (Don) river[30] and Mette sees no reason to doubt him.[31] He was especially interested in the ocean itself, both inside and outside Gibraltar, and in its powers. Notable are his views on the peculiar effects of the cold barrier in the north (he referred to it as a "chain"), which was compacted of sea, earth, and air.[32] It had movement, and he compared it to a "sea lungs" or "jellyfish" ($\pi\lambda\epsilon\acute{\upsilon}\mu\omega\nu$). Similarly, he writes about the volcanic islands off the Sicilian coast and of the "cooking" action of the sea there.[33]

Returning to the Pliny passages, we are annoyed by their brevity. This may be entirely Pliny's fault, or it may be that Pliny knew Timaeus only through some intermediary, perhaps Philemon.[34] The statement about *Ictis* as "an island on the inside [*i.e.,* toward the continent] six days' sail from Britain," is obviously wrong, but correcting it is not easy. The six days suggest confusion with Thule, which was six days' sail beyond the north end of Britain (Pyth. F 6a = Strabo I, 4, 2). *Ictis* is also mentioned in Diodorus, and there too as a source of tin. But the tin is so near the shore that at low tide men drive out to collect it by the wagon load (D.S. V, 22, 2). In the Pliny passage, however, they use leather boats (*N.H.* IV, 104).[35] That Timaeus is said by Pliny to have called the amber-producing island *Basilia* instead of *Abalus* as does Pytheas[36] lends support to the view that Diodorus' account also comes from Timaeus. Mette, noting the differences in detail between Pliny and Diodorus, concludes that Diodorus did not use Timaeus direct.[37] Yet the explanation may lie, rather, in the cavalier way both writers used their sources. An obvious example of Pliny's alterations is: "Pytheas says the Guiones, *a German tribe*" (*N.H.* XXXVII, 35 = Pyth. F 11a); as Mette sees, the original probably had *a Scythian tribe*.[38] In general, the Pliny passages do not give us a very high opinion of Timaeus' grasp of Pytheas' work. Sensational touches, like the use of amber as fuel, are not reassuring (Tim. F 75b = Pliny *N.H.* XXXVII, 35). However, it is to Timaeus' credit that he did accept Pytheas' account as genuine, and in doing so he appears in a more favorable light than his detractor, Polybius.[39]

The following fragment suggests Timaeus' limitations in the field of geographic theory (F 73 = Aetius *Plac.* III, 17, 6 p. 383 Diels):

Timaeus of Tauromenium holds responsible [*i.e.* for the tides] the rivers which pour themselves through the Celtic mountains into the Atlantic, thrusting forward the water by their flow, drawing it back when they subside.

Evidently, like Strabo, he lacked the mathematical training to appreciate Pytheas' observations on the tides and the reasons for their occurrence. No fragment of Timaeus attempts to fix the latitude of a place by measuring the inclination of the sun, yet this is what, basically, made Pytheas a Captain Cook rather than a Lief Ericson. Timaeus was interested in color. Later, in discussing his account of the Argonauts, we will see why he found Pytheas' work so attractive. Meanwhile, let us return to the inner sea and Timaeus' description of Pythecussae (or Pythecussa), an island off the Campanian coast of Italy (F 58 = Strabo V, 4, 9):

And Timaeus says many wondrous things were told by the ancients about Pythecussae; and that not long before his day the hill in the center of the island, Epomeus, was shaken by an earthquake and belched forth flames; and that it even pushed back the intervening land into the sea, but that the burnt land rose once more, and rushed back on to the island like a whirlwind while the sea retreated three stades; and then, not long after its withdrawal, the sea turned and overran the island in a flood, and the fire was extinguished. People on the island fled away from the noise, inside Campania and away from the coast.

This is indeed a remarkable passage which, in its attempt to describe the spectacular effects of an earthquake in historic times, reminds us of Callisthenes' account of how two Achaean cities, Helice and Buris, were overrun by the sea (Callisth. 124 FF 19; 20; 21). Callisthenes, however, had an earthquake theory,[40] but the passage under consideration is limited to telling what occurred. Pytheas had views about volcanic islands and the "cooking" action of the sea. Can this have originated with Pytheas? Diodorus says nothing about it—an indication of the many things Diodorus left out in his own remarks about islands. Somehow, the description is so lively and circumstantial that unless Timaeus, too, was a Bergaean romancer, it is hard to resist the impression that he picked up his information on the spot. The earthquake no doubt was a real earthquake, as the "not long before my day" indicates; and it must have been an impressive one. A generation or so of experience in describing the horrors to visitors might account for the clear sequence of events found in Strabo.

Many of the geographical notices preserved from Timaeus are so brief that we cannot judge them fairly, lacking a context. A few examples will illustrate. Pliny has something to say about two islands near Gades, Spain, but fails to indicate clearly what his main source is (*N.H.* IV, 120 = Tim. F 67). He says Timaeus called the smaller island, the one where Gades was first built, *Aphrodisias*. In this Timaeus and Silenus were agreed, while Philistides and Ephorus called the island *Erythea* instead. The natives called it *Juno's Island*. The larger island, according to Timaeus, was named *Cotinusa* from the wild olive tree (the κότινος), while the Phoenicians named it *Gadir* from a word of their own meaning "hedge" (*saepes*); the Romans referred to it as *Tartessos*. Pliny may well have obtained this from one late source. Timaeus, with his special interest in the Phoenicians and with Pytheas' account as well as the Tyrian histories at his disposal,[41] undoubtedly had much more to say. The same thing applies to his description of Corsica, the only direct allusion to which is an unfriendly one by Polybius (XII, 3, 7 = Tim. F 3).[42] Polybius tells us that he mentioned the wild animals, as well as the people who lived on the island while hunting them, and that he wrote badly and carelessly. Massilia, too, was evidently treated at some length by Timaeus, as his remarks about the five mouths of the Rhone (F 70 = Strabo IV, 1, 8)[43] and about the origin of the name of the city seem to suggest (F 72 = Steph. Byz. *s.v.* Μασσιλία).[44] It would be natural for Pytheas to have said a good deal about Massilia, but his only known remark concerns the latitude of the city[45]—and of that there is no trace in Timaeus.

Another passage (F 57 = Antig. *Hist. mir.* 152) is slightly more illuminating. It is about Lake Avernus, and may be translated as follows:

Heracleides writes that no birds fly over the Sarmatian swamp, for whatever comes near it dies from the fetid odor. This seems to be true of Aornitis [*i.e.* L. Avernus] and this report has usually been accepted. However, Timaeus regards it as false, for most creatures living near it do well. He says this, moreover: "The surrounding area is very woody, and the multitude of branches and leaves—now driven together, now pushed apart by the wind—nothing can be seen above it; but it appears to be deserted."

Here we find Timaeus on the side of the angels, insisting on a reasonable explanation rather than a sensational one. But the context is far from clear. If some other writer had applied Heracleides' argument about the Sarmatian swamp to Lake Avernus, Timaeus, who had no respect for Heracleides,[46] would certainly not have been convinced. As is characteristic of Greek historians in general, Timaeus assumes the report about Lake Avernus to have a basis (the name itself is proof of that), but does not take what would seem to us the more direct method of saying that he, or someone he knew about, had gone to Lake Avernus and had seen birds flying over it. Instead, according to the rules of the game, he accepts the report, then seeks to rationalize it. Like other historians, he is greatly impressed by etymologies.

Somewhat different are three references, each to a river. The first is very brief (Tim. F 46 = Antig. *Hist. mir.* 134): "Timaeus, writing about Italian rivers, says the Crathis dyes one's hair a tawny color." Aristotle, no less, held that animals sometimes change the color of their hair with a change of water (*Hist. An.* III, 12). In number 169 of *De Mirabilibus Auscultationibus* (*On Marvellous Things Heard*), a treatise falsely assigned to Aristotle, we read about two rivers, the Sybaris and the Crathis. The former makes people timid, the latter makes them *tawny-haired*. The pseudo-Aristotelian *Physiognomica* is filled with data on the relationship between the color of a man's skin, hair, or eyes, and his character—whether he is courageous or cowardly, and so on.[47] Probably Timaeus is attempting to give some scientific-sounding explanation for the character and the history of the people he is describing.

The second river is the Althaenus in Apulia. Its name comes from its power to heal (ἀλθαίνειν) wounds. Apparently this healing quality is connected with a legendary tale about Podalirius (a Greek hero who came to Italy after the Fall of Troy), and therefore should not be judged as primarily geographical.[48] Likewise, Timaeus' account of the Po, for which Polybius upbraids him, was probably a part of the legend about Phaethon and his unhappy attempt to manage Apollo's chariot (Tim. F 68 = Polyb. II, 16, 13).[49]

Perhaps the best-known geographical howler attributed to Timaeus concerns the fountain of Arethusa on Ortygia, the famous island fortress of Syracuse. Three writers have mentioned it, but we will content ourselves with Strabo's version (VI, 2, 4 = Tim. F 41c):[50]

Ortygia, being close in, is connected with the mainland by a bridge, and it contains the fountain of Arethusa, which immediately empties itself into the sea as a river. The story goes that this is the Alpheius, which rises in the Peloponnese and then crosses the sea, its stream remaining underground until Arethusa. They reason on the basis of the following: that a bowl thought to have fallen into the river reappeared in the fountain, and that the fountain becomes clouded up by the sacrifice of cattle in Olympia. Accepting this, Pindar wrote: "Sacred resting place of Alpheius, offspring of illustrious Syracuse, Ortygia." And Timaeus the historian follows Pindar in this.

Strabo refutes this, not on theoretical grounds, but on the basis of observation. The mouth of the Alpheius is well known, and the river clearly does not sink into the ground. Evidently, Timaeus cannot find it in his heart to question a report linking Syracuse with Olympian Zeus. That Pindar had accepted it made the interpretation almost official. Yet surely Timaeus, who had visited Olympia, did not believe this story;[51] nor could he have expected any of his educated readers to do so. But Strabo and Polybius were both inclined to be literal-minded, showing perhaps that same lack of delicacy toward an old myth for which Arrian later rebukes Nearchus (Arr. *Ind.* 31, 9).[52] Our judgment is hampered by not knowing the context, and Timaeus is entitled to the benefit of a doubt.

To Timaeus geography and history were intimately connected, and in his treatment of the early legends he seems to belong to the Herodotean tradition, rather than to that of Thucydides, or Polybius for that matter. Polybius congratulates himself on his choice of the period to be described in his history, not merely because of its significance, but also because he had played a part in it and had lived through most of it (Polyb. III, 4, 12–13). The inference is that the historian, as such, confines himself to the period of his own experience, and Polybius despises any writer who merely reads over the earlier histories at his leisure and finds fault with them (Polyb. XII, 27, 3–4). The idea that experiences of a later age help in the interpretation of an earlier one is foreign to his way of thinking about history. Instead, his real interest lies in influencing future events by correctly interpreting the past. He believes strongly in the educational value of the study of history for future statesmen (I, 1, 2).

In his treatment of legendary material, Timaeus probably made a conscious distinction between history and prehistory, as indeed others had done before him.[53] Whether he drew the line at the first Olympiad may be doubted, in view of his having assigned a precise date to the founding of Rome, "the thirty-eighth year *before* the first Olympiad" (Tim. F 60 = Dion. H. *A.R.* I, 74, 1), though that is not conclusive. Perhaps he tried to equate what he found in the Tyrian histories with Olympic dates. Did he, like Herodotus, leave a "no man's land" between the two epochs, or like Hellanicus did he attempt a continuous narrative?[54] These questions, easy to ask but hard to answer, may be kept in mind as we go along.

One of the tales in which Timaeus took particular interest was that of Jason and the Argonauts. Our informant is Diodorus (D.S. IV, 56, 3–6 = Tim. F 85):

Not a few of the old writers and also later historians, including Timaeus, say that after they had snatched up the fleece, the Argonauts were found out by Aeëtes, and the outlet from the Pontus secured by ships; but that the Argonauts performed an amazing exploit worthy of being remembered. For they sailed up the Tanais river to its source, and then, hauling their ship overland to a certain place, descended another river that flows into Ocean, and embarked upon the sea, changing course from north to west, and keeping the land on their left. In the neighborhood of Gades they entered our sea. (4) And they offer proofs of this account, saying that the Celts who live by Ocean show special regard for the Dioscuri among their deities. For the arrival of these gods from Ocean has been handed down to them from ancient times. Also, there were not a few place names in the countries beside the sea derived from the Argonauts and the Dioscuri. (5) Likewise, the mainland inside Gades bears tokens of their return. For when they were near Etruria, they sailed across to the island named *Aethaleia* [*i.e.* Elba], and its harbor, the finest in those parts, they called *Argous* after their ship; and the name has endured to the present day. (6) In addition to the places mentioned in Etruria, they also named one harbor *Telamon*, and the port of Formiae in Italy they called *Aeëtes*—now Caiëta. Further, cast forth by winds on the Syrtes, and learning about this sea from Triton, who was ruling in Libya at the time, and escaping from their perils, they presented the bronze tripod inscribed in antique letters, which remained among the Euesperitae until recent times.[55]

This passage illustrates beautifully the plasticity of legend, always lending itself to new interpretations. Timaeus, writing about the west, is interested in making his subject as attractive as possible by transplanting legendary material wherever he can. In this he is aided by the existence of many variants in the stories and also by the vagueness of the geographic setting. The age of scientific geography had come, and it seemed as natural to try to locate the Cave of Polyphemus as it does for us to concern ourselves with the geographic background for Beowulf's adventures. And Timaeus has shown great ingenuity in this field of myth-historiography. The golden fleece had long since been associated with Colchis on the eastern shore of the Black Sea—in the Caucasus—but the details of the return voyage of the Argo had not been standardized. Everyone had assumed, however, that they returned by a circuitous route. To have come through the Bosporus and the Dardanelles would have been most unheroic, like the *purchase* of rights in the Holy Land by Frederick II. They are deterred not by Aeëtes and his squadron but by the law of their own being. They must return by some unusual and spectacular route, one that would lead to a fresh series of adventures. Since Alexander and Patrocles, there had been a revival of interest in the northeast and the problem of the Caspian,[56] while Pytheas had aroused men's curiosity about the northwest and Thule. Timaeus cleverly combines the two in his version of the Voyage of the Argonauts. The *join* is quite clear when he says, with convenient lack of precision: "For they sailed up the Tanais river to its source, and then, hauling their ship overland *to a certain place*, descended another river that flows into Ocean." A portage truly worthy of that boatload of heroes! But he also offers proof of a myth-historiographical kind—place names to show the passage of the Argo, documentary evidence in the form of a "bronze tripod inscribed in antique letters," though unhappily this tripod has recently disappeared. This is no attempt to hoodwink the reader. Timaeus is following the rules of myth-historiography and in writing about the Argo he is entitled to be as "Bergaean" as he likes;[57] his object is plausibility, still the chief requirement for writing prehistory. Briefer notices from the scholiast on Apollonius add a few details. The marriage of Jason and Medea, assigned by Antimachus of Colophon to the Colchian land and by Dionysius of Miletus to Byzantium, was boldly transferred by Timaeus to the western island of Corcyra, where annual sacrifices in the temple of Apollo still commemorated the original sacrifice offered by Medea.[58]

But if the west was to hold its own with the Greek world of the Aegean, its legendary past must be connected with the traditions about the Trojan War. The fragments are less satisfactory here, but their tendency is unmistakable. Timaeus evidently had little admiration for Homer, whom he condemns on the basis of a favorite theory of his that writers reveal their own character by what they like to write about. The fondness of the Homeric heroes for barbecued ox proves that Homer was a glutton (Tim. F 152 = Polyb. XII, 24). We may, perhaps, see some reflection here of the iconoclastic views of the witty Xenophanes, who unquestionably had a claim to Timaeus' admiration on two counts—he was a very famous man and, even more important, he emigrated to the west.[59] Timaeus seems to have used the Fall of Troy as a springboard in dealing with colonization. Since no one believed the Greeks originated in the west, the next best thing was to bring them west as early as possible and under the most distinguished leadership.[60] Most of what he wrote on this can no longer be identified, though much probably survives in Strabo, Diodorus, and, indirectly, Virgil. However, we have one good example of his methods in the following tale about Diomedes (F 53 = Schol. Lycophr. *Al.* 615):

When Troy was taken Diomedes placed stones from the city wall in his ship to serve as ballast. Reaching Argos, where he was driven off by his wife, Aegialea, he went on to Italy. There, finding the Scythian serpent ravaging the Phaeacian land, he slew it acquiring the golden shield of Glaucus, which the serpent had mistaken for the ram's golden fleece. Held in high honor for this deed, he made statues [*i.e.* of himself] from the stones of Troy. Timaeus relates this, as does Lycus, in his third book. Later, Daunus killed him, and threw his statues into the sea. However, buoyed up by the waves, they returned to their pedestals. Such is the tale.

The remarkable behavior of the ocean waves is a little reminiscent of that magic lake described by Polycritus of Mende. This lake, at first no larger than a shield, obligingly expanded to permit fifty men or beasts to bathe in its waters. But when that number had been reached, it would swell up and hurl the bathers back on to dry land.[61] Timaeus seems to have taken quite an interest in the dismantling of the battlements of Troy. The other known example concerns Periander, who is said to have aided Pittacus of Mitylene to erect defenses against the Athenians with stones from Troy. In making this statement Timaeus ran afoul of Demetrius of Scepsis (F 129 = Strabo XIII, 1, 39), an expert on Troy who, according to Strabo, wrote thirty books commenting on some sixty lines in Homer (Strabo XIII, 1, 45). Demetrius is said to have been contemporary with Aristarchus of Samos and with Crates of Mallus (Strabo XIII, 1, 55), and must have found himself frequently in disagreement with Timaeus. He had his own views about the Argo. Relying on a passage in Mimnermus he transfers Aeëtes and the golden fleece to the outer sea east of Asia (Strabo I, 2, 40). In general, his legendary world lies in the east. He is quoted by Strabo in opposition to those who held that Aeneas left Troy for the west at the end of the war (XIII, 1, 53). Ti-

maeus may have been the most influential writer who made extensive
use of the Trojans to people the western world, but he was not the first
to do so. We have a provocative bit from Alcimus the Sicilian, preserved
by the Roman grammarian Festus, which reads as follows (Alcim. 560
F 4):[62]

Alcimus says that Tyrrhenia bore Aeneas a son, Romulus, and that Romulus was the
father of Aeneas' granddaughter, Alba, whose son, Rhomus by name, founded the
city of Rome.

An interesting point here is that through Tyrrhenia's marriage with
Aeneas, Alcimus has linked Rome both with the Etruscans and with
Troy. He may have been the first to connect Aeneas with Rome; Anti-
ochus of Syracuse, at least, seems not to know of such a relationship.[63]
But Timaeus accepted it, and the popularity of his work may explain
why we have so few references to Alcimus' *Sicelica*. Characteristically,
Timaeus supports his version by appealing to a religious ceremony, as we
learn from a fragment preserved by Polybius (XII, 4b = Tim. F 36):

In his *Pyrrhus*, again, he says that the Romans, still mindful of the destruction of
Troy, on a fixed day shoot down a war horse in the place called *Campus* before the
city—because Troy was taken by means of the so-called Wooden Horse.

This shows not only that Timaeus connected Rome with the Trojans,
but also that he knew enough about Rome to have heard of the *Campus
Martius*. This is a local touch missing in the fragments of earlier writers.
Polybius interprets the horse sacrifice differently, as a form of hippomancy widely practised among the barbarians, but he does not deny
Timaeus' statement of fact (Polyb. XII, 4b). Evidently the account was
based on accurate local information, then interpreted along the lines
suggested by Alcimus. Further proof of his theory was found by Timaeus
in the Trojan artifacts, "sacred *caducei* of iron and bronze, and Trojan
earthenware vessels lying in the innermost shrines of Lavinium." And
Dionysius tells us Timaeus said he got his information "from the inhabitants of the area" (Dion. H. *A.R.*, I, 67, 4 = Tim. F 59). It may be
doubted whether anyone had a clear idea about Trojan artifacts so
many years before Schliemann, and it may also be doubted whether the
"inhabitants of the area" were responsible for the identification. But old
sacred objects there must have been, which Timaeus interpreted as he
chose. Incidentally, this bit of Roman archaeology, like the horse sacrifice, probably belongs to the last part of Timaeus' work. We find the
following statement by Pliny about Roman coinage (*N.H.* XXXIII, 43
= Tim. F 61):

King Servius was the first to coin bronze; before that Timaeus relates that they used crude metal in Rome. It was stamped with the image of a cow (*pecus*) and so came to be called *pecunia*.

Pliny remarked just before that "the Roman people did not even use silver coins before the defeat of King Pyrrhus," and it is possible that he also got this from Timaeus. If he did, then Timaeus may have worked up his Roman archaeology when he came to write the continuation of his *History*, which dealt with Pyrrhus. It is possible that he visited (or revisited?) Italy after his return from Athens. He must, at any rate, have known something of the traditions about Servius Tullius.

Like Alcimus, Timaeus also goes back to the founding of Rome, as reported with some misgivings by Dionysius of Halicarnassus:[64]

The final colonization, or foundation, or whatever it ought to be called, of Rome, says Timaeus the Sicilian, took place at the same time as the founding of Carthage— though I do not know what system he used—in the thirty-eighth year before the first Olympiad [*i.e.* 814/3 B.C.].

Dionysius is mystified by the conflicting testimony that Rome was founded either right after the Fall of Troy or fifteen generations later. To complete his bafflement, Antiochus of Syracuse recorded a Rome even before the time of Aeneas and the Trojan refugees.[65] No wonder Timaeus' date, which coincided with none of the others, is a source of embarrassment. What interests us here is the association between the founding of Rome and of Carthage, a happy coincidence inspired by events late in Timaeus' life. The determining factor for him is apt to have been Carthage. As a Sicilian historian he must have been concerned with Carthage from the beginning. In fact, his claim to have consulted the Tyrian histories bears this out (F 7 = Polyb. XII, 28a, 3). It is with considerable interest, therefore, that we read the following fragment, preserved by an anonymous writer (F 82 = Anon. *De mul.* 6, p. 215 West):

Theiosso: Timaeus says this is what Elissa was called in the Phoenician tongue, the sister of Pygmalion, King of Tyre; and he says that she founded Libyan Carthage. When her husband was slain by Pygmalion she put her possessions on shipboard and fled with some of the citizens, reaching Libya after many sufferings. Because of her extensive wanderings she was called *Deido* locally, by the Libyans. When she founded the aforementioned city, the Libyan king wished to marry her, but she refused him; however, she was pressed by the citizens. On the pretext of carrying out a rite to release her from her oaths [*i.e.* not to marry], she constructed a huge pyre near her house; when it had been lighted, she threw herself from her chamber on to the pyre.

The synchronism between Rome and Carthage, adopted by Timaeus, left a gap between the Fall of Troy and the founding of Rome, and thus provided Aeneas with the opportunity for many heroic deeds once assigned to Odysseus, and also left an interval of several centuries for the adventures of his pre-Roman descendants. But Timaeus represents a transitional stage. There is no reason to doubt that he is the source for Diodorus' picturesque account of the Liparian (or Aeolian) islands, particularly since the combination of legend and common sense suits Timaeus so well. Diodorus writes (V, 7, 7 = Tim. F 164):

Now this Aeolus is the one the mythologers say Odysseus visited during his wanderings. They say he was pious and upright, and that he was kind to strangers; also that he introduced the use of sails for his ships, and that by observing the indications of the fires [*i.e.* the volcanic ones] he could accurately predict the local winds. They say that he was called the friend of the gods because of his great piety.[66]

In Diodorus' account there is an idyllic interlude in the islands under Aeolus and his descendants, following which comes the known Greek colonization from Cnidus and Rhodes, which will be discussed in the following chapter.[67]

Another welcome survival of Timaeus' description of early Italy was best preserved for us by Aulus Gellius (*N.A.* XI, 1, 1 = F 42a):

Timaeus, in the history he wrote about the deeds of the Roman people, and M. Varro, in his *Antiquities of Human Affairs*, say that the land of Italy was named from a Greek word; for cattle were called *italoe* in ancient Greek. There were a great number of them in Italy, and the pastures in that land were wont to produce and breed many cattle.

This might suggest that much of what Timaeus wrote on Italian archaeology was connected with his account of Rome, and that for this reason it was introduced into the sequel of the *History*. But Timaeus wrote extensively on Locri and other Italian cities, and he cannot have failed to discuss the meaning of *Italy* early in his work. The implication that he was primarily a Roman historian is, of course, demonstrably false. It is worth noting that here Timaeus rejects the mythological interpretation that Italy was named for *Italus*, the bull pursued by Heracles across the straits from Sicily to Italy.[68]

But Timaeus was also interested in the ancient Etruscans. This was already a familiar topic in Greek historiography.[69] Timaeus belongs with those who upheld an eastern origin for the Etruscans, bringing them west from Lydia under the leadership of Tyrrhenus.[70] Their luxury (τροφή) was proverbial, and perhaps Timaeus had a theory that the older cities of Magna Graecia were ruined by soft living, and he held the Etruscans responsible. At least he does speak of the great admiration for Etruscan ways felt by the much-maligned citizens of Sybaris (F 50 = Athen. XII,

17, p. 519B); there may have been some connection between the Etruscans and the debauched city of Siris (F 51 = Athen. XII, 25, p. 523C). Of the Etruscans themselves, we have Timaeus' rather cryptic remark about their naked maidservants, which can best be understood by referring back to the clearer references in Theopompus and Alcimus.[71]

It may seem strange that so little remains in the Timaean fragments about prehistoric Sicily. We may note, however, that Timaeus disagrees with Philistus, who held that the earliest inhabitants, the Sicans, crossed over from Spain.[72] Timaeus regarded them as authocthonous[73] and he is probably responsible for Diodorus' elaborations. At first they occupied all Sicily, then because of the severe eruptions of Mt. Aetna, they retreated from the eastern coast, leaving the way open at a later time for the Sicels, their future enemies (D.S. V, 6, 3 = F 164). It is also probable that Diodorus followed Timaeus in localizing the Rape of Corē (Persephone) in Sicily (D.S. V, 4, 2), and also in awarding Sicily the honor of being the first grain-growing land (D.S. V, 2, 4). Heracles, too, came to be intimately connected with Sicily and Timaeus probably wrote about him in some detail.[74] But we cannot be sure that what remains in Diodorus comes from his pen. The attested fragments are meager. Here is an example (F 90 = D.S. IV, 22, 6):

When Heracles reached the Straits and the narrowest part of the sea, he transported his cattle to Sicily. He, himself, seizing a bull by the horns, swam across the Straits, a distance of thirteen stades, according to Timaeus.

Is Timaeus responsible for anything here except for the distance across? We cannot tell. He does describe Heracles' adventures in Italy, including his battle with giants on the Phlegraean Plain (F 89 = D.S. IV, 21), and he mentions the activities of Hyllus (Heracles' son) as a colonizer in Dalmatia (F 77 = Ps. Scymnus *Perieg.* 405). But we lack details comparable to those about Jason and the Argonauts. We may mention, in passing, a graceful little tale preserved by Parthenius about a mortal who fell in love with a nymph (Parthen. *Narr. am.* 29 = F 83). The setting is on the slopes of Mt. Aetna and the theme is the familiar one of jealousy and retribution. The human lover proved unfaithful, despite stern warnings from his immortal mistress. He fell from grace after "one of the Sicilian queens," as she is called, had plied him with wine. His outraged spouse then blinded him. Perhaps this is the sort of thing Clement of Alexandria had in mind when he wrote:[75] "But they charge Theopompus and Timaeus with myths and calumnies." On the other hand, Theopompus prides himself on his tall stories and sometimes, like

Plato, he invents myths for his own purposes.[76] Timaeus, however, seems to have had genuine feeling for folklore as such.

Before concluding this survey of Timaeus' remarks about the mythological or prehistoric period, we need to question his attitude toward the primitive. Can he be trusted to describe backward peoples as they actually were, or is his account deflected by the effort to be entertaining and by the desire to paint an exciting picture of the west? Does he regard the outer world only through the film of Greek literary associations? Does he know how to distinguish the primitive from the legendary? The long Diodorus passage printed by Jacoby as an appendix to the fragments contains much ethnographical material which, if Timaeus could be proved to be the source, would help to answer these questions. This is particularly true of the descriptions of the Balearic islands (D.S. V, 17–18), of Corsica (V, 13, 3–14, 4), and of Sardinia (V, 15). And some of this must come from Timaeus. In mentioning Majorca, Diodorus refers to it as (V, 17, 1), "the largest of all the islands except for the seven—Sicily, Sardinia, Cyprus, Crete, Euboea, Cyrnus [Corsica] and Lesbos." According to Strabo, this same remark about Majorca was made by Timaeus (Strabo XIV, 2, 10 = F 65), and since it is both unusual and wrong, Diodorus must here be following Timaeus. Furthermore, Diodorus reports that there were over 30,000 inhabitants on these islands (D.S. V, 17, 2). In speaking of Corsica he also says "their numbers amount to upwards of 30,000" (V, 14, 4), a resemblance that suggests the same source. Also, the interest shown in Etruscans (V, 13, 4) and Carthaginians (V, 15, 4–5; 17, 4), as well as the references to Heracles (V, 15, 1–2; 17, 4) would be appropriate for Timaeus.[77] Let us take a closer look at Diodorus' account of Sardinia:[78]

15. Next [*i.e.* following Corsica] is the island named Sardinia, comparable in size with Sicily, and inhabited by barbarians called Iolaeis, thought to be descended from the Thespiaeans who settled there with Iolaus. In the period when Heracles was accomplishing his celebrated labors he had many children by the daughters of Thespius, and in accordance with an oracle he sent them off to Sardinia, along with a considerable force of Greeks and barbarians, to establish a colony. (2) Iolaus, Heracles' nephew, was in charge; he seized the island and built worthy cities on it. Portioning out the land, he called the people Iolaëis after himself, and he built gymnasiums, temples to the gods, and everything else to make life agreeable—indications of which (ὑπομνήματα) remain to our time. For the fairest plains are called Iolaëia, getting their name from him; and the people, even now, keep its name derived from Iolaus. (3) The oracle concerning this colony promised those who participated that the colony would preserve its independence forever, and it is remarkable that up to now the oracle has preserved unbroken self-government for the inhabitants. (4) For the Carthaginians, growing powerful and ruling the island, were unable to enslave those who first possessed it, for the Iolaëis fled to the mountains and built houses underground. They raised many herds of cattle, for which there is abundant pasturage, and lived on milk, cheese and meat. Withdrawing from the lowlands they abandoned the unpleasantness of hard work, living an agreeable life in the mountains, and subsisted on the foods mentioned above. (5) Although the Carthaginians often marched against them with considerable forces, they remained free, thanks to the rough terrain and the difficulties of getting at them underground. [Finally, when the Romans took over and frequently marched against them, they remained unconquered by a hostile army, for the same reasons.] (6) Nevertheless, [in the early days] Iolaus returned to Greece after arranging matters in the colony, and the Thespiaeans, having governed the island for many generations, were finally driven out to Italy, where they settled down in the region near Cyme. The rest of the population, being entirely barbarian, chose the best men from among the inhabitants as their leaders, and kept their independence up to our own times.

If we disregard what are obviously interpolations by Diodorus, we see that the Sardinia described here was still under Carthaginian rule, and the natives were entirely non-Greek. Yet this had not always been so. The island was once occupied by a mixed Greek and barbarian population sent out under Heracles' nephew, Iolaus, in accordance with an oracle. We find the hero performing the usual civilizing functions, building gymnasiums and temples, "indications of which remain to our time." These "indications" appear to consist entirely in the alleged name of the inhabitants—the Iolaëis.[79] The physical description of Sardinia, aside from its size and shape,[80] is vagueness itself, plains on the coast, mountains inland. There were "many herds of cattle, for which there is abundant pasturage," and the inhabitants live on "milk, cheese and meat." The detail about "underground houses" is also no true description, but merely a rationalization from the assumption that, in accordance with the oracle, the Sardinians remain free, despite losing the open country to Carthage. Diodorus solemnly affirms that the Sardinians are still free despite Roman attempts to subdue them.[81] There is nothing in this generalized account of Sardinia that Timaeus could not have written in an Athenian library. The whole approach is bookish. Yet perhaps Timaeus read the right books. The fanatical resistance of Sardinians to outside domination is a historical fact based, as we see here, on the inaccessibility of the rugged interior of the island. Also, he is correct in bringing the Carthaginians in at a later date, rather than the Phoenicians of Tyre at an earlier one. The impression is of genuine local tradition, smoothed and polished for literary purposes until the original is almost obliterated. The likelihood that Timaeus did write about Sardinia in detail and therefore the Diodorus passage comes from him is increased by the following attested fragment (F 64):

Sardonic (Σαρδάνιον): proverbial of those who laugh at their own destruction. Timaeus says that the inhabitants of Sardinia, when their parents grow old and are thought to have lived long enough, lead them to the spot where they intend to bury them. Digging holes there, they seat those who are to die at the very edge, and then each strikes his own father with a stick, and thrusts him off into the pit. The old men greet the approach of death happily, and they are destroyed with laughter and cheerfulness. When there is laughter, and yet laughter at something not altogether pleasant, the aforementioned expression is used by the Greeks.

The excerptor is making a collection of various explanation of "sardonic laughter," and that is the only reason he happens to select this precious bit from Timaeus. But surely in the original the situation was reversed, with "sardonic laughter" being put in merely by way of decoration. A little thought may enable us to restore the context of this passage. In the Greek epic tradition, primitive or remote peoples were described in one of two ways, either as living an idyllic life and possessed of every virtue, or as leading a rude, uncivilized, barbarous existence. Of the former, the Ethiopians are the prototype, of the latter, Polyphemus and his fellow Cyclopes. Developments in philosophy, as well as in history and science, led to a subtle elaboration of these two main themes about the primitive,[82] and the expansion of geographic knowledge kept this interest alive, as more and more non-Greek peoples came to be known at first hand. Thrift had been bred into the early Greeks as a virtue necessary for survival. When they met and defeated the opulent Persians, it was not unnatural to attribute their own superiority to a relatively frugal life, and Persia's defeat to effeminacy induced by living off the fat of the land and to luxuriousness (τρυφή). The Greeks came to feel that their frugality had been deliberate, the result of conscious moral choice (the choice of Heracles). Then, alas, luxury also began to make itself felt in the Greek world, and in those sinful days the moralist found his ideal personified in some remote, primitive people. This people, he was prone to believe, like the old Greeks, deliberately avoided gold, silver, and high living.[83] The Cynics urged a return to this primitive natural life so once more man might be master of himself and his fate. Onesicritus, in a very clever passage, puts this Cynic doctrine of the corrosive influence of luxury into the mouth of an Indian sage.[84] But sometimes the Cynic did not keep to an enlightened primitivism; he threw the baby out with the bath water, sacrificing civilization itself in favor of complete individual freedom, however brutish.[85] An opposite tendency was one which traced the development of society from rude beginnings to a civilized state, largely by a series of discoveries or inventions (εὑρήματα).[86] And of course the two views might well be united in any of a succession of cycle theories. In this context an attempt can be made to understand Timaeus' account of Sardinia.

He began, evidently, with a description of the island, which he said was shaped like a sandal (F 63 = Pliny *N.H.* III, 85), and was comparable in size with Sicily itself. He probably made some general remarks about its location, the distance from Corsica,[87] the fertility of the soil, and other natural features. Whether he mentioned any inhabitants before Heracles' day is uncertain. One remembers that the Sicans were autochthonous, but no such theory is needed to explain the population of Sardinia in Timaeus' day. He tells us that Heracles sent both Greeks and barbarians under his nephew, Iolaus, and nothing suggests they met resistance in the island.[88] The oracle led Heracles to choose this site for his settlement by its promise of perpetual freedom. Iolaus establishes no rude primitive society, but a civilized one, building "gymnasiums, temples to the gods and everything else to make life agreeable." Chronologically, the next event is the departure of Iolaus, who "returned to Greece after arranging matters in the colony." All went well for a time, but then the barbarians turned on the Greeks and drove them out, setting up instead an aristocratic government of their own. This still does not suggest a primitive society. But what happens next? The Carthaginians are the villains in the piece. The Iolaëis, relying on the oracle guaranteeing them their independence, withdrew, abandoning "the unpleasantness of hard work, living an agreeable life in the mountains." But although they remained free, the Iolaëis gradually lost the civilized ways of the old colony. The temples were neglected, life became rude and brutish. One example of this latter-day primitivism is their practice of putting the old men to death. And here we are on familiar ground, for this was a practice that had shocked Alexander in Sogdiana and Bactria (see Onesicritus 134 F 5 = Strabo XI, 11, 3), and it shows up in the utopian literature of the day, sometimes as a kind of euthanasia.[89] Timaeus, then, had a theory of progressive deterioration. This began, probably, with the expulsion of the Greeks, but was accelerated by the arrival of the Carthaginians. Perhaps it is not too fanciful to imagine the wrath of Apollo when the barbarians who had driven out the Greeks still relied on his oracle for protection. But, as in the case of Cassandra, Apollo was able to obtain satisfaction without breaking his word. True, the Sardinias remained free, but in doing so they lost everything that makes freedom worth having. In a sense, too, they succumbed to indolence in abandoning "the unpleasantness of hard work, living an agreeable life in the mountains." An examination of Diodorus' account of the Liparian islands[90] and the Timaeus fragment on Dalmatia (F 77)[91] suggests the conclusion that this theory of progressive deterioration was a favorite with him.

To end this examination of Timaeus' account of the prehistoric period with the "sardonic laughter" question, the dispute essentially is about the derivation of the expression: did it come from a word meaning "gaping" or "grinning" (that is, from σαίρειν and σαρδάνιον) or did it owe its origin to Sardinia? Should it be written *sardanic* with a small "s," or *Sardonic* capitalized?[92] The older form probably was *sardanic* and the modern spelling of our own word is in part a tribute to the popularity of Timaeus' innovation. Discussion here will be restricted to three writers, nearly contemporary: Timaeus, Clitarchus, and Demon. Clitarchus describes the practice of the Phoenicians, particularly the Carthaginians, of sacrificing their children to "Cronus" (Melkart). The child was placed in the arms of a bronze image of the god, which then tilted him into the firebox burning brightly underneath. In the process the child's face was contorted so that he appeared to be grinning. This was the origin of "sardonic laughter."[93] Demon in his *Atthis* says that the descendants of the Carthaginians in Sardinia "used to sacrifice their finest prisoners and also the men over seventy years of age to Cronus," who "laughed in order to seem brave."[94] How are these accounts related to one another? If the argument presented earlier for pushing back Timaeus' dates is valid, and also the view defended elsewhere for an early Clitarchus dating,[95] then it is possible, even likely, that Clitarchus and Timaeus wrote independently of one another, and highly probable that Demon wrote with a knowledge of both. His version represents an awkward combination of the Carthaginian sacrifice to "Cronus" and the Sardinian practice of putting old men to death. But the final step in confusing the issue came with the Hannibalic historian, Silenus, who described a plant growing in Sardinia which caused those who tasted it to make a wry face![96]

CHAPTER III

THE GOOD OLD DAYS

REAL PEOPLE and the historical events stretching all the way from the foundations of the Greek colonies in the west down to the renewed Carthaginian offensive of 409 B.C. form the subject of this chapter.

There is no reason to think that Timaeus treated these matters in strictly chronological order, or even that he wrote a continuous narrative for the whole period. Diodorus in his famous description of the palmy days of Agrigentum, just as that city is about to be destroyed by the Carthaginians (XIII, 81, 4), was imitating Timaeus; at least we know that Timaeus also wrote about Acragantine luxury in the corresponding part of his own history (Tim. 566 F 26 = D.S. XIII, 83, 2),[1] and that in the same fifteenth book he also has something to say about that city's famous citizen, Empedocles (Tim. F 26b = D.L. VIII, 51). However, we also learn that he wrote about Empedocles in Books I (F 2 = D.L. VIII, 66),[2] IV (F 6 = D.L. VIII, 67),[3] and IX (F 14 = D.L. VIII, 54); and he may have written about him as late as Book XVIII.[4] This would be exasperating if we were trying to restore the plan of Timaeus' work, but it does not interfere at all with a discussion of the fragments arranged chronologically in accordance with the persons or events to which they allude.

The reasons for calling this second period the "Good Old Days" lie in the fragments themselves. In the prehistoric period the gods and goddesses, heroes and heroines, by their very presence redeem Sicily and the west from the charge of barbarism, of belonging to an outer world, foreign, non-Hellenic. But historic Magna Graecia was not the heart of Hellenism, and well Timaeus came to realize that fact during his long years of exile. Despite Lysander with his Spartans and despite Philip and Alexander with their Macedonians, Athens remained what she had become after the Fall of Miletus, the intellectual and spritual center of the Greek world. An intelligent Sicilian like Timaeus, living in Athens most of his life, could not fail to be impressed by the contrast between the city he knew and her reputation. That reputation, he might well persuade himself, depended to a large extent on the distortion of the facts of history by men of genius like Herodotus and Hellanicus, or even the more objective Thucydides. He may have felt, in modern parlance, that Athens owed her preëminence to favorable publicity. As he studied fur-

---

[1] For notes to chap. iii, see pp. 124–131.

ther, he became more and more convinced of the important yet neglected contribution made by the Greeks in Sicily and the west, and decided to do for them what had already been done for Athens, Sparta, Thebes, and the other Greek cities of the east. It was not enough for the west to share in the glories of a legendary past; her statesmen, philosophers, poets, and soldiers must also be given their due. But Timaeus was not merely a loyal Sicilian, he was also enough of a realist to recognize that Sicily had fallen on evil days, and was anxious, as a historian, to find the reasons for it. He was far too much under the influence of prevailing philosophic views to leave out moral causes and he seems particularly to have favored τρυφή, the luxuriousness and effeminacy that come from too much prosperity, as an important factor. But he was perhaps more interested in external causes and in the influence of individuals for good or ill. "The Good Old Days" mark the rise of Sicily and particularly Syracuse to a position of great importance politically and culturally. The resounding victory over Carthage at Himera corresponds with eastern victories over Persia, and the architect of victory, Gelon, is idealized despite doctrinaire objections to tyranny as such. Equally creditable was the dogged defense of Syracuse against the Athenians, with characteristic underestimation of Spartan aid.[5] Shortly afterward, however, came the Carthaginians, whose destruction of Selinus, Himera, and Agrigentum brought the period abruptly to a close.

Fragment 12, one of the longest in the whole collection and one which, like so many others, we owe to Polybius (XII, 5, 1 ff.), deals with the colony of Locri in southern Italy, and Polybius' interest in the subject is personal as well as professional. He had himself been on particularly good terms with Locri and its citizens, whose gratitude he won by obtaining their release from certain burdensome military obligations to Rome (Polyb. XII, 5, 1–2). But above every other consideration he is interested in refuting Timaeus. The latter had come to the defense of Locri against what he regarded as the slanderous statements made about that colony by Aristotle. In addition to this long fragment there are several others having to do with Locri, which can be grouped together for discussion— FF 11; 130a; 130b; 146a; 146b. After explaining his own cordial feeling toward Locri, which has had the effect of prejudicing him in their favor, Polybius goes on to say (XII, 5, 4–8):

(4) Nevertheless, I have not hesitated to say and to write that the history of the settlement handed down by Aristotle happens to be more reliable than that of Timaeus. (5) For I am convinced by those who agree that the report of the colonization given by Aristotle, but not that by Timaeus, has been transmitted to them from their fore-

fathers. They offered the following proofs of this. (6) First, that all the honors of descent among them derive through the female, and not through the male line—such, for instance, as the descendants of the One Hundred Houses being regarded as noble. (7) For these were the One Hundred Houses chosen by the Locrians in the period before the colony was sent, and from which the Locrians, in accordance with the oracle, intended to select the maidens to be sent to Ilium. (8) Some of these women went along with the colony, and their descendants are even now regarded as noble, and called the descendants of the One Hundred Houses.

So far, Polybius has brought out only one significant fact—that noble lineage was traced from the One Hundred Houses through the female line. This peculiarity of Locri had to be explained by the usual device of an aetiological myth. Timaeus, too, must have explained the custom, though obviously his explanation differed from Aristotle's. But there is a common background in the legend about the maidens sent to Ilium. We are fortunate here in having Timaeus' account preserved in another fragment, which may be translated as follows (F 146b = Tzetz. Lycophr. *Al.* 1141):

Locrian Ajax, being cast ashore near the Gyrae, was buried in Tremon, a part of Delos. The Locrians, managing to escape, reached their home. Death and plague gripped Locris after the third year, because of Ajax' impious treatment of Cassandra. And the God said in an oracle that they should propitiate the Goddess Athena in Ilium for 1,000 years, sending out two maidens chosen by lot. The Trojans intercepted them, and when they got their hands on the maidens slew them, burning their bodies with wood from uncultivated non-fruitbearing trees; their bones they threw from Mt. Traron of Troy, and their ashes they cast into the sea. But the Locrians sent others. If they got through, they were to enter the temple of Athena by stealth and to sweep and sprinkle it. But they were not to approach the goddess, nor initiate their rites except at night. Their hair was cut short, they wore no sandals and only one garment. The first Locrian maidens to arrive were Periboea and Cleopatra. At first the Locrians sent grown maidens, then one-year-olds with their nurses. When 1,000 years had gone by, at the end of the Phocian War, they stopped this sacrifice, as Timaeus the Sicilian says.

Here Timaeus gives us what must be accepted as historic fact—the Locrian priestesses at Ilium and their withdrawal after the Phocian War. Evidently the origins of this cult were lost in obscurity and the Ajax story adopted by way of explanation. The 1,000 years results in an earlier date for the Fall of Troy than the date later canonized by Eratosthenes.[6] Presumably this legend was official and would have been given by Aristotle just as it was by Timaeus, that is, Timaeus also must have said that the priestesses always came from the One Hundred Houses. But here agreement ends. Following Aristotle, Polybius says: "Some of these women went along with the colony, and their descendants are even now regarded as noble. . . ." Since Polybius, too, survives only in fragments, this statement has to be explained by remarks made elsewhere.[7] The explanation given by Polybius-Aristotle was that the Locrians assisted Sparta in the Messenian War, and while the Locrian men were away the women consoled themselves by forming alliances with the slaves, whom their masters had left behind. Consequently a difficult social problem loomed when at last the army returned, but was solved by sending a colony to Italy, composed of young women from the One Hundred Houses along with their slave paramours.

But Aristotle offers one more bit of evidence, of historic fact, which Polybius summarizes (XII, 5, 9–11):

Again, a similar story has been handed down to them [*i.e.* the Locrians in Italy] about Phialephorus (Cupbearer). (10) For at the time when they drove out the Sicels, who held that part of Italy, and whose sacrifices were conducted by the noblest best-born youth, they adopted a number of Sicel customs *because they had no ancestral customs of their own*—and also they adopted this practice from them. (11) But they revised the custom, not making one of their *boys* Phialephorus, but choosing a *girl*, because their lineage was based on the female line.

This is historicizing at its worst. It has no independent value, being introduced merely to bolster up a preconception based on the one tangible fact about female ancestry. What follows in Polybius describes Locrian sharp practice in evading their oaths to uphold their treaty with the Sicels (XII, 6, 1–6).[8] Aristotle, then, held that Locri began by making a treaty with the Sicels, and next, according to him, a constitution and laws were drawn up for the new colony by the famous lawgiver, Zaleucus (*Pol.* 1274a).[9] Timaeus, starting out in agreement about the Locrian priestesses at Ilium, systematically attacks the other chief points made by Aristotle: (1) That Locri was a colony of former slaves and their paramours; (2) that they broke their treaty obligations with the Sicels; (3) that Zaleucus drafted laws for the new colony. Let us see what can be recovered of Timaeus' refutation of Aristotle. The most serious charge was the one about the slaves. Here Timaeus uses a variety of arguments, some very dubious. He tries to throw Aristotle's account out of court on the general grounds that when the colony was founded the Greeks did not recognize slavery as an institution, as the following passage will demonstrate (F 11a = Athen. VI, 86, p. 264CD):

Timaeus of Tauromenium says in the ninth book of his history: "It was not customary for the Greeks in ancient times to be ministered to by purchased slaves." And he writes: "In general, they blamed Aristotle for being wrong about Locrian *mores*. The Locrians were not accustomed to owning male or female slaves, nor were the Phocians until recent times—for the wife of Philomelus, the man who seized Delphi [*i.e.* in the

Sacred War], was the first to be accompanied by two handmaids. Likewise, Aristotle's friend Mnason, who had 1,000 slaves, was criticized by the Phocians for depriving so many citizens of the necessities of life. It was their custom to have domestic services performed for the older men by the young.

This passage is specially interesting because it preserves Timaeus' own wording and enables us to recapture his point of view. Perhaps nothing in Aristotle is better known than his examination of the institution of slavery in the *Politics*, in which he maintains that slavery is *natural* because some men are fitted by nature to rule, others to serve, and, therefore, it is better for the natural slave to be a slave rather than to be free (*Pol.* 1253b–1255b).[10] Not everyone agreed with Aristotle at the time he wrote;[11] and in the period that followed, antislavery sentiment can be traced in some utopian literature, such as the popular romance of Iambulus.[12] Greek feelings in general about slavery seem not to resemble thse of the nineteenth century, that is, they are not based primarily on humanitarian grounds and individual rights; rather, they are concerned with the bad effects of slavery on the free man. Slavery is treated as a form of τρυφή,[13] of luxury, and as such it has a corrosive influence. Opposition to slavery parallels Puritan objections to bearbaiting. The sturdy Cynics took the lead. When Diogenes was captured by pirates and put up for sale, he is supposed to have pointed with his finger at a wealthy Corinthian, and then to have told the auctioneer: "Sell me to that man— he needs a master!" (D.L. VI, 74.)[14] Timaeus shows his views by appealing to the ancient times when there was no slavery. But menial tasks had to be performed, and his solution of having them carried out by the young people is also a familiar solution, and in the utopian tradition. In his idealized account of the Land of Musicanus on the lower Indus, Onesicritus describes a slaveless society in which the young men do the menial work (Onesic. 134 FF 24 and 25).[15] But Timaeus is not content with refuting Aristotle, he cannot resist the temptation of making a personal remark as well. Therefore, he accuses Aristotle's friend, Mnason, of owning 1,000 slaves. It is interesting that his objection is a practical one, based on the hardship caused the citizens by Mnason's cheap labor force. The slaves, as such, interest him no more than the machines, as such, interested the Luddite rioters.

But Timaeus has another argument against Aristotle's account of Locri which he regards as the clincher (F 12 = Polyb. XII, 9, 1–4):

For he says in the same book [*i.e.* Book Nine] that he no longer relies on arguments based on probability, because he has actually visited the Locrians in Greece, and investigated the matter of the colony. (3) First, they showed him a written treaty with the exiles, which still survives, and which begins with: "As parents toward their children." In addition, there were decrees according to which each enjoyed citizenship rights with the other.

There can be no doubt that Timaeus had seen the treaty he describes, but it is extremely unlikely that the treaty he saw dated back to the establishment of the colony. Oldfather regards the phrase "as parents toward their children" (ὡς γονεῦσι πρὸς τέκνα) as unsatisfactory. As he suggests, it may be a forgery[16] or, as seems more likely, the document may represent a later attempt to commit to writing what had previously been a matter of oral tradition. Presumably the text of the treaty was inscribed at the time when isopolity was established, and perhaps it may have helped to justify this arrangement. Polybius tries to discredit Timaeus as a liar on the grounds that he fails to state *which* Greek Locrian state he visited, which town it was where he saw the treaty, or who was responsible for showing it to him (Polyb. XII, 10, 1–3). Polybius argues persuasively. He points out that Timaeus was always careful to indicate his sources of information when they were good ones. As an example of this, Polybius refers to Timaeus' statements about Italian Locri (XII, 10, 7–9):

(7) For he backs up his testimony by mentioning Echecrates by name, with whom he says he had a conversation on Italian Locrian affairs, (8) and whom he questioned on the subject. Then he adds, lest he be thought to be relying on some chance person, that Echecrates' father had earlier been honored as an envoy by Dionysius. (9) Would such a writer have been reticent about a public document or a commemorative decree if he had got hold of it?

But Polybius is not logical. There was every reason for Timaeus to tell us about Echecrates because Echecrates, not the document, was his source. He did not get his information on the spot, but from an exile. On the other hand, he is giving the substance of public documents he had seen himself while in the mother state. No added support was needed. If Timaeus did not mention whether he found this material in East Locris or West Locris, he is guilty of deplorable carelessness, because there was a difference of opinion as to whether Italian Locri had been founded by the Eastern or by the Western Locrians.[17] Strabo upholds the claims of West Locris, while stating that the contrary view had been maintained by Ephorus (VI, 1, 7). Polybius did not always play fair with Timaeus, if we are to accept the testimony of Athenaeus. Athenaeus tells us that Polybius had refuted "Epitimaeus" on slavery by quoting his own words about Mnason and his 1,000 slaves (VI, 103, p. 272 AB = F 11b). Yet we have seen that Timaeus was speaking only of the very early days when he denied slavery in the Greek world.[18] One would prefer to think that Athenaeus has made a mistake rather than be forced to believe Polybius capable of such gross misrepresentation. The chances are that if Timaeus did not mention which Locris he had visited, it was because he assumed that everyone who had read Aristotle and Ephorus would know he meant East Locris. Had he posited West Locris as the mother country, no doubt Polybius would have included this deviation from the Ephorus party line in his indictment of Timaeus.

Timaeus, then, answered Aristotle's vague references to a treaty between Locri and the Sicels with the text of a treaty between Locri and the mother country. And that was sound historical procedure. But how are we to explain Timaeus' refusal to recognize the work of Zaleucus, when he is usually so anxious to claim all great men possible for the west?[19] We may, perhaps, acquit him on the very respectable ground that he did not find good historical evidence for Zaleucus' existence. Beloch, among the moderns, argued vigorously against the historicity of Zaleucus, and those who disagree with Beloch find rather heavy going. For example, Oldfather says that almost every notice about Zaleucus is apocryphal but none is mythical. He argues that: "The period is late enough to permit the survival of the name of a striking personality, but so early that the actual tradition about the details of his life will certainly have disappeared."[20] How very convenient! But according to Oldfather, just one fact rings true—Zaleucus did attribute his laws to Athena.[21] But with all respect for the grey-eyed goddess, this seems rather a slender basis for accepting the laws as the work of a truly great historical personage. However, Timaeus gives us a clue when he cites Echecrates as his authority for statements about Locri (Polyb. XII, 10, 7–8), and here Oldfather's discussion is helpful.[22] He identifies Echecrates with the Pythagorean, Echecrates of Phlius,[23] a banished nobleman very likely connected by birth with the One Hundred Houses. There had been a bitter struggle in Locri during the time of Dionysius II, culminating in a successful revolt. The nobility had become very unpopular, and no doubt there was an outpouring of abuse on both sides. The dim figure of Zaleucus must have taken on new substance, claimed as an aristocrat by the nobles, and, according to Oldfather, held to have been a slave in the democratic version.[24] It seems more likely that once Zaleucus had become identified with the popular cause, he was painted as a slave in the aristocratic counter-propaganda. Thereupon the democrats retaliated with their scandalous story about the servile origin of the nobility.[25] Timaeus, examining the evidence, rejected the propaganda on both sides for what it was, and came to the sensible conclusion that Zaleucus was not a real person at all.[26] It is unnecessary to deal with the subsidiary arguments used by Timaeus and answered by Polybius.[27] They add little force one way or the other to the main arguments. Our conclusion about this whole controversy must be that the honors go to Timaeus, though his documentary proof no longer carries much weight. Moreover, the identification of Echecrates with the Pythagorean living in Phlius suggests that he may also have been Timaeus' leading source on Pythagoras and the early philosophers of Magna Graecia.

Timaeus mentioned other early philosophers, such as Epimenides (F 4 = D.L. I, 114)[28] and Xenophanes,[29] but he seems to have been especially interested in Pythagoras (FF 13; 14; 16; 17; 131; 132) and Empedocles (FF 2; 6; 14; 26; 30; 134). This is understandable in a western Greek, since they were undoubtedly the most famous of all the western intellectuals, and for a historian there was the additional attraction that they had also taken part in politics. The Pythagoreans were finally killed or driven out of Italy, but for the time they constituted an important force, controlling Croton and other cities.[30] Pythagoras and the Pythagoreans are among the most fascinating subjects in Greek history, although it is almost impossible for us now to separate fact from fancy because of the neo-Pythagorean movement that transformed or obliterated the original. Unhappily, the fragments of Timaeus contribute virtually nothing to our knowledge of the philosophy of Pythagoras. However, though they give us no clue to the early Pythagoreans, still, together with the fragments of Dicaearchus of Messene[31] and Aristoxenus of Tarentum,[32] they do give us something of the earlier stages of the legends about him. We have not yet reached the extravagances of Porphyry or Iamblichus.[33]

In one of the Plato scholiasts we find the following statement (F 13a = Schol. T Plat. *Phaedr.* 279C):

Now Timaeus writes as follows in the ninth book: "When young men approached him [*i.e.* Pythagoras], and wished to stay with him, he would never accept them right off, but told them that all who joined must have their property in common." Then somewhat later he remarks: "They were the first in Italy to say, 'Friends have things in common.'"

Evidently, as with "sardonic laughter," various explanations of the origins of the phrase (κοινὰ τὰ τῶν φίλων) were given. The scholiast also cites Aristotle on the matter, but the passage does not link the phrase with Pythagoras.[34] After placing their possessions in the common pool the neophytes spent five years studying Pythagoras' doctrines. Only after this testing period were they admitted to the presence of the great man

(F 13b = D.L. VIII, 10). Another fragment relates particularly to the divine names bestowed by Pythagoras on women at the four stages of a woman's life (F 17 = D.L. VIII, 11).[35] There is also an obscure fragment which indicates approval of Pythagoras and an extreme dislike for Heraclitus (F 132 = Schol. Eurip. *Hecabe* 131).[36] Pythagoras' daughter is also mentioned, probably with a view to emphasizing the high rank of the family (F 131 = Porphyry *V. Pyth.* 4).

One rather odd passage from Athenaeus is worth quoting (F 16 = Athen. IV, 56, p. 163EF):

In the ninth book of his history Timaeus of Tauromenium writes as follows: "Diodorus, an Aspendian by birth, introduced a bizarre way of dressing, and pretended to have lived with the Pythagoreans. When Stratonicus sent him a message, he instructed the messenger to address himself, "To the client of Pythagoras, the man who draws a crowd by his mad animal-skin dress and by his insolence."

Here we may credit Echecrates as a likely source. This sounds like the gossip one might expect about true and false believers at the time the sect was breaking up. Diodorus must have been quite notorious. He was probably referred to in a play by the fourth-century comic poet, Anaxippus;[37] and the third-century biographer, Hermippus, attributes the so-called Pythagorean style of wearing hair to Diodorus (*FHG* III, p. 42 F 26 = Athen. IV, 56, p. 163E). Timon the philosopher alludes to him contemptuously as a Pythagorean vegetarian (Athen. IV, 56, p. 163D). Sosicrates, who probably lived into the second century B.C., says he carried the famous Cynic wallet and staff, and wore his hair long (D.L. VI, 13 = *FHG* IV, p. 503 F 19). Iamblichus still knows about him in the fourth century A.D., as a man reluctantly admitted to the Pythagorean fellowship by Aresas, then head of the society, for lack of men properly trained in Pythagorean doctrine (Iambl. *V. Pyth.* 266).

The Empedocles of the fragments has a strong individual personality, and Timaeus attempts a critical evaluation, which he seems not to have done with Pythagoras. We may begin with the following fragment from Diogenes Laertius (VIII, 66 = F 2):

And later Empedocles dissolved the body of 1,000 [*i.e.* in Acragas], reconstituting it on a three year basis so that it included, not only the wealthy but also the democratically minded. But Timaeus, who often mentions him, says in the first and second (?) book that he displayed opposite views in politics and in his poetry; for though in the former he seemed modest and reasonable, in the latter he was boastful and conceited. For he says, "Hail! I come among you, not a man but an immortal god,"—and the like. While he lived at Olympia he was the object of much attention, and no one was so much talked about when people met, as Empedocles.

In explaining how such a haughty man could have become politically a
democrat, Timaeus relies on his imagination. Aristotle had said that
Empedocles was a free man who hated any kind of rule and had even refused the kingship (D.L. VIII, 63). The opinion of Xanthus of Lydia
that Empedocles was a man of admirably simple tastes also carries special weight because Xanthus takes us back close to Empedocles' day;
Ephorus says Xanthus lived early enough to influence Herodotus.[38] But
Timaeus, perhaps seeking some novel interpretation, traces Empedocles'
political conversion to his irritation over a dinner party. His host was a
member of the Council, and when it was learned that another guest,
also a state dignitary, would be late, the host refused to allow the wine
to be brought in before his arrival. Empedocles objected. When the great
man finally appeared, he was pronounced Master of the Feast. Empedocles, who had demanded wine loudly when there was none, now protested
against being forced to drink at the behest of the Master of the Feast.
He was told to drink up or have the wine poured over his head, where-
upon Empedocles accused his host of setting up a tyranny. The sequel
was that the host and his friend were hauled into court and sentenced to
death (F 134 = D.L. VIII, 63). The merit of the story is that it may have
been a fairly good caricature of the real Empedocles. The extravagance
of the punishment and the generally boisterous behavior of the leading
persons suggest that Timaeus has been reading some pasquinade, perhaps something from one of the comedy writers. Dialogues of this kind,
involving famous men, have a long literary history coming down through
Lucian all the way to Walter Savage Landor. Perhaps Timaeus did not
take the story seriously, and Diogenes Laertius was the first to do so.

Another anecdote shows us Empedocles as the inventor, the man of
many contrivances (F 30 = D.L. VIII, 60):

Timaeus says in the eighteenth book that the man [*i.e.* Empedocles] was admired for
his many inventions. When the Etesian winds were blowing violently and ruining
the crops, he bade them flay some donkeys, and place their hides around the hills
and ridges, and then he stretched them out to hold back the wind. When he was
successful, he was nicknamed "Wind-Stopper" (Κωλυσανέμας).[39]

When Timaeus wrote, the work of arranging the famous philosophers
in schools had begun, along with an awakening interest in the biographies
of illustrious men;[40] but that work was far from complete. The assump-
tions of the doxographer may have been naive, but with their emphasis
on tangible external facts and with their dogmatism they proved effective. Briefly stated, the major premise was that every philosopher was
influenced by a teacher, and he in turn exerted a moulding influence on

at least one student. Once this assumption has been accepted, it becomes possible to construct genealogical trees of philosophers, the branches representing the various sects. Two separate and stately spiritual genealogies of this sort were known to Diogenes Laertius, an Ionian tree stemming from Thales and an Italian one beginning with Pythagoras (see D.L. *Prooemium* 13). Very convenient for the young scholar who needed pegs on which to hang his bits of information, it was often a source of confusion to the historian of philosophy. Timaeus contributes to this literature by telling us that Empedocles was the pupil of Pythagoras (F 14 = D.L. VIII, 54), though others had made him Parmenides' student, and some, probably on chronological grounds, attributed his training to the later Pythagorean, Archytas.[41] More interesting is Timaeus' statement that Empedocles was excluded by Pythagoras because, *like Plato*, he was guilty of plagiarizing (F 14 = D.L. VIII, 54). This reference to Plato suggests that here, as perhaps elsewhere, Timaeus was under obligations to Alcimus.[42] Despite this reflection on Empedocles' character, Timaeus vouches for his distinguished family background, mentioning his grandfather in particular, also an Empedocles (F 26b = D.L. VIII, 51). This grandfather is said to have won a victory in the seventy-first Olympics (496 B.C.) according to Eratosthenes who, like Timaeus, wrote an *Olympionicae*. It is noteworthy that he cites Aristotle rather than Timaeus as his authority (F 26b).[43]

But Timaeus deserves credit for rejecting the sensational stories about Empedocles' death. As in his debate with Aristotle over Locri, his reasoning is sound, but here too he adds trivial considerations that have the effect of blunting the edge of his legitimate arguments. Heracleides Ponticus tells a tale about Empedocles raising a woman from the dead, following which demonstration of his abilities he invited a group of friends to take part in sacrifices in the Field of Peisianax. After the festivities they all retired to sleep; when they awoke, Empedocles was not to be found. One of the servants remembered hearing a loud voice calling Empedocles in the night, and he also noticed a light in the sky and the glow of torches. Subsequently one of the company, Pausanias, made an investigation which led him to conclude that divine honors should be paid to the departed philosopher (D.L. VIII, 67–68). Hippobotus' version is the famous one: Empedocles had thrown himself into the crater of Mt. Aetna to persuade his followers of his divinity, but later one of his sandals had been thrown back from the depths. This version Pausanias is said to have denied.[44] The Timaeus fragment (F 6 = D.L. VIII, 71–72) reads as follows:

(71) Timaeus, however, denies these things, saying positively that he emigrated to the Peloponnese and never returned, and that as a result his ending was obscure. He contradicts Heracleides by name in the fourth (?) book. For Peisianax was a Syracusan, and had no field in Acragas. But Pausanias may, as the report goes, have erected a memorial to his friend, either some sort of statue or shrine, as though to a god—for he was a wealthy man. "But how," he asks, "can he have leaped into the crater when, though it was in the neighborhood, yet he never once alludes to it? Therefore, he died in the Peloponnese. (72) It is not surprising that his tomb is unknown; neither are the tombs of many others known." After several remarks to this effect, Timaeus adds: "But Heracleides is such a thorough-going marvel-monger that he says the man fell out of the moon."

The argument that all the highly colored stories about his death derive from the fact that he died obscurely, a long way from Sicily, is clear and convincing; so is his explanation about the tomb. And that is where he should have stopped. The argument about Peisianax being a Syracusan is weak, and the notion that Empedocles would not have jumped into a crater to which he never referred is senseless—at least as reported by Diogenes Laertius.

But Empedocles was forced to share the honors in Acragas (Agrigentum) with the famous tyrant, Phalaris. Everyone had heard of him when more substantial figures in the Greek past were entirely forgotten, but mostly they were thinking about his famous bull. Timaeus had his own views about the Bull of Phalaris. His opinion carried weight and is reported, apparently with approval, by the scholiast on Pindar's *Pythian Odes*. After referring to the usual story that Phalaris had ordered a bull to be made with a firebox inside, he goes on to say (F 28c = Schol. Pindar *Pyth.* I, 185):

The Acragantines threw the Bull of Phalaris into the sea, according to Timaeus. For the one exhibited in the city is not that of Phalaris, as most people think, but an image of the River Gela.

The scholiast adds that Perilaus, who made the bull for Phalaris, was the first to be burned in it, but here he may no longer be following Timaeus.[45] At the time Timaeus wrote, the Carthaginians still retained the loot they had taken from Acragas in 406/5 B.C. However, in 146 the Romans took Carthage, and Polybius was there with his friend the Younger Scipio when that city was looted and destroyed. As a historian he was very much interested in checking up on Timaeus' story. To his delight a bull was found, complete with a door for introducing the victims. Polybius remarks that there was nothing to suggest that the bull had been made in Carthage. Then he adds (Polyb. XII, 25, 4 = F 28b):

Still, Timaeus attempted to discredit the common report, and to give the lie to the statements of poets and historians, saying that the bull in Carthage did not come from Acragas, and that there had been no such bull in the city.

A century later Diodorus Siculus commented happily on the episode (XIII, 90, 5 = F 28a):

But Timaeus, affirming in his history that this bull never even existed, has been refuted by a chance happening. For about 260 years after this siege Scipio captured Carthage, and sent the bull back to the Acragantines, along with other objects kept by the Carthaginians; and the bull was in Acragas at the time this history was being written. (6) I have been all the more eager to mention the matter, because Timaeus was so sharp in his criticism of the historians who preceded him.

As we examine these passages more closely, we become aware of inconsistencies. No version comes through unscathed. It may help to clarify the situation if we enumerate all possible bulls. Number one is Timaeus' Bull of Phalaris, which he says has been thrown into the sea; number two is the bronze bull transported to Carthage from Acragas by Himilco in 406/5 B.C.; number three is a bull sacred to the River Gela, seen by Timaeus in Acragas in the period between Himilco and Scipio; number four might be a bull known by Timaeus to be on display in Carthage, yet not from Acragas; number five is the bull seen by Polybius, the same bull which, according to Diodorus, was restored to Acragas, where it remained in his time. Now Timaeus, Polybius, and Diodorus, however they may differ in ability and in point of view, should not be regarded as deliberate falsifiers. When any one of them makes a statement of fact based on his own observation, we have no choice but to accept it. Therefore, we must agree that there was a bull in Acragas when Timaeus was there late in the fourth or early in the third century B.C., and again a bull must have been there in the first century when Diodorus was writing his history. We must also agree that the Romans found in Carthage a bull provided with a door for introducing victims, because Polybius saw it. These three animals, then, appear to be attested by the best possible evidence. But Polybius' bull and Diodorus' bull are identical if we are to believe Diodorus, which leaves us with only two bulls vouched for by eye-witnesses, the bull with doors and the bull in honor of the River Gela. They cannot be identified except on the gratuitous assumption that the Carthaginians acquired their bull, not in 406/5 when they sacked Acragas, but at some date after Timaeus and before Polybius, and it is difficult to conceive of a raiding party, however resourceful, stealing the bronze monster some dark night and carrying it off to Carthage undetected. However, it is quite possible that Diodorus and Timaeus saw the same bull, whereas only Polybius saw the bull with doors. Thanks to the scholiast, we know that Diodorus read Timaeus' account carelessly because he thought Timaeus had denied there had ever been a Bull of Phalaris. May he not have been equally careless in stating that Scipio sent the bull back from Carthage to Acragas? This, at least, is not said in what remains of Polybius' account. Naturally, when Diodorus visited Acragas he was shown "The Bull of Phalaris." That is what every tourist expected to see, just as later Arrian, a distinguished Roman official and man of letters, was shown the anchor of the Argo,[46] and the modern visitor to Cos is shown "Hippocrates' Tree." Timaeus, too, had been shown the famous bull, but Timaeus had questioned the identification. Diodorus, however, was not skeptical enough to examine the bull to see if doors were between the shoulder blades; he would have taken the guide's word for it that this was the original bull, captured by the Carthaginians and returned a century earlier by Scipio. And we cannot prove that the guide was lying; we can only wish that Diodorus had borrowed a stepladder. But what of Polybius and his triumphant refutation of Timaeus? Historically, they stand on the same footing; both admit the existence of a Bull of Phalaris, but Polybius' reasoning is not impeccable. He says there is no evidence that his bull had been made in Carthage, *ergo* it came from Acragas. But surely we require more than the absence of a "Made in Carthage" stamp on the bronze to prove its manufacture in Acragas? Carthage was no Greek tourist center. However many stories had been told about the Bull of Phalaris and its theft by the Carthaginians, it is probable that the bull itself only became known to the Greeks after the Fall of Carthage. How is all this to be explained?

There is first of all the story about Phalaris, accepted by both historians. How did it arise? Despite one reference that shows a Phalaris capable of mercy toward his enemies,[47] he is usually depicted as a cruel and inhuman tyrant. Clearchus of Soli, whom Athenaeus refers to as second to none among Aristotle's students (Athen. XV, 62, p. 701C), said that Phalaris was in the habit of devouring infant children (Athen. IX, 54, p. 396E = *FHG* II, p. 309 F 17). Clitarchus tells us that the Phoenicians generally, and particularly the Carthaginians, were accustomed in times of great emergency to sacrifice children, burning them alive inside a bronze statue of Cronus (Clitarchus 137 F 9). Philo of Byblus, who lived during the Roman empire but whose sources on Phoenician history were respectable,[48] also speaks of the Phoenicians as sacrificing their own children to placate outraged divinities (*FHG* III, p. 570 FF 3 and 4). But Philo mentions slaughtering them at an altar, and has nothing to say about burning them inside a statue; perhaps he suppressed this particular barbarism as outmoded and shocking to the public for which he wrote. Given the Greek imagination, is it not likely that the tale about the Bull of Phalaris was a product of early relations with the Phoenicians? They *did* sacrifice children and burn them alive. It would be natural for the Greeks to suggest vengeance rather than atonement as the motive—atonement not having a strong appeal for the Greek temperament—and then to attribute this practice to a shadowy figure like Phalaris, the tyrant of tradition? Returning to the statue of the bull, we cannot decide definitely for or against Polybius. But since his bull had doors in it, and since it is unlikely that this mode of sacrifice was ever used at Acragas, the chances are that it was of Punic manufacture. However, the recovery of a bronze bull from Sicilian waters would certainly reopen the discussion, particularly if an expert could be found to restore Περίλαος ἐποίησε ("Perilaus Made It") on the base.

Behind the Phalaris story probably lay something of Timaeus' theory of history, not, so far as we can see, a theory elaborated separately such as Polybius gives us in his sixth book, but a theory implicit in Timaeus' account of the period. One clue here is the statement that the citizens of Acragas threw the statue into the sea. Perhaps we can supplement this from the Peripatetic writers. Aristotle speaks of Phalaris as having seized power, like the Ionian tyrants, by means of a magistracy (Arist. *Pol.* 1310b 28); and Heracleides says he was justly punished by the people and Alcamenes took over his duties, followed in turn by Alcander, a man of integrity. The consequence was the growth of Acragantine wealth and prosperity. The inhabitants took to wearing expensive clothes dyed with the famous purple dye (*FHG* II, p. 223 F 37). Luxury had arrived full blown, and this would doubtless lead to degeneration and disaster. The question is, how many cycles of luxury, decline, and revival did Timaeus present? His sarcastic remarks about the democratic views of Empedocles do not suggest that he was a strong believer in popular government (F 134 = D.L. VIII, 63). But he has words of praise for Theron of Acragas and his family. For instance, we read (F 92 = Schol. Pindar *Ol.* II, 15a):

The ancestors of Theron held Acragas, the abode of the Acragas river, and the city was given the same name. For the Acragantines are colonists from Gela, so that when he [*i.e.* Pindar] says, "an honor to his forebears," he is speaking of Theron's ancestors, who did not simply go to Gela, but went direct from Rhodes to Acragas. And this is clear from Pindar himself, as Timaeus points out.

The high point of this period was the annihilation of the Carthaginian

invaders by Gelon and the Sicilians. Theron of Acragas was allied with
Gelon's family by marriage, and evidently Timaeus went to the trouble
of tracing Theron's family back to Rhodes and even dwelt on the reasons
that led them to try their fortunes in the west.[49] It is possible that
Timaeus portrayed the original Geloan colony in Acragas as falling on
evil days because of the luxury in the period after Phalaris, and as being
rescued by the benevolent rule of the newcomers from Rhodes. The examples that survive of his description of Acragas and its luxury, however,
probably belong to the good times following the removal of the Cartha-
gininan threat. But he did dwell on the evils of luxury in the early period
as well, as will be seen when his remarks about Sybaris are discussed.
What needs to be noted here is the possible emergence of a pattern of
change: (1) barbaric despotism of a tyrant; (2) overthrow of that tyrant
by "the people"; (3) strong beneficent rule of one man; (4) period of
growing prosperity, symbolized by wearing rich clothes; (5) popular agi-
tation, here associated with Empedocles; (6) evil days, ended by the appearance of a new beneficent ruler from without—here, the Rhodian
ancestor of Theron. All this is rather vague and some of it is guesswork,
but two points may profitably be kept in mind. First, Timaeus appears
to have had much more faith than Polybius in the power of the individual
ruler for good or for evil.[50] Second, Timaeus stresses the part played by
the introduction of new blood by way of colonization as a vitalizing or a
disintegrating factor.

The history of colonization must have formed an important part of
any history of the west. This was a field already explored by Antiochus
and Philistus before Timaeus came along, and in the absence of corresponding fragments from all three historians it remains most difficult
to distinguish his contribution from theirs. Timaeus' account of the
colonization of Locri has already been discussed,[51] and therefore Corcyra
will be considered next. Timaeus says the Bacchiad, Chersicrates, led a
colony to Corcyra 600 years after the Fall of Troy (F 80 = Schol. Ap.
Rhod. IV, 1216). If we accept Tzetze's statement that the Locrian priestesses were withdrawn from Troy at the end of the Phocian War and 1,000
years after the priesthood had been established, we arrive at 1346 B.C.
for the date when the first priestesses reached Troy. Allowing for the
events immediately preceding their installation, we reach 750 B.C. or
thereabouts for the colonization. Strabo, who may well be following
Timaeus here, mentions that Chersicrates was left behind by Archias to
settle Corcyra, while Archias went on to Syracuse (Strabo VI, 2, 4). The
original inhabitants of Corcyra, the Liburnians, were driven off.[52] There

is little doubt that Timaeus will also have connected the colonization of Corcyra with the internal situation in Corinth, in which he always took an interest.[53] What we deplore most is the loss of his account of the founding of Syracuse. Only one fragment deals with events before the tyranny of Gelon; this contains a reference to the overthrow of the Geomoroi by the Callicyrii in 595/4 B.C. (F 8 = Phot. *Sud.* s.v. Καλλικύριοι). The name Callicyrii had become proverbial for a large number of anything, and it is this fact that interested the lexicographers. Timaeus said that the Callicyrii had been slaves of the Geomoroi, whom they expelled—and Aristotle has the same opinion (*FHG* II, p. 170 F 219). Such a slave revolt is unlikely to have occurred, if for no other reason than the assertion rests on the untenable hypothesis that there were far more slaves than masters.[54] Therefore, this story, like the one about the origins of Locri,[55] was probably the product of party vituperation. Presumably the overthrow of the Geomoroi led to the development of constitutional government in Syracuse, overthrown once more when Gelon took control (Arist. *Pol.* 1302b 32).

Diodorus gives us an account of the Aeolian (or Liparian) islands.[56] Following the death of Aeolus, Odysseus' host, his sons succeeded to his possessions, dividing up the empire amicably among themselves. Astyochus was the one who obtained Lipara. Then time passes very rapidly (D.S. V, 8, 3):

For many generations their descendants succeeded to these kingdoms, but finally the kings of Aeolus' line were eliminated in Sicily. *9.* After this the Sicels entrusted the rule to the best men, and the Sicans, disputing about the government with one another, waged war for a long time. (2) Many years after this, when the islands were becoming more and more deserted, some Cnidians and Rhodians, vexed by the harshness of their Asiatic rulers, decided to send out a colony.

Here we see the familiar pattern: (1) colonization by a hero in the days following the Fall of Troy; (2) extinction of the true heroic line; (3) anarchy, leading in this instance almost to the extinction of the colony; (4) the decision to send out a new colony from the east. Then, as we have grown to expect in Timaeus, Diodorus comments on the circumstances that led the Cnidians and the Rhodians to send out a colony. Pentathlus the Cnidian, also vouched for by Antiochus (Antiochus 555 F 1), left for Sicily in the fiftieth Olympiad (that is, 580 B.C.—another point suggesting Timaeus as the source) and landed in the west near Lilybaeum. But here disaster almost terminated the expedition. Egesta and Selinus were at war. The colonists took sides with Selinus and were soundly beaten in battle, losing many men, including their leader. They decided to return to Asia, choosing new leaders from among the kinsmen of Pentathlus. On the way back they touched at Lipara. Diodorus continues (V, 9, 4):[57]

(4) When they reached Lipara they met with a friendly reception, and were persuaded to live there along with the native population; for about 500 descendants of Aeolus' expedition remained. Later, because of Etruscan piracy on the sea they went to war, and built a fleet. Then they divided themselves into groups, some farming their common islands, others arraying themselves against the pirates. Making their property common property, and grouping themselves into eating clubs (*syssitia*), they continued this communal life for some time. They used to divide up all the islands for twenty years, and when that period had ended they would redivide them into allotments. Subsequently, they defeated the Etruscans in numerous naval engagements and often dedicated considerable tithes in Delphi from the booty.

Here there is a significant difference from Antiochus' account. Antiochus says nothing about the 500 survivors of the colony of Aeolus, but writes instead that either the islands were deserted or else the newcomers drove out the natives (Ant. 555 F 1). We have already come to suspect that the fusion of new and old populations is a favorite theme with Timaeus.[58] And there is added the desire to preserve some continuity between modern times and the age of heroes. Pausanias mentions the spoils of victory over the Etruscans dedicated by the Liparaeans at Delphi, and he may have learned this by reading Antiochus.[59] The notion of common property is a regular feature of fourth-century utopian writing and also appears later.[60] There follows a description of the natural resources of the islands, including their famous hot springs, some details about which recur in Strabo.[61]

Timaeus is interested in Phoenician as well as Greek colonization, and it is much to be regretted that so little remains. We do know that he wrote about Gades, but the relevant passage in Pliny is obviously of complex origin, and it is not easy to see just what he got from Timaeus.[62] However, Diodorus evidently got hold of a fairly comprehensive account of Phoenician colonization, and that account, though he has abridged it, probably comes from Timaeus. Something of the flavor of the original may perhaps be recovered from the following passage (D.S. V, 19–20):[63]

19. . . . . Off Libya there is an island on the open sea which is large enough to be worth mentioning. It lies many days' sail west of Libya. (2) It is a productive land, much of it mountainous, but with a sizable plain of surpassing beauty. Traversed by navigable rivers which irrigate it, there are many parks planted with all sorts of trees, and there are numerous gardens intersected by sweet running waters. This land offers its abundance for enjoyment and for luxury. (3) The mountains have many large oak groves, and all sorts of fruit-bearing trees, and for mountain living there are many gullies and springs. The island as a whole is watered by sweet streams which not only give great pleasure to those who live there, but also contribute to their health and strength of limb. (4) There is much hunting of game and animals of all kinds, and since they are so well supplied with game from these beasts, they lack nothing in reaching the height of luxury and magnificence. Also, the sea that washes that island has quantities of fish, because Ocean, by its very nature, everywhere teems with all sorts of fish. (5) And, in general, this island is surrounded by a benign atmosphere; most of the year it yields many nuts and other seasonal fruits, so that it seems the abode of gods rather than of men, so exceedingly prosperous is it.

20. In ancient times this place was not discovered, because of its remoteness from the inhabited world, but it became known later in this way. The Phoenicians, who were always making trading voyages from earliest times, planted many colonies in Libya, and no small number in the western regions of Europe. Their revenues increasing to their satisfaction, they accumulated great wealth, and took a notion to sail the sea called Ocean, outside the Pillars of Heracles. (2) First they founded a city on the Straits, by the Pillars and on the European side, which they named Gadira. . . . (3) Now the Phoenicians, for the reasons given, explored the coast outside the Pillars, and sailing along by Libya, they were carried out by heavy winds on a long voyage through Ocean. Driven many days before the storm, they reached the island mentioned. Observing its characteristics and its prosperity, they made it known to everyone. (4) But when the Etruscans gained control of the sea and planned to colonize there, the Carthaginians prevented them. They also took precautions to prevent large numbers from going out there from Carthage, attracted by the virtues of the island. But their plan was, at some future time to make it their refuge from the uncertainties of Fortune. For as masters of the sea they would be able to sail off to this island with all their goods, unknown to their conquerors.

The antiquity of Diodorus' source is guaranteed by the reference to the Carthaginians as "masters of the sea." Timaeus' interest in remote parts of the Ocean has already been shown by his use of the narrative of Pytheas.[64] But here he is evidently following a truly "Bergaean" chronicle. Its utopian nature is not proved so much by the accidental discovery of the island, which is reminiscent of the voyage of Cabral, but by the vagueness of all the details. Nothing pleasant is lacking, nothing unpleasant mars the idyllic conditions of the island. Nor is its position with reference to Libya indicated with any clarity. Ostensibly, such details are withheld because the Phoenicians wish to keep them secret. However, beneath the conventional language there may be some account of actual discovery made by Hanno or some unknown Phoenician navigator, then dressed up for popular taste with details borrowed from stories about the Blessed Isles or the Hesperides.[65]

Timaeus' interest in great men, which, as we have seen, led him to attach more significance to the actions of individuals than to constitutional change, brings us back once more to Syracuse. Gelon was the dominating figure of this whole period for Timaeus, as he was for Antiochus and Philistus before him. But he was also a hero who needed support, for he had been a tyrant, and a tyrant whose conduct at the time of the Persian invasion had been widely criticized. What remains in the fragments on Gelon is of the slightest, but the spirit in which he was treated can be inferred. Ample space was given to Gelon's distinguished family background.[66] Furthermore, and this is in the encomiastic tradition, Gelon was distinguished from others by clear evidences of divine favor while still a boy. For this we have only a wretched fragment from Tzetzes, which may be accepted with some reservations as probably based on Timaeus (F 95 = Tzetz. *Chil.* IV, 266):[67]

Gelon of Syracuse cried out in his sleep, for he dreamed he had been struck by lightning. His dog, noticing he was seriously disturbed, continued barking until he aroused him. Once a wolf saved him from death. When still a boy, sitting in school, the wolf appeared and snatched his writing tablet. He ran after the wolf and the tablet, and in the meantime the school was shaken to its foundations and collapsed, killing all the pupils along with their master. The historians proclaim the number killed— *Timaeuses*, Dionysiuses, Diodoruses and Dion—as amounting to over one hundred.

As he grew into manhood he attracted the attention of Hippocrates, tyrant of Gela; his bravery in battle as well as personal popularity among his fellow citizens won him the command of the cavalry against Syracuse (F 18 = Schol. Pindar *Nem.* IX, 95a). We also hear of his friend and companion, Chromius of Aetna, a distinguished man and a well-known competitor in the games (F 18).[68] The only other exploit of Gelon's before he became ruler of Syracuse, for which we have a fragment, is the destruction of Camarina about 490 B.C.[69] But our best evidence comes from Polybius and concerns the request for aid against Persia. Polybius sums up the negotiations in Corinth and the message from Gelon promising 20,000 men and 200 ships if he were put in command either of the land or of the naval forces. To this, according to Polybius, the Greeks made a statesmanlike reply, urging Gelon to compete with them on friendly terms for the prize of valor, for on that doubtless the future supremacy would depend. There was no desperation, just a manly feeling of self-reliance. Polybius goes on to say (XII, 26b, 4–5 = F 94):

Nevertheless, Timaeus introduces such long speeches and shows such zeal in making Sicily the greater part of all Hellas, and the deeds there more conspicuous than those in the rest of the world, and Sicilian men as wisest among those most distinguished for wisdom, and Syracusans as the greatest and most outstanding leaders among the statesmen. (5) So that he does not lack the exaggeration of youths in their exercises, when they attempt paradoxes, such as writing in praise of Thersites or casting reproaches on Penelope, and subjects of that sort.[70]

One more fragment belongs to the same context. In commenting on a line in which Pindar praises Syracuse for her warlike exploits, the scholiast remarks that not only were the Carthaginians and the others who attacked Sicily wiped out by Gelon and Hieron, but also Carthage became subject to Gelon's orders. After citing Theophrastus as his authority for the statement that Gelon forced the barbarians to give up human sacrifice, he adds that Timaeus wrote in his eleventh book that he also ordered them to pay tribute (F 20 = Schol. Pindar *Pyth*. II, 2). Examining Polybius and the fragment from the Pindar scholiast, we find little support for Polybius' charges. In fact, that historian is guilty of playing down the anxiety of the Greeks assembled in Corinth. They would have been glad to settle for a great deal less before the fighting began than after Salamis had been won. They were certainly not inviting Gelon over in the pious hope that virtue would triumph. What probably irritated Polybius is the rhetorical embellishment with which Timaeus insisted on adorning his narrative. Polybius knows that this is not the language in which practical statesmen carry on negotiations, and in this we must agree with him, since Cicero implies the same thing (*De or*. II, 55/8; *Brut*. 325). But it is a matter of taste what form of ostentation is suitable and what is unsuitable for a historical narrative. Gibbon and Macaulay write in a manner of their own and either, on occasion, may be tedious. But we do not judge them as historians on the basis of style. Yet that is what Polybius seems to be doing. The scholiast attributes only one statement definitely to Timaeus—that Gelon demanded tribute from Carthage. That is probably correct. Naturally we know, just as Timaeus knew, that if tribute were ever paid by Carthage, it was not for long.

Such are the unsatisfactory remnants of what was once a detailed account of the exploits of Gelon and the great war against the Carthaginian invaders. The fact that Philistus is cited more than once as agreeing with Timaeus and not once as disagreeing with him about Gelon serves to remind us that Timaeus was entirely dependent on earlier writers for his account of fifth-century Sicily, writers whose works we no longer possess. When he disagrees with someone we occasionally hear about it, but when he does not, there is no way to separate out his account from his sources.

We have already noted that Timaeus was interested in correcting what he regarded as the distorted, though popular interpretation of Ephorus.[71] One fragment of Ephorus proves him to have advanced the seductive hypothesis of a formal alliance between Carthage and Persia in order to synchronize their attacks on the Greeks (Ephorus 70 F 186 = Schol. Pindar *Pyth*. I, 146b). This same view is also presented in Diodorus (XI, 1, 4; 20, 1), but is not even hinted at in Herodotus, whose special interest in the west would surely have led him to include this suggestion if he had heard it.[72] Herodotus' silence is enough to condemn the alleged alliance as unhistorical, but it is one of those obvious misrepresentations which was bound to recommend itself at some later date, just as it was inevitable that the death of Scipio Aemilianus from natural causes should later be called murder.[73] The fragments of Ephorus do not suggest a historian with much imagination or capacity for working out new theories. That is probably why Jacoby suggests that this interpretation must be earlier than Ephorus, that it may even go back as far as Antiochus of Syracuse.[74] This seems rather libelous. Antiochus was in as good a position to get at the facts as Herodotus was, and we have no reason to doubt his honesty. Only in the fourth century could a conscientious historian "discover" this unholy alliance, and even a mediocre writer like Ephorus could hardly fail to notice the coincidence when he drew up his general table of events; we have no right to deny him the ability to draw the wrong conclusions. The question becomes important in discussing the sources on the west that lie behind Diodorus' eleventh book. The view adopted here, and developed elsewhere,[75] is that Diodorus used a number of sources, including Timaeus, but that these sources are so combined that we can no longer separate them out, much as we need to supplement the fragments of Timaeus. It remains quite possible that Timaeus followed Ephorus in his error about a Persian-Carthaginian alliance.[76]

The tyranny in Syracuse did not last long[77] and we have no other fragments dealing with it. Gelon remained a popular hero, and even in the difficult period of Timoleon the Syracusans, desperate for money though they were, spared the statue of Gelon.[78] Hieron was also admired for defeating the Etruscans, but Laqueur has argued that Timaeus changes his tone in describing Hieron, whom he regarded as a typical tyrant.[79] But the fragments are inadequate, unless we supplement them from Diodorus. Timaeus does write about a struggle between Hieron on one side and his brother Polyzelus, supported by Theron, on the other. But the quarrel was patched up, thanks to the good offices of the poet Simonides. Hieron is said to have envied his brother's popularity, but this is no basis for assuming a systematic vilification of Hieron as a tyrant by Timaeus (F 93b = Schol. Pindar *Ol.* II, 29d). He did allude to Hieron's victory in a chariot race (F 141 = Schol. Pindar *Pyth.* II, inscr.), and he is probably responsible for the statement that: "Hieron, wishing to be a city-founder rather than a tyrant, renamed Catane, after he had destroyed it, as Aetna, and denominated himself as the founder."[80] So far as the fragments go we have no reason to see in Timaeus a bitter enemy of tyranny as such. His concern, no doubt, was to explain the decline of Syracuse following the glorious period of Himera, but it is unlikely that he sought for an answer in the constitution.

In the period that followed the overthrow of the tyranny in Syracuse, the Sicilian cities resumed their ancient wars and friendships, but more and more they grew alarmed over the increasing power of Athens and her expanding trade empire. But of this the fragments give us no hint until the time of the Congress of Gela in 424 B.C., except for a brief reference to the arrival of an Athenian admiral in Naples.[81] Timaeus' account of the famous congress would be lost entirely except for the happy accident that it annoyed Polybius, who gives us a summary of the circumstances leading up to the congress, as described by Timaeus (F 22 = Polyb. XII, 25k, 3–4).[82] Eurymedon had come out from Athens to stir up the other cities to make war on Syracuse and her allies. Then Gela, tiring of this war, approached Camarina on the subject of an armistice. When the proposal was welcomed, both cities consulted with their allies, and this led to the peace conference meeting at Gela. Here Polybius is brief, just where we wish he had been detailed, but he reserves fuller coverage for the opening speech made by Hermocrates (XII, 25k, 5–26, 8). There is no reason to doubt that Polybius gives an accurate summary of the speech, nor can he be blamed for his indignation. It is inappropriate, trivial, and pretentious. After one or two fulsome compliments to the Geloans and Camarinans for calling the conference, particularly because they chose the method of negotiating with delegates in private rather than before a popular assembly, Hermocrates becomes reflective:

. . . he imagines that at the outset he must warn the delegates that in time of war sleepers are aroused at dawn by trumpets, in peacetime by birds. (2) That in founding the Olympic games and the truce, Heracles gave proof of his own disposition; for when he made war, anyone he hurt, he hurt by necessity and under orders, while of his own free will he caused harm to no one. (3) Next he mentions Zeus in a rage with Ares as exclaiming "You are to me most hated of the Gods who live on Olympus, for discord, wars, and fighting are ever dear to you." (4) Likewise, the wisest of heroes said, "Clanless, lawless, heartless is he who longs for dreadful internecine war." (5) Also Euripides agrees with the Poet when he says:

> "Oh, wealthy Peace
> Fairest of the Blessed Gods.
> I long for thee, that thou may'st linger.
> I have feared old age will overwhelm me
> 'Ere I look upon thy lovely season
> And garlanded revels."

(6) In addition to this he says that war resembles sickness, and peace health, for the latter restores the sick while by the former the healthy are preserved. (7) Also, in peace old men are buried by their sons as is natural, while in war the opposite occurs. (8) And most important, in war there is no security even as far as the walls, while in peace it stretches as far as the national boundaries.

No, we cannot quarrel with Polybius. We need only compare this with Thucydides' report on the congress[83] to feel the full force of Plutarch's remark that Timaeus shows himself in a very unfavorable light when he tries to surpass his great predecessor (Plut. *Nic.* 1). There can be no doubt that Plutarch's criticism applies here, but some measure of blame was inescapable. Even today historians find it difficult to add anything significant to the acute observations on men and policies made by Thucydides almost on the spot.[84] Timaeus strove for originality, and was castigated; Philistus, who chose to follow his author closely, was dubbed a "pint-sized Thucydides" for his pains![85]

Although temporarily effective, the peace patched up at Gela did not endure, and finally the Athenians arrived in overwhelming force. There are a few references in the fragments to the leading figures connected with the expedition. Cornelius Nepos professes astonishment at the praise bestowed on Alcibiades by Thucydides, Theopompus, and Timaeus, particularly because the two latter are ordinarily such abusive writers (Nep. *Alcib.* 11, 1 = F 99). But Nepos probably followed some Peripatetic biography of Alcibiades and owed the references to Theopompus and Timaeus to that biography.[86] The Hellenistic period was one capable of valuing Alcibiades. Timaeus' contemporary, Duris of Samos, went even further. Not only did he praise the Athenian scapegrace, but he also claimed to be related to him (Duris 76 F 70). Timaeus' known remarks about Hermocrates (aside from the speech given above), Demosthenes, and Nicias are confined to trivialities. He disagrees with Philistus and Thucydides in that he exonerates the Syracusans from the charge of putting Demosthenes and Nicias to death. Instead, he says Hermocrates first opposed the death sentence in the assembly, then warned the victims in time to permit them to take their own lives.[87] No doubt the temptation to correct Philistus proved irresistible. Timaeus also indulges in a tiresome play on words, connecting Hermocrates with the vengeance of Hermes, and pointing out that Nicias, whose name meant "victory," had opposed the expedition (F 102b = Plut. *Nic.* 1, 2).[88] His references to Gylippus are rather contemptuous, but Gylippus actually seems to have been an unusual combination of rogue and hero, and it may be that Timaeus did justice to his undeniable military talents.[89] Then there is the interesting assertion that Thucydides lived in Italy during his exile and was buried there;[90] but we have no way of testing his information. And that is all we have on the famous Syracusan expedition. The fragments are very disappointing and probably not at all representative of the original. We could do with an account criticizing Thucydides and rooted in Sicilian tradition. But both Philistus and Ephorus chose to follow Thucydides here, and Diodorus seems not to have made any use of Timaeus at this point. Consequently, we do not know whether Timaeus merely reinterpreted the same old facts to suit himself or whether he introduced fresh material, perhaps including documents not available to Thucydides. Probably he added few facts, since he was writing in Athens, but his reference to Hermocrates' distrust of popular assemblies does sound as though he had got hold of something new. But here the Athenian tradition proved too strongly entrenched to be dislodged.

It is a melancholy fact that while so little of Timaeus' account of the leading figures at this moment of dramatic crisis survives, we do have an abundance of detail about one of the captives, the courtesan Lais, whom Thucydides does not mention. Athenaeus cites no less than four writers who concerned themselves about her antecedents and her fate. The circumstances of her death are given in detail, and the epitaph on her tomb beside the Peneius river is quoted verbatim. But Athenaeus is hopelessly confused. There was an earlier and a later Lais, both famed for their beauty. Obviously the young girl who charmed Apelles and with whom the orator Demosthenes' name was connected cannot be the Lais taken captive in 415. Whether Timaeus described one or both we, of course, no longer know.[91]

The Syracusan victory over the Athenians was not only the turning point in the Peloponnesian War, but also it upset the balance of forces in the west. Like Athens, Syracuse was more esteemed by her neighbors when fighting for her very existence than in her days of triumph. The departure of Hermocrates for the Aegean removed the leading exponent of Sicilian Greek unity, and the familiar disputes between individual Greek states, as well as fierce partisan struggles inside them, followed as a matter of course. Thus it came about that within four years Carthage felt strong enough to renew her operations against the Greeks in Sicily. This in turn was directly responsible for the rise of Dionysius and the creation of the Syracusan empire, whose achievements were so highly regarded by Philistus. Timaeus, with the wisdom born of hindsight, thought differently. For him, the policies of Dionysius, however successful, were ultimately disastrous to the cause of Hellenism in the west. The good old days came to an end with the arrival of Hannibal and his invading Carthaginians. But Carthaginian victories had been made possible by the insidious effects of great prosperity on the Sicilian Greeks.

There are five fragments about Sybaris, destroyed by her neighbor, Croton, about 510 B.C.[92] Sybaris had become a favorite example of moral turpitude and its consequences,[93] and Timaeus probably added nothing new to the indictment. Gluttony, drunkenness, laziness, and vanity, all are represented in the fragments, sometimes with humorous exaggeration. We are told that on solemn public occasions at Sybaris, as in other Greek cities, it was the custom to present gold crowns to those who had served the city well. But in Sybaris those honored were the men who spent the most on public feasts; frequently cooks were crowned for preparing the most appetizing dishes (F 50 = Athen. XII, 17, p. 519E). Then there is the following, written long before Oblomov was heard of (F 48 = Athen. XII, 15, p. 518D):

And Timaeus says that at one time a Sybarite had been walking in the fields. He happened to remark that he had ruptured himself, just watching the laborers at work. One of his friends exclaimed: "And I feel a sharp pain in my side just from hearing you!"

But not all his remarks are in this vein. He seeks for some rational explanation for the riotous living in Sybaris, and finds at least a partial answer in the climate. Supposedly it was unbearably hot there except at night and during the early morning. Therefore, drinking was adopted as a health measure on the ground that "anyone in Sybaris who did not wish to die before his time, should neither see the rising nor the setting sun" (F 50 = Athen. XII, 18, p. 520A). But, as usual, there are too many explanations. At one time we are told that the Sybarites had a taste for Milesian woolen cloaks, and that this had a bearing on their relations with other states, such as the Etruscans (F 50 = Athen. XII, 17, p. 519B). Yet elsewhere he speaks of Sybaris as isolated, forced to produce only for the domestic market because they had no good harbor for exporting (F 50 = Athen. XII, 18, p. 519F).[94] Then, too, there is the inevitable Delphic oracle which seemed to promise them everlasting prosperity, but which, of course they had misinterpreted (Athen. XII, 18, p. 520A). But the isolation of Sybaris, misguided though it may have been, was truly a "splendid isolation" of large estates where wine reached the cellars by canal direct from the vineyards (Athen. XII, 17, p. 519D), where the young men went off to live in luxuriously appointed caves during the hot season, and where the city cavalry wore bright yellow tunics over their armor (Athen. XII, 17, p. 519C). The Sybarites reached such a scandalous pitch of high living that they even indulged themselves in steam baths (Athen. XII, 17, p. 519E). And in their isolation they came to feel a mild contempt for the outside world. "They jeered at those who left their native land, and took pride in growing old on the bridges of their own rivers" (Athen. XII, 17, p. 519E). Surely there is as much here of regret as of moral indignation.

But Sybaris had fallen long ago at the hands of another Greek city. Much more shocking was the fall of Acragas, second among Sicilian cities only to Syracuse, shocking in itself, and more so because it fell to Carthage in the full light of history. Timaeus' description of Acragas is more specific, less generalized, than of Sybaris. He must have known the later city and have seen the ruins of the disaster of 406/5. Most splendid of the public buildings in the city was the Temple of Olympian Zeus. It had not yet been roofed over when the Carthaginians came, and it was not completed afterward because the later city lacked resources to carry out so large a project. But Timaeus takes pride in giving us its dimensions as some 340 feet long, 60 feet wide, and 120 feet high. He tells us that a man could easily squeeze his body inside the flutings of the great exterior columns—a graphic way of bringing the size home to us (F 26a = D.S. XII, 82, 3). He also writes about an artificial lake near the city, well stocked with fish, swans, and all other sorts of birds, "so as to give joy to those who beheld them" (F 26a = D.S. XII, 82, 5). As is done in modern Kentucky, they set up monuments to their race horses; inscriptions commemorated the little pet birds cherished by the children of Acragas. Timaeus says these memorials could still be seen in his time (D.S. XII, 82, 6).

Although luxury began early in Acragas—the children wore soft garments and even the young bloods "used scrapers and oil flasks of silver and gold"—there was no evidence of a loss of vigor on the athletic field. Timaeus tells us that before the troubles began, in the ninety-second running of the Olympics (412 B.C.) an Acragantine citizen, Exaenetus, won a victory. He was brought home in style, riding in a chariot escorted by 300 pairs of white horses (D.S. XII, 82, 7–8). But the crowning touch in his description of luxury concerns a rich man, Antisthenes, and the magnificence with which he celebrated his daughter's wedding. The bridal procession consisted of 800 carriages plus the entire cavalry of Acragas and guest cavaliers from surrounding towns. Everyone in the city was feasted, the food and drink being taken around to each separate street. Then we read (D.S. XII, 84, 2):

But the most extraordinary feature was furnishing lights for all the temple altars, while those in the streets throughout the city were provided with fuel, and tinder and fagots were handed out to men from the shops who were ordered to kindle fires when the flame was lit on the acropolis. (3) They carried out their instructions just as the bride was being escorted, and many went ahead carrying torches and the city was filled with light; the public streets could not hold the crowd following along in order and joining together in honor of the man's magnificence.

Despite his extravagance in the matter of lighting the streets, Antisthenes is said to have been as shrewd as he was rich. His son, impatient to force a poor neighbor to sell his farm, kept threatening and abusing him. Antisthenes rebuked his son. The proper thing to do, he pointed out, was to help the poor man to become rich; then he would want a larger farm and would be glad to sell the small one to his neighbor (D.S. XII, 84, 4).

But the happy days were numbered, ending with Timaeus' account of the drastic measures taken by the Acragantine government to provide for the defense of the city when the Carthaginians were at the gates (D.S. XII, 84, 5):

The great prosperity of the city bred such luxury among the Acragantines, that after the siege had been going on for some time they passed a decree concerning the night watch, to the effect that no one should have more than one bolster, one coverlet with fleece, and two pillows.[95]

CHAPTER IV

MODERN TIMES

HERE, IF ANYWHERE, we would expect Timaeus to have given a straightforward narrative of events in chronological order, beginning with the Carthaginian invasion and continuing on down to the intervention of Rome in 264 B.C. But unsatisfactory though the fragments are, enough remains to prove that Timaeus did no such thing. His delight in anecdotes continues, as does his penchant for picking up odd bits of information and inserting them when he chooses to do so. His method of writing makes it quite impossible to restore the table of contents for this part of his work with any degree of accuracy.[1] Lacking the original, the next best thing would be an intelligent summary by a later writer, but unfortunately Photius has not done for him what he did for Ctesias, very likely because when he wrote, it was no longer possible to get hold of a copy of Timaeus' works.[2] Diodorus Siculus has given us by far the best narrative of Sicilian events which we now possess, a narrative that can be pieced out from Books XIII–XVI and XVIII–XX of his *Historical Library*, with some not unimportant additions from the fragments of the later books. What is needed badly is a careful study of the sources of Diodorus, book by book. At first sight Book XIII seems to be a happy hunting ground for recovering the lost account of Timaeus, because it contains no less than eight attested fragments. All of them are related to the Carthaginian attacks on Greek Sicily between the years 409 and 405 B.C.,[3] and they may profitably be considered first in a discussion of the modern period.

Diodorus has described the arrival of a military force from Libya in 409/8 B.C., a force that Hannibal had just succeeded in bringing safely to shore at Lilybaeum. Diodorus continues (XIII, 54, 5 = Tim. F 103 = Ephorus 70 F 201): "Altogether, Hannibal had, according to Ephorus, 200,000 foot and 4000 horse, but according to Timaeus not more than 100,000." The next reference concerns the same expedition. Hannibal has moved on Himera and the Greeks sallied out to meet him. Then we read (XIII, 60, 5 = F 104):

They fought splendidly, and the barbarians . . . turned in flight. While they fled in disorder toward those who were camped in the hills, the others pursued, exhorting one another not to take prisoners, and they slew more than 6,000, as Timaeus says, but 20,000 according to Ephorus (Eph. 70 F 202).

---

[1] For notes to chap. iv, see pp. 131–134.

Was Diodorus' main source here Ephorus or Timaeus, or an intermediary who used both historians? Ephorus and Timaeus lived long enough after the event to be dependent on still earlier writers for their information. This is particularly true when it comes to statistics about the Carthaginians; even in Sicily official government figures would hardly be obtainable. The Sicilian tradition about the numbers of Punic forces was like that in Greece on the Persians. They seemed to come in overwhelming numbers, and the actual estimates were left pretty much to the imagination of the historian. There was a natural tendency to exaggerate in order to enhance Greek prowess. Whereas this was still true in Herodotus' day, Xenophon obtained more accurate information about Persian armies as a result of his own observation of them on the march. He must have realized the ineffectiveness of enormous forces in battle, as well as the impossibility of maintaining them in the field over a long period. Therefore, if the figure of 200,000 comes from him, it is a serious reflection on his integrity; this actually represents a larger army than the combined efforts of Seleucus, Antigonus, Demetrius, and Lysimachus were able to bring together to fight for world dominion at Ipsus, the greatest battle in the whole Hellenistic age.[4] Wherever Ephorus obtained his information, it must have derived from a patriotic western source. Timaeus, whose figures were not always accurate,[5] deserves credit here for sound judgment. And this is true whether he cut down the earlier numbers on the general grounds of probability or on the basis of an earlier account now lost. He would have liked correcting Ephorus, and if he could at the same time have thrown discredit on Philistus, his enjoyment would not have been lessened. The armchair historian is sometimes more trustworthy than his fire-breathing colleague.

Timaeus is not mentioned again on the expedition of 409/8, but Diodorus cites him for the more ambitious invasion of 406. This time there were two commanders, Hannibal, who had been so successful before, and Himilco. Diodorus, after describing the Carthaginian plan to attack Sicily, goes on to say (XIII, 80, 5 = F 25):

Finally, when the forces gathered in Carthage they amounted altogether, cavalry included, to not more than 120,000 according to Timaeus, but 300,000 according to Ephorus [Eph. 70 F 203]. The Carthaginians repaired all their triremes and assembled more than 1,000 merchantmen for the crossing.

As before, the references to both historians are such that we do not know whether Diodorus owes his main account to Timaeus or to Ephorus, but once more the figures of Ephorus are very much larger; and also they are evidently inflated figures. The campaign that follows cannot be discussed in detail here, for we are interested only in what belongs to Timaeus. The first action was a naval engagement in which the advance force of forty triremes was very roughly handled by the Syracusans off Eryx. Some fifteen Carthaginian vessels were destroyed. This, however, did not prevent Hannibal from crossing with 50 ships and landing his troops successfully (D.S. XIII, 80 *ad fin.*). Diodorus then turns to the preparations made by the Greek states to meet the invaders and prepares the way for the siege of Acragas, whose citizens correctly surmised that they were to be the first Carthaginian objective (XIII, 81, 1–3). This is the setting for the Timaeus fragment on the splendors of Acragas discussed in the preceding chapter,[6] but it is also the setting for Fragment 27, which may be translated as follows (D.S. XIII, 85, 3):

And Dexippus the Lacedaemonian helped them [*i.e.* the Acragantines], for he had recently arrived from Gela. As Timaeus says, this man was a resident of Gela at the time, highly regarded because of his nationality. (4) For this reason the Acragantines requested him to hire as many mercenaries as he could, and then to proceed to Acragas. In addition, about 800 Campanians, formerly in the service of Hannibal, were hired. These troops occupied the hill above the city called the Athenaeum, which is favorably located with reference to the city.

This passage about Dexippus may serve to illustrate the complexity of the problem of Diodorus' sources. He mentions Dexippus four times later, and it is evident when we put all these references together that Diodorus got his information from two different writers. The passage just quoted and the three subsequent ones follow a pattern already familiar to us from Timaeus' remarks about that more famous Spartan, Gylippus.[7] The statement that Dexippus was "highly regarded because of his nationality" surely fits well with the later statement that the citizens of Acragas upbraided Dexippus for not attacking the Carthaginian camp at the proper time, "since he was held to be no novice in military matters" (D.S. XIII, 87 *ad fin.*). As a Spartan he had no right to plead inexperience and must therefore have been a traitor. We are not surprised later when we read: "Dexippus the Lacedaemonian is said to have been bribed with fifteen talents" (XIII, 88, 7). This is evidently a malicious interpretation, as the phrase λέγεται ("it is said") suggests, being based only on the fact that Dexippus advised evacuating Acragas when the food supply was almost exhausted. What facts emerge about Dexippus? He was a professional soldier, living in Gela, whose services were obtained by Acragas, and he was able to raise a small army. His task was to keep the Carthaginians from taking possession of a hill from which they might threaten the city—and he seems to have carried out his

assignment. However, when the Syracusans defeated an advance force
of Carthaginians sent ahead to intercept them, a force that was obliged
to fall back for support on the main Punic camp before Acragas, some in
the city felt that this was their chance to take advantage of the confusion
of the enemy and to launch a sharp counterattack from the city. Whether
this was sensible or not, we have no way of telling. Diodorus says that
the Acragantine generals were accused before the assembly by Menes of
Camarina, and punished (XIII, 87, 4). Dexippus had attended the meeting of the assembly—where he was abused—but unlike four other gener-
erals he was not deprived of his command. Perhaps that lay outside the
power of the assembly. Later, when the supplies from Syracuse were
intercepted, he advised abandoning Acragas. The charge of corruption
is probably invented by Timaeus, who was devoted to Acragas, and
Timaeus here anticipates the method of Tacitus. The facts are not
altered, but unpleasant insinuations about Dexippus are introduced.
Later we find this same Dexippus sent packing by Dionysius for fear he
might seize the chance to restore freedom to Syracuse. And here, it is
evident, Diodorus is no longer following Timaeus, but some other author
who held different views about Dexippus (XIII, 96, 1).[8]

The three remaining references to Timaeus in the thirteenth book can
be dismissed more rapidly. The first is clearly inserted by Diodorus as a
variant from his main source and concerns the Bull of Phalaris, discussed
in the previous chapter (XIII, 90, 4–6 = F 28a).[9] The second is a typical
example of Timaeus' fondness for synchronisms, and it, too, is about a
statue (XIII, 108, 4 = F 106). We are told that outside Gela there was
a large statue of Apollo, set up there by the Geloans in accordance with
an oracle. The Carthaginians, whose enthusiasm for monumental sculp-
ture seems to have been quite undiscriminating, carried Apollo home
with them, then presented him to their mother city, Tyre. When Alexander later laid siege to Tyre, Apollo proved unfavorable and was duly
cursed by the Tyrians. By a strange coincidence Tyre fell on the same
day of the month, the same hour even, in which the statue of Apollo
had been abducted by the sacrilegious Carthaginians![10] The conquering
Greeks then paid honor to the statue of the god, since it was Apollo to
whom they owed the capture of Tyre. One wonders which of the various
Greek calendars was used to synchronize these events—and whether the
chronometer consulted was running on Sicilian or Phoenician time. The
only other reference in Book XIII is to a statement about the numbers of
soldiers recruited by Dionysius at the outset of his tyranny, to oppose
Carthage (F 107 = D.S. XIII, 109, 2). Timaeus' figures are contrasted

with what "some writers say" (ὡς μέν τινες . . . ὡς δὲ Τίμαιος). Whether by the other writers he means Ephorus is hard to tell, but as usual the figures of Timaeus are smaller. This time, however, even the higher figure of 50,000 is not incredible.

In looking back over Book XIII we notice how much Diodorus is pre-occupied with Sicily,[11] though he does not cite Timaeus until chapter 54. It is unlikely that he made use of him at all in his narrative of the Athenian expedition against Syracuse (XIII, 2–35). It can also be shown that Timaeus was not responsible for the long speech made by Nicolaus, an old man who pleaded for mercy toward the Athenian prisoners despite having lost two sons in the war (XIII, 20–27). Timaeus would never have spoken in such glowing terms about the Athenians as the people who introduced civilization to the rest of Greece.[12] Also, Gylippus' speech against showing mercy contradicts a Timaeus fragment in two particulars: the Gylippus of the fragment is shouted down by the Syracusans; also, the fragment represents Gylippus as pleading for the lives of the generals, not as demanding their blood.[13] It is all the more remarkable, then, to find eight references to Timaeus for the period 409/5 B.C., a greater concentration by far than anywhere else in Diodorus.[14] Perhaps Timaeus' special interest in Acragas made what he wrote about that city particularly attractive, but even for the siege of Acragas Diodorus did not rely on his account alone. The task of separating one source from another is extremely difficult, demanding as it does familiarity with the historical fragments as a whole in addition to a thorough knowledge of Diodorus and the other extant accounts for each period.[15]

In following up these fragments from Book XIII, we have reached the time of Dionysius I, a landmark in Timaeus' *History*, because with Dionysius he and Philistus reach the parting of the ways. Constitutionally speaking, Philistus is the more consistent writer, since we have reason to believe that he defended not only Dionysius as a person, but tyranny as a form of government.[16] Timaeus, however, is a believer in great men, crediting them with the chief responsibility for success or failure. Without Dionysius there could not have been the disorders of the following period, when the empire passed into the nerveless grasp of his incompetent son. Out of these disorders came the triumph of Timoleon, but too soon after Timoleon's retirement another and more terrifying threat appeared in the person of Agathocles, who in his turn left a legacy of strife behind him. Then came Pyrrhus and finally Rome—and Sicily found itself the prize in a battle between the two giants, with the Romans taking over. Before that, however, Timaeus had died. But even in his life-

time, and before the Pyrrhus adventure, it must have struck him that
Hellenism was waging a losing fight in the west. For this he put the blame
partly on the Carthaginians whom he detested, but also and with more
conviction on internal factors and bad leadership, beginning with Dionysius.

Philistus ushers Dionysius on the stage with dreams and other por-
tents. Something of the spirit of his presentation can still be felt in the
following excerpt (Philistus 556 F 57a = Cic. *De div.* I, 39):

> According to the writings of Philistus (a learned and a conscientious man who lived
> in those days), the mother of the Dionysius who became tyrant of Syracuse, when she
> was pregnant, carrying this same Dionysius in her womb, dreamed that she gave
> birth to a baby satyr. The interpreters of omens, called the Galeotae in Sicily at that
> time, told her, as Philistus says, that the son she bore would be very famous in the
> Greek world and that his fortune would long endure.[17]

But Timaeus, too, heralded the coming of Dionysius with a dream. We
read (F 29 = Schol. Aeschin. II, 10):

> In the sixteenth (?) book Timaeus writes that a certain woman, a Himeraean by
> birth, had a dream in which she was transported to Heaven and conducted by some-
> one to view the homes of the gods. And there she saw Zeus sitting on his throne, but
> a large red (πυρρός) man was chained and pilloried underneath. She asked her guide
> who he might be, and the guide replied: "That is a criminal from Sicily and Italy,
> and if he were released he would ruin the country." She awoke, and at a later date
> happened to meet Dionysius the tyrant with his spearbearers. When she saw him,
> she cried out that he was the criminal she had seen earlier in chains. And as she said
> this she fell to the ground in a faint. After three months had passed the woman was
> not seen again, having been secretly murdered by Dionysius.[18]

The description of Dionysius strikes one at first as quite vivid, since
πυρρός can mean "red-headed," and it would be interesting to know that
Dionysius was a big man with bright red hair. But it is unusual for writers
of the period to give us the physical traits of their characters. When we
turn to Pseudo-Aristotle's *Physiognomica* we see what Timaeus was
about. For there we find that "red [or red-headed] men are great rascals";[19] and later, for good measure, that "very big men are dull [or
illiterate]."[20]

This is not the only fragment announcing the arrival of Dionysius,
but the other one contains one of those synchronisms dear to Timaeus.
In its present form it is quite ridiculously wrong, and wrong in a way un-
thinkable for Timaeus. Perhaps the fault lies with our source, Plutarch,
or more likely some copyist is to blame. What it says is that Euripides
died on the day Dionysius the Elder was born, "Tyche, as Timaeus says,
removing the imitator of tragic deeds and introducing their perpetrator

at the same moment" (F 105 = Plut. *Quaest. conv.* VIII, 1, 1, p. 717C). Timaeus evidently said that Dionysius entered on his career as tyrant at the same time that Euripides died.

These monitory statements about Dionysius before he appears on the scene were probably aimed primarily at Philistus, who had been Dionysius' strongest defender. But Timaeus also criticized Ephorus' account, a piece of information that we owe to Polybius, who as usual sides against Timaeus. The passage is not without interest, and may be rendered as follows (F 110 = Polyb. XII, 4a, 3):[21]

... and again when he [*i.e.* Timaeus] tells lies about Ephorus, saying that he wrote that Dionysius the Elder seized the power when he was twenty-three years old, that he ruled forty-two years, and then took leave of life after living sixty-three years. (4) For no one would call this the historian's fault; it was obviously a scribal error.

Polybius has missed the point entirely. Timaeus is not challenging Ephorus on a mistake in elementary arithemetic. He is not disturbed because Ephorus implies that $23 + 42 = 63$. Not at all. His objection is to the date when Ephorus said Dionysius became tyrant. And here the *Parian Marble* helps us out. In that document Dionysius enters on his tyranny in the archonship of Euctemon (that is, in 408/7), whereas Timaeus synchronizes the beginning of Dionysius' tyranny with the death of Euripides (406/5 B.C.).[22] It is also interesting to note that Timaeus and Philistus agree perfectly on this date. Polybius, who does not understand what Timaeus' criticism was about, still has no hesitation in rebuking him. This is just one more example of Polybian prejudice and it does not square with his insistence that the historian must be fair to everyone.[23]

Dionysius was not firmly established as tyrant for some years. The war with Carthage had ended ingloriously for Syracuse, and the citizen cavalry, no doubt recruited from the wealthy families, refused to put up with their new ruler. Leaving the city they seized the little town of Aetna as a base. When in 404/3 B.C. a popular uprising came to a head in Syracuse, Dionysius' position was precarious indeed. His later successes, like those of Justinian after the Nika riots, added piquancy to his alleged indecision during the crisis itself. Timaeus tells us that one of his advisers had urged him to jump on a fast horse and try to escape, but Philistus had said a tyrant ought not to run away, rather he should relinquish his power only if dragged away by the leg (F 115 = Plut. *Dion* 35, 6). It is fortunate that in this same passage Plutarch corrects Timaeus. According to this prince of biographers, Philistus had merely recorded the remark in his history as made by someone else. We are not justified in doubting Plutarch's word.[24] Therefore, if anything is certain, it is that the account of this episode in Diodorus' fourteenth book comes from Timaeus; it is unlikely two writers, independently, would have misinterpreted Philistus in the same way. The passage in question, which deserves to be treated as a fragment of Timaeus, reads as follows (D.S. XIV, 108):

Dionysius, finding himself cut off from access to the interior and abandoned by his mercenaries, called his friends together to discuss the situation. He had so completely lost hope of ruling, that he was not even trying to find a way of overcoming the Syracusans; he was merely looking for some way to die so that the end of his rule would not be entirely without honor. Now Heloris, one of his friends—some say his foster father—told him that tyranny makes a fine winding sheet. Then his kinsman, Polyxenus, said he ought to take the fastest horse he had and gallop off to the Campanians in the Carthaginian territory. For Himilco had left them to protect their Sicilian holdings. But Philistus, who later wrote the history, disagreed with Polyxenus. "Dionysius," he said, "you ought not to run away from your tyranny on a swift horse, but fall only if dragged off by the leg!" Dionysius was impressed, and he decided to risk everything rather than abandon his rule willingly.

The temptation was too great for Timaeus. He has deliberately shaded the account of Philistus for dramatic effect. Later on he is able to allude to Philistus' own death, being dragged through the streets of Syracuse by a mob, as an appropriate end for the man who had given such advice to Dionysius (F 115). At the time Timaeus wrote, undoubtedly Ephorus' history of the period was most widely read, and it was his influence that Timaeus was so anxious to counteract.[25] Ephorus had an account of Philistus' death which makes him commit suicide rather than fall alive into the hands of his enemies (Eph. 70 F 219 = Plut. *Dion* 35, 3). However, Timonides of Leucas, who must have known the facts,[26] says that Philistus was captured alive and mistreated by the Syracusans. His head was cut off and his body dragged through the Achradina section (by the children!), and then thrown into a stone quarry (Timonides 561 F 2 = Plut. *Dion* 35, 4–5). Timaeus, familiar with both accounts, accepted that of Timonides and then adapted the story of the advice given Dionysius to fit his ending.

How much Diodorus borrowed from Timaeus in writing the history of the tyranny of Dionysius the Elder is uncertain, because he cites him only once in Book XIV (XIV, 54, 6 = F 108). In that passage he is describing Dionysius' invasion of Carthaginian Sicily against the forces of Himilco, and the campaign takes place in 396/5.[27] Diodorus, citing Ephorus, gives the numbers of the Carthaginians as 300,000 foot, 4,000 horse, 400 chariots, 400 warships, and over 600 other vessels to carry the troops, supplies, and war machines over from Libya. Then he adds:

Timaeus, however, says that the forces crossing over from Libya were no more than 100,000, and he shows that 30,000 more were enlisted in Sicily.

Here, as in Book XIII, Timaeus continues to win our respect by rejecting the highly exaggerated figures for the Carthaginians he found in Ephorus. The exaggeration here is even greater than in the earlier passages. If Philistus is responsible, then we must assume that he wrote tongue in cheek, perhaps hoping to win his way back into favor; but one is reluctant to think this of a historian of his reputation. At least, it is gratifying to know that when Timaeus makes mistakes, whether inadvertent or deliberate, they are not dictated to him from above.

Little else remains of Timaeus' account of Dionysius I. We are told that the historian drew conclusions about his character—unfavorable no doubt—from his interest in finery (F 111 = Polyb. XII, 24, 3). This is part and parcel of Timaeus' belief that character reveals itself in what a man talks and writes about, that Aristotle was an epicure, Homer a glutton (F 152 = Polyb. XII, 24, 2). Then there is another fragment giving us a deathbed scene, the atmosphere of which reminds one a little of Tacitus. Certainly the bit we still have is suggestively grim. The fragment may be translated as follows (F 109 = Plut. *Dion* 6, 2):

When Dionysius seemed ill beyond recovery, Dion tried to talk to him about the children of Aristomache. (3) But the physicians, to gratify the man expected to inherit the kingdom, gave him no opportunity; Timaeus says that when he asked for an opiate, they rendered him unconscious, joining sleep with death.

How accurately Tacitus reflects this same spirit in his insinuating remarks on the deaths of Augustus and also of Tiberius (*Ann.* I, 5; VI, 50)! Dionysius had been the object of so many plots that it seemed incredible he should die peacefully in his bed. Timaeus may also have been influenced by his own peculiar ideas of morality. No man as wicked as Dionysius could possibly have died a natural death. It was bad enough for him to have died painlessly, but at least his days had been shortened! All that remained was for the tyrant to be given a suitable burial. We hear that Timaeus "was astonished at the pyre prepared for Dionysius, the Sicilian tyrant" (F 112 = Athen. V, 40, p. 206E). Since he was not alive when Dionysius died, his admiration must have been for the size of the burial mound or, more likely, at the reports of his funeral in earlier writers. That it was a magnificent burial we also learn from the fragments of Philistus (556 FF 28 and 40b). Timaeus' interest in funerary pyres has already been noted in the instance of Dido.[28]

The fragments about Dionysius the Younger deal chiefly with scenes from court life. One of these, which is concerned with Democles, one of the courtiers of Dionysius, deserves to be quoted in full (F 32 = Athen. VI, 56, p. 250AD):

In the twenty-second book of his *Histories* Timaeus speaks of Democles, the flatterer of Dionysius the Younger. There being a custom in Sicily of offering sacrifices at home to the Nymphs, and to spend the night feasting in front of their images and dancing drunkenly around them, Democles, spurning the Nymphs because he said one ought to pay no attention to lifeless divinities, went off to dance around Dionysius. Later, taking part in an embassy . . . the members all travelled on a trireme, he was charged by his fellow envoys with seditious conduct abroad, and with damage to the state business. When Dionysius flew into a rage, Democles explained that a quarrel had arisen between him and his fellows, and for the following reason. After dinner his fellow envoys chose songs from the repertory of Phrynichus and Stesichorus, some of the sailors sang a song of Pindar's, but he and those who so desired attempted the songs of Dionysius. He added that he could give clear proof of what he said, for his accusers would be unable even to name these songs, while he was prepared to sing them all in succession. And when Dionysius had put aside his anger, Democles spoke once more: "Do me a favor, Dionysius, and ask someone who knows it to teach me the song in praise of Asclepius, for I hear you have written a song on that subject." And on another occasion Dionysius' friends had been invited to dinner, and Dionysius came into the room saying: "My friends, a letter has come to us, sent by the leading men in Naples." Interrupting, Democles exclaimed, "By the gods, they have done well, Dionysius!" The latter said, looking at him, "How do you know whether what they write is satisfactory or not?" "By the gods, you have rebuked me well, Dionysius!" Timaeus also writes about a certain Satyrus, the flatterer of both Dionysiuses.

This is one of the most useful fragments we have for studying the author's style. It bears a certain resemblance to that other passage about Empedocles (F 134),[29] but here we are privileged to see something of Timaeus' subtlety in composition, since here there is more continuity; not one episode, but a series of related incidents has been preserved. The whole is constructed rather in the form of a satyrical comedy and the atmosphere is not unlike that of Ben Jonson's *Volpone*. It is an utterly ruthless satire and a cold, hard light plays upon the stage. There are really only two actors. Everything not essential to the plot has been swept aside. The thought is developed in four episodes. First comes our introduction to the two leading characters. As the curtain rises we find ourselves watching the festival night in Syracuse. All is gaiety, laughter, the drinking of wine, and, in accordance with ancestral custom, we see the citizens enjoying themselves in their homes and dancing in traditional fashion around the images of the Nymphs. We also see the palace of the tyrant where Dionysius stands apart. Then we hear Democles speak out loud and clear: "Why bother with the lifeless images of the gods?" And off he goes, whether from his own house or from somwhere in the palace, until he finds Dionysius and dances round and round the silent figure. The observer sees Democles as he is—impudent, shameless, and contemptuous of the gods. What of Dionysius? We are told only by indirection, for when the curtain rises once more the scene has changed. Democles appears now, strutting his importance as the member of a state embassy, and promptly shows himself, as one would expect, to be a traitor, gain his only object. Only with the third scene does Dionysius begin to play an active role. Furious with Democles, he summons him in anger, clearly planning some drastic punishment. This is Democles' great scene. By playing on Dionysius' poetic vanity he turns the tables on his enemies. Instead of witnessing his well-deserved fall from favor, they find themselves in disgrace for failure to know the tyrant's poems by heart. This remarkable scene ends with Democles' insincere request for someone to teach him the lines of Dionysius' latest song about Asclepius. At this point we may imagine the ruler smiling fatuously. But this will never do, the rogue must not triumph. So there is a final episode in which Democles, like Satan in *Paradise Regained*, is reduced to his proper size. We see him once more as a mere buffoon and a parasite. Clever though he is, foolish though Dionysius is, there can be no dignity or self-respect for a man in Democles' position. But what a scathing judgment on the character of the tyrant, all the more effective because it is not explicit! Whether it is a fair judgment may be doubted. But he has presented Dionysius unconventionally. He is weak rather than vicious, and in the last episode he begins to see the light.

Not all the men at court were parasites. Timaeus has only praise for the philosopher, Xenocrates, whom he describes as winning a golden crown offered by Dionysius to the first guest who drained his stoup of wine at the Pitcher Feast. Xenocrates dedicated his prize to the statue of Hermes as he departed, and was more highly regarded for despising wealth than Dionysius was for giving such a lavish entertainment. This anecdote was evidently popular. Both Athenaeus and Philodemus picked it up from Timaeus, and Aelian tells the same story without, however, citing his authority.[30] Xenocrates is a well-known figure from the Academy, and Diogenes Laertius tells us he went to Syracuse with Plato (D.L. IV, 6). The Socrates of Plato's *Symposium* had set an embarrassingly high standard for drinking and holding one's liquor. But Xenocrates satisfied two requirements at once, demonstrating his contempt for wealth as well as his imperviousness to alcohol. The Philodemus version

is helpful in that it alone shows us the point of the story, that is the superiority of the philosopher who needs no money to the tyrant who
spends it so freely. There is also the contrast between the man of principle who cannot be bought and a rogue like Democles.

So far we have seen a foolish though well-meaning Dionysius, and also
we have seen him as a royal spendthrift. But we have had no real criticism of his public acts. With Fragment 113, however, we touch on his
statecraft (F 113 = Plut. *Dion* 14, 4–7). A letter sent by Dion to the
Carthaginians had been intercepted, a letter in which Dion urged the
Carthaginians to insist that he be present in any peace negotiations that
might take place with Syracuse. Here, too, Dionysius is putty in the
hands of a persuasive adviser. The adviser in this instance is Timaeus'
bête noire, the historian Philistus. Philistus suggests a ruse by which
Dionysius allays Dion's suspicions and then manages to exile him from
Sicily.[31] So sudden was Dion's departure that he had no chance to take
his family with him. We do learn, though, that Dionysius permitted the
writing of letters back and forth. But Plutarch cites Timaeus only incidentally, to note that he said Dion's son was named Aretaeus after his
mother, Arete. But the biographer adds that he prefers to follow Timonides, who "is more to be trusted in such matters" (Plut. *Dion* 31, 2–3
= F 114). Since Plutarch evidently prefers Timonides on this period it is
regrettable that Diodorus, who gives so much about Sicily in Books
XIII and XIV, is so disappointingly brief in the two books following.
Books XV and XVI, which cover the entire period between Artaxerxes'
war against Evagoras (386/5 B.C.) and the death of Philip (336 B.C.),
thus include most of the reign of Dionysius II as well as the activities
of Dion and Timoleon.[32]

The only other fragment on Dionysius II has to do with his abdication
in 343/2 and comes to us through Polybius. It may be translated as
follows (XII, 4a, 2 = F 117):

He [*i.e.* Timaeus] upbraids Theopompus over this because Dionysius made his withdrawal from Sicily to Corinth in a warship (ἐν μακρᾷ νηί), while Theopompus says
Dionysius went in a merchantman (ἐν στρογγύλῃ).

We must agree with Polybius that Timaeus need not have stressed such a
minor correction of Theopompus' version, but *a fortiori* why does Polybius find it worth while to say so? He has not even the excuse of making
any correction at all. The fragment assumes more importance, however,
when we turn to the account in Diodorus and read that he sailed off to
Corinth "in a small merchantman" (ἐν μικρῷ στρογγύλῳ πλοίῳ—D.S. XVI,

70, 3). Not only does this suggest that Diodorus was not following Timaeus here as his "western" source, but it also raises the question of Diodorus' use of Theopompus in Book XVI. Whatever his source here may have been, the reference in the same context to the tyranny left by the elder Dionysius as "fastened with adamantine chains" reminds one of this same phrase used in connection with the events of 356/5 B.C. (XVI, 5, 4). But this is by no means conclusive evidence that Diodorus was following the same author in both passages. The fact that we know Diodorus got the same Dionysius story from two authors, using one version in one book and one in another, warns us from jumping to conclusions.[33]

The gaps in the fragments do not permit any appreciation of Timaeus' narrative of the complicated events of the tyranny of the younger Dionysius. We do not, regrettably, know what his judgment was of Dion, though presumably it was favorable. But we have a little something left of his portrayal of Timoleon. In addition to the fragments there can be little doubt that much of what we read in Plutarch's *Life* must come, directly or indirectly, from Timaeus.[34] Timoleon was by no means a hero without blemishes before Timaeus became his apologist, and Polybius might have helped us by pointing out specific errors of interpretation or emphasis. Instead, although he writes at some length, his criticism is confined to generalities (Polyb. XII, 23, 4–7 = F 119a). He objects to Timaeus on the mote and beam principle. Whereas he convicted Callisthenes of flattery—and Callisthenes, after all, was writing about Alexander—Timaeus proceeded to exalt his own hero above the gods. In effect, Polybius says that Timoleon was a second-rate performer given first-rate billing because of the exaggerated importance attached by Timaeus to Sicilian history. Plutarch, after his own fashion, is more helpful. He writes as follows (*Timol.* 36, 2 = F 119b):

> But of Timoleon's acts, if we leave out of discussion the distressing business about his brother, there is nothing, as Timaeus says, which does not serve to call to mind those words of Sophocles: "Oh, Gods, what love, what affection were joined in him!"

Cicero, writing to L. Lucceius the historian, exclaims over the good fortune that would be his if his friend would undertake to do for him what Timaeus had done for Timoleon, or Herodotus for Themistocles (*Ad fam.* V, 12, 7 = F 119c). Marcellinus, too, had remarked that Timaeus praised Timoleon beyond measure because Timoleon did not overthrow his father's rule in Tauromenium (*V. Thucyd.* 27).[35] Polybius, the exponent of *Realpolitik*, cares not a fig whether Timoleon was a fine man, but belittles his achievements; Plutarch, less interested in what he did, is worried about how so fine a man could have brought himself to kill his brother; Cicero, characteristically, wishes someone would glorify his own deeds; and Marcellinus suggests a prosaic reason for Timaeus' idealization of his hero.

Timaeus' account of the assassination of Timophanes, Timoleon's brother, who had set himself up as tyrant of Corinth about 365 B.C. (F 116 = Plut. *Timol.* 4, 5–8),[36] reads:

Timoleon took this hard, regarding the man's wrongdoing as his own misfortune. He tried to reason with him . . . (6) But when he repulsed him and showed his contempt, then Timoleon enlisted Aeschylus from among his relatives—for he was the brother of Timophanes' wife—and from his friends the diviner whom Theopompus calls Satyrus but whom both Ephorus and Timaeus call Orthagoras. Allowing a few days to go by, he went up again to see his brother. (7) The three men stood around him and begged him to listen to reason and to change his mind. At first Timophanes laughed at them, but then he grew angry and became violent. Timoleon withdrew a short distance from him, and stood there weeping with his face covered, while the others drew their swords and soon dispatched him.

There are two other accounts of this event: one that of Cornelius Nepos, who agrees substantially with Plutarch;[37] the other is in Diodorus, and it shows some important differences (D.S. XVI, 65). But the Plutarch passage itself proclaims the agreement of Theopompus, Ephorus, and Timaeus that a soothsayer took an active part in the assassination; Theopompus called him Satyrus, although the others said his name was Orthagoras. A number of years ago H. D. Westlake made an intensive study of the two biographies of Timoleon,[38] in which he tried to show that their close resemblances spring from the use of a common source—a Peripatetic biography, used exclusively by Nepos, but which in Plutarch supplemented by direct reference to the *History* of Timaeus. Such a hypothesis can neither be demonstrated nor refuted. The argument would be more plausible if in fact Nepos never disagreed with Plutarch, for then it would be reasonable to assume that Nepos had used just one of the sources used by Plutarch. But since they do disagree occasionally, the author is forced to account for these irregularities by the inventiveness of Nepos,[39] thus adding an element of speculation. But the idea that there was a Peripatetic biography of Timoleon in the background and that Plutarch knew about it is a likely suggestion. Furthermore, it is just possible that this biographer can be identified. A short but enlightening statement by Clement of Alexandria reads as follows (Clem. Alex. *Strom.* I, 135, 1):[40]

Theopompus and Ephorus and Timaeus write about a certain soothsayer, Orthagoras, just as Pythocles the Samian writes about Caius Julius Nepos in the fourth book of his *Italica*.

Is it not strange to find all three writers cited here writing about Orthagoras while in the Plutarch passage Theopompus mentions a soothsayer other than Orthagoras? But let us suppose a name had fallen out of the text of Plutarch, probably an error in copying. Then we might restore the text thus:[41]

... τῶν δὲ φίλων τὸν μάντιν, ὃν Σάτυρος μὲν * * *
Θεόπομπος, Ἔφορος δὲ καὶ Τίμαιος Ὀρθαγόραν ὀνομάζουσι ...

This would give us Satyrus as the name of the Peripatetic biographer, and there was a Satyrus who is known to have written biographies of many illustrious men, including some kings and generals.[42] Is not the dispute over small details, such as this one over the name of the soothsayer, a characteristic of the so-called Peripatetic writers in the later Hellenistic period?

However this may be, Plutarch records no major differences in his sources on the assassination of Timophanes. It was a carefully planned, coöperative undertaking in which Timoleon played the leading role, though he stood aside while the deed was done, no doubt on grounds of family feeling. The variation here in Nepos is interesting. Instead of covering his face, Timoleon is keeping a sharp lookout lest the conspirators be interrupted (Nepos *Timol.* 1, 4; *cf.* Plut. *Timol.* 4, 8). If this is an example of Nepos' inventiveness it does him credit. The Plutarchan version (surely that of Timaeus) is touching, theatrical even, but not at all convincing. It shows that neither Plutarch nor Timaeus had ever planned an assassination. Timoleon's later success as a practical man cries out against his having stood blindfolded at the crisis of his life while others acted for him. Nor is it likely that Aeschylus, himself a kinsman, would have consented to such a proceeding. The object, evidently, is to attempt to remove the stain of fratricide from the man who could do no wrong. Timaeus would probably have been horrified had he known that his hero was to serve as an inspiration for murder inside the family as late as the Italian Renaissance.[43]

How different is the account in Diodorus (D.S. XVI, 65, 3 ff.)! Timophanes was a very rich man who surrounded himself with a crowd of ne'er-do-wells and never walked abroad without an escort of ruffians. He made no secret of the fact that he was and intended to remain the tyrant of Corinth. We find Timoleon impelled to intervene because of his own personal aversion to one-man rule. As in Plutarch, he tries first to persuade his brother to give up his power willingly. But when this was of no avail, Diodorus' Timoleon proves that he is a man of action. He kills his brother, not in the house but in public, not by proxy but without any help from fellow conspirators. Then follows the account of the stir caused in Corinth and of the dilemma of the court as to whether Timoleon should be praised as a tyrannicide or punished as a fratricide. The appeal from Sicily arrived at just the right time, and it was decided to let Timoleon go. Should he succeed in overthrowing tyranny in Syracuse, he would automatically have cleared himself of all charges. Thus, in addition to other differences, the Diodoran account puts the assassination in 346/5 B.C. instead of about twenty years earlier, and in this Diodorus is clearly wrong.[44] How can these differences be explained?

His account of the assassination of Timophanes is so fundamentally opposed to the account in Plutarch–Nepos that the discrepancies cannot be accounted for by the presence of Satyrus as an intermediary between Timaeus and Plutarch–Nepos, and his absence in Diodorus. Diodorus must have had an entirely different source than the others, and because Plutarch's authorities were in general agreement, that source cannot have been Theopompus or Ephorus, neither of whom would have displaced this event by twenty years. Westlake's interpretation is sensible as to what actually happened—that Timoleon withdrew into private life and that many years later the Corinthians, not wishing to refuse help to their colony in its time of trouble, yet unwilling to risk a valuable military man, sent Timoleon, a comparative unknown and rather elderly. This may well have set tongues wagging about the sinister episode some twenty years back and may have led someone to remark that now they would find out the truth about Timoleon.[45] At the time his great abilities, both diplomatic and military, could not be suspected. But how can we explain the chronological blunder in Diodorus? Probably it came about because his source, also favorable to Timoleon, was a Sicilian historian who mentioned the assassination only in passing, as an introduction to Timoleon's activities in Sicily, which is why Diodorus himself brings it in. The error is so embedded in Diodorus' account that it should not be attributed to carelessness in transcribing. Certainty is out of the question where so many writers have disappeared without leaving a trace, but an attractive possibility is the historian Athanis (or Athanas) of Syracuse. He was known to Diodorus, who tells us that he wrote a work in thirteen books beginning with Dion's activities in 362/1, with a preliminary book summarizing events during the seven years between that date and the end of Philistus' history (D.S. XV, 94, 4). If he is also the *Athenis* who was chosen as one of the two leaders of Syracuse in 357/6 (Steph. Byz. *s.v.* Δύμη = Athanis 562 T 1), then he was a man with practical experience who would be able to appreciate Timoleon's qualities. Enough remains to show that he wrote favorably about him.[46]

Another fragment illustrates Timoleon's quick thinking in what might have been a dangerous situation. It reads as follows (F 118 = Plut. *Quaest. conv.* V, 3, 2, p. 676D):

Timaeus the historian relates that when the Corinthians were marching along to fight the Carthaginians over Sicily, they came on some mules laden with parsley. Most regarded this as a bad omen because parsley is associated with funerals, and when someone is desperately ill we say he is in need of parsley. Timoleon, on the contrary encouraged them, reminding them of the parsley with which the Corinthians crown the victors in the Isthmian Games.

We are able to supplement this from Diodorus, who was evidently following Timaeus here (XVI, 79). We learn that Timoleon's men accepted this as an indication of victory, and that at his bidding they continued their march wearing crowns of parsley in their hair. Incidentally, Diodorus mentions that just before this Timoleon had called the soldiers together and addressed them. His object, which he attained, was to arouse their fighting spirit by filling them with contempt for the enemy. Diodorus is very brief, but he brings out two points, the cowardice (ἀνανδρία) of the Carthaginians and the glory of Gelon. At the end of the speech the soldiers clamored to be led against the foe. This must be the speech that has been summarized by Polybius. One passage, supposedly copied verbatim from Timaeus may be given here (XII, 26a, 3 = F 31b):

"For who . . . can be at all afraid of men who, when nature has given them something superior to the other animals—I mean hands—carry them about uselessly all their lives inside their sleeves? But this is even more amazing; they wear underclothes beneath their tunics for fear that if they fall in battle they may expose themselves to the enemy!"

Polybius quotes this in order to ridicule Timaeus. Is it so ridiculous? There is something here of the rough humor of an Agesilaus when he showed his Spartans the kind of men they had to contend with in the underdeveloped Persians (Xen. *Hell.* III, 4, 19).

No other fragments about Timoleon have survived.[47]

The history of Agathocles for the first time presents the Hellenistic period with all that implies in the way of source problems. Beloch makes one of his sweeping generalizations when he asserts that no certainty is possible about the relationships between extant accounts and contempo-

rary sources, because only the *Parian Marble* actually goes back beyond
the Roman empire;[48] but this does not deter him from making pronounce-
ments of his own. Diodorus' account of Agathocles, according to Beloch,
rests on an intermediate source (*Mittelquelle*) which in turn made use of
Timaeus and of Duris.[49] Were he still living, Beloch would no doubt be
one of the first to rejoice over the recovery of a new fragment from
Oxyrhynchus on the history of Agathocles, written in a hand that suggests the middle of the first century B.C.[50] Three columns can be read
with some degree of completeness. The fourth column is poorly preserved,
and the fifth is a detached piece whose position has to be determined by
the context. There are also five other bits, with a few words still legible.
The first column concerns Agathocles' campaign in Africa; the others
have to do with events in Syracuse during his absence, including a very
stormy meeting of the Syracusan assembly. Considering Timaeus' reputation in antiquity and the law of averages, we would rather expect the
fragment to come from him. However, despite the fact that the text has
not yet been published and that the editor may hold a different opinion,
it would be fainthearted not to record my own conviction that whoever
the author may have been, it was not Timaeus. There is neither praise
nor blame of Agathocles to guide us, but there is one villain. So far as I
have been able to learn he is a man otherwise unknown, "Diognetus who
is called the Phalaenian" ("Monster"? "Whale"?).[51] He is said to have
been corrupted both by Hamilcar and by the exiles to attempt to overthrow the government.[52] Diognetus tries to rouse the people by an in-
cendiary speech, but he is opposed by Antander who makes charges
against him and against Hamilcar.[53] So far as one can tell, the tone is
favorable to Antander. This in itself should eliminate Timaeus, and it is
at least an obvious possibility that here, at long last, we have a genuine
extract from Antander's history.[54] Neither the details given by the papyrus on the Libyan campaign nor those on events in Syracuse match
what we have in Diodorus or in Justin's epitome of Trogus. Therefore,
we apparently have more evidence for Diodorus' sins of omission, as well
as fresh material to be fitted into a new study of Agathocles. The text
should arouse considerable interest when it appears in print.

Timaeus made fun of Agathocles for his humble origins. Polybius writes
(XV, 35, 2 = F 124c): "Agathocles, as Timaeus scoffingly says, began
as a potter, but abandoned the wheel, the clay and the smoke to come
to Syracuse as a young man." We cannot feel much confidence that this
is not a libelous statement. There always seems to have been a certain
amount of satisfaction in this sort of thing, nor have we outgrown it. It

may be noted here that both Duris and Timaeus evidently enjoyed referring to Socrates as a common laborer.[55] Therefore, the story that Agathocles started out as a potter would probably have appealed to them both and since each wrote about Agathocles, it is not easy to determine which account Diodorus is more likely to have adopted. Diodorus tells us quite an interesting story about Agathocles' childhood, which may be summarized as follows (XIX, 2–3):

Carcinus of Rhegium was exiled and settled down in Thermae, then under Carthaginian rule. He married there, and after his wife became pregnant he began having most distressing dreams. Because some Carthaginians were about to visit Delphi, he persuaded them to question Apollo about his unborn child. The oracle said that the boy would cause great unhappiness to the Carthaginians and to all Sicily. Carcinus, therefore, exposed the infant at birth and set watchers nearby to wait until he died. The watchers proved careless, and the mother managed to remove the child. She named him Agathocles after her own father, and turned him over to her brother, Heracleides, to look after. Years later Carcinus visited Heracleides and was charmed by the young Agathocles, who was stronger and more handsome than other boys his age. Learning who the boy was, Carcinus acknowledged him. But he knew the Carthaginians would be angry, so he took his family to Syracuse. Being a poor man, he taught young Agathocles the trade of potter. Then, when Timoleon offered Syracusan citizenship to anyone who wished it, Carcinus had his own name and that of his son added to the citizen rolls. Soon afterwards he died. The mother—we are not told her name—dedicated a statue of her son in some sacred spot, and a swarm of bees built their nest around the hips of the statue. Expert interpreters saw in this an indication of coming greatness. Young Agathocles was not to remain poor long. A rich Syracusan named Damas was smitten by his charms and helped him to acquire a competence. When Damas died he left all his money to his widow and Agathocles very soon married the widow, thus becoming one of the richest men in Syracuse.

This story has a number of the earmarks of Timaeus. The use of dreams and the fortunes predicted for Sicily remind one of his account of the youthful Dionysius.[56] Also, the omen of the swarm of bees is an interesting one. Philistus, a writer Timaeus knew thoroughly, spoke of bees swarming in the mane of Dionysius' horse as an indication of his coming rule (Philistus 556 F 58).[57] Also, the handsomeness of Agathocles is twisted into evil by the unscrupulous use he makes of his beauty, first with Damas, then with the rich widow.[58] But Duris cannot be eliminated as a possibility merely on the convenient assumption that he would have said nothing derogatory about a fellow monarch.[59] The fragments of his *Agathocles* do not settle the question, and he did write critically of at least one other ruler, Demetrius of Phalerum (Duris 76 F 10). There could, naturally, have been personal reasons for this, but so could there have been for his portrait of Agathocles; he was a contemporary, too. We can only say that the story in Diodorus suits Timaeus well, we cannot say he wrote it.

There are two attested fragments from the twentieth book of Diodorus, both of which touch on Agathocles' relations with Deinocrates. Deinocrates was the leader of the exiles in Sicily, largely Syracusans, who were out to overthrow Agathocles and restore free government to the Sicilian cities. The movement had gained headway as the Carthaginian danger lessened after Agathocles' invasion of Libya. The undertaking began in an idealistic spirit, but Deinocrates proved to be, as Tillyard calls him, "a shifty partisan."[60] The first fragment concerns peace with Carthage, concluded by Agathocles in 306/5, when it became apparent he could not reach a settlement with his Greek enemies because of Deinocrates (F 120 = D.S. XX, 79, 5). We cannot tell from the text whether Diodorus is following Timaeus for his main narrative of events or only for the detail about the money paid by Carthage to Agathocles as a part of the treaty. The other fragment has to do with events in the following year, after Agathocles had inflicted a crushing defeat on Deinocrates. It tells how Agathocles butchered a body of soldiers who had surrendered their weapons on the promise that their lives would be spared (F 121 = D.S. XX, 89, 4–6). This is the only example of a passage where Timaeus' figures are cited as larger than those of some other author. He says 7,000 men were massacred; some unnamed source says 4,000. There are no other fragments on Agathocles until the end of his life. Discrepancies over how old he was when he died have already been alluded to.[61] We do not know what lies behind the words (D.S. XXI, 16, 5 = F 123a): "He ended his life in a manner fitting his wickedness." But we can be sure that Agathocles' death was just as indicative of divine displeasure as that of Herod!

This, unfortunately, is as far as the fragments take us, though we would like some day to recover excerpts from Timaeus' history of Pyrrhus and of the outbreak of the First Punic War. For that our chief, perhaps our only, hope lies under the soil of Egypt.

CHAPTER V

TIMAEUS AND HIS CRITICS

THE HELLENISTIC PERIOD, as has been pointed out so often, resembles the modern in the variety of its literary production. Books were relatively cheap, private libraries no longer a curiosity but a necessity, and authors wrote more and more consciously to suit the tastes of a growing reading public. Greeks who found themselves living far from home in an alien environment were greatly assisted in preserving their identity, from generation to generation, by the steady flow of cheap papyrus from the state-controlled mills of Ptolemaic Egypt and by the rival parchment output of the Attalids. The written word, of growing importance from the fifth century on, now outstripped the spoken word in influence, not only on serious subjects, but also in the field of entertainment. Increasingly, books came to be designed for silent reading rather than for recitation. They were produced on various levels for recreation or instruction, each making its particular appeal to like-minded persons over a wide geographic area. The book, for the first time, had come into its own. Works like the histories of Herodotus and Thucydides, or the *Cyropaedia* of Xenophon lent themselves to being read aloud, but productions such as those of Timaeus and Theopompus, or the specialized collections of a Craterus[1] or a Diodorus Periegetes,[2] must have been intended at the outset for perusal in private or for reference. There came to be a growing interest in detail, fostered in part by the fact that learned men wrote for other learned men, who could and did check one author against another in their well-stocked libraries. It was in this atmosphere that the literary polemic grew to maturity and Timaeus contributed to its growth, both directly and through inspiration to those who came after him.

Some fifty years after Timaeus' death the historian Istrus wrote a polemic against him. The work has disappeared but not without leaving its mark, for Istrus was apparently the man who first referred to Timaeus as "Epitimaeus" or "Fault-Finder" (Istrus 334 F 59 = Athen. VI, 103, p. 272B). Istrus, who also wrote an *Attica*, was probably annoyed with Timaeus for his anti-Athenian viewpoint and for his disregard for the authority of the insipid but ever popular Ephorus.[3] As Jacoby indicates, Istrus was chiefly interested in the early days of Greece, and more in antiquarianism than in history proper, which had lost its *raison d'être* in

[1] For notes to chap. v, see pp. 134–136.

Athens with the end of the Chremonidean War.[4] His local pride shows itself particularly when he mentions Egypt,[5] but we cannot know whether this entered into his feelings about Timaeus.

During the second century—the exact date is uncertain—Polemon of Ilium wrote what must have been a substantial work about Timaeus' *History*.[6] Athenaeus, although we sometimes deplore his taste, is invaluable. He cites his sources carefully and often reproduces long passages verbatim. And it is Athenaeus who mentions a statement made by Polemon in Book XII of his Πρὸς Τίμαιον (*Against Timaeus*). It is very useful to know that in the second century B.C. Timaeus was sufficiently popular to justify consideration on such a generous scale. Nor was Polemon an amateur in the field of polemics. He also attacked Timaeus' earlier critic, Istrus, though perhaps not in a separate treatise,[7] and he is known to have written a work in two or more books against Eratosthenes, another against Neanthes, and an attack on Adaeus and Antigonus in at least six books.[8] Polemon is especially noted for his periegetic writings. Whether his studies were unrelated or formed parts of a general work is uncertain and need not be considered here.[9] He evidently had a particular interest in Attica, and his search for inscriptions won him the appropriate nickname of Στηλοκόπας ("Devourer of Tablets").[10] His curiosity seems to have been world-wide; he wrote about the foundation of cities in Italy and Sicily and also about Sicilian rivers (*FHG* III, Polemon, FF 37–38; 81–83). Although only eight fragments of his *Against Timaeus* survive, they show an interesting range of subject matter. The first four have to do with cult statues and religious observances in Sicily and also in other parts of the Greek world.[11] Two of the topics dealt with, Demeter the Bringer of Grain and the Erinyes (Polemon FF 39 and 41), have been noted already as subjects that interested Timaeus.[12] But the fragments offer no clue as to how Polemon differed with his predecessor. The fifth fragment is an odd bit informing us that quinces were known in Crete as "Cydonian apples" (Polemon F 43). Perhaps this relates to Timaeus' special interest in "inventions" or "discoveries" (εὑρήματα).[13] The sixth fragment is about the famous courtesan, Lais. Strangely Polemon and Timaeus are cited as being in agreement (Polemon F 44).[14] The last two fragments are concerned with parody and with the history of comedy (Polemon FF 45 and 46). Müller suggests this may have been inspired by something Timaeus had written about a famous Sicilian writer of parody, Boeotus, who was exiled by Agathocles.[15] The evidence is insufficient to give us any idea of the *Against Timaeus* as a whole, but when considered along with other Polemon fragments it becomes likely that the author was interested in correcting Timaeus on matters of detail, rather than in criticizing his general historical interpretation. Polemon has been judged unfavorably for his extremely bald style and for the way he crowded together masses of facts into a colorless narrative, condensed to the point of obscurity.[16] This judgment is substantiated by the passages Athenaeus quotes.[17] It is likely that such a writer found Timaeus an encyclopedia of information on which he drew freely, preserving his independence by criticizing his benefactor for minor slips. At least Polemon's work demonstrates that Timaeus was regarded as a very important writer, indeed—a conclusion that is strengthened when we remember that Polybius, who also lived in the second century, devoted almost the entire twelfth book of his own history to an attack on Timaeus. Surely it was no mean accomplishment to have drawn the concentrated fire of two such different antagonists, the dry-as-dust compiler and the practical political historian. Incidentally, Timaeus' other nickname, Γραοσυλ-λέκτρια ("Gossip-Monger"), can hardly have been invented by Polemon, for that would have been too much like the pot calling the kettle black.[18]

The remarks of Polemon and Istrus about Timaeus have largely been forgotten. Not so those of Polybius, for enough remains of Book XII of his history to make his attitude toward Timaeus perfectly clear. Polybius' reputation is high, usually insuring him of at least third place among the leading Greek historians, ahead of Xenophon but behind Herodotus and Thucydides. For only these four survive from the period of independence in sufficient bulk to be read consecutively; and later historians cannot be weighed in the same balance. Greek historical writing was a city-state product, and when the city-state drooped, it drooped too. Polybius' own position in this tradition is assured by his survival, but it does need to be redefined. The relevant facts about his life are well established and need only be referred to briefly. As the member of a leading family in Megalopolis he was cut out for a political career and served the Achaean League in various capacities, no doubt expecting ultimately, like his father before him, to obtain the highest office. But his life was shaped differently when, along with some thousand other Greeks, he was sent to Italy as a hostage following the Third Macedonian War (approximately 167 B.C.). By great good fortune he became closely associated with Scipio Aemilianus, and had unrivalled opportunities for learning about the details of Roman administration as well as the intricacies of military organization. He became a historian when, at some time unknown, he first conceived the brilliant idea of writing a general history, concentrating on the fifty-three years between 220 and 167 B.C., during which Rome became the dominant power in the Mediterranean world (see Polyb. III, 1, 9–11). This was his leading idea, though he found it necessary to write two preliminary books to set the stage, carrying the story back to the First Punic War where Timaeus breaks off (Polyb. I, 5, 1). Later he extended his account to the Fall of Carthage and the destruction of the Achaean League in 146 B.C.[19] Polybius was a man impressed by political power. His own experiences had taught him that Rome's series of triumphs was not the result of accident, and he sought to find an explanation in her governmental institutions.[20] Since political history alone interested him, and primarily contemporary history, he had little patience with what he no doubt regarded as an unrealistic admiration for the heroic deeds of the remote past. Also, he felt contempt for the civilian, the man of letters without military experience. Polybius was a painstaking writer. He worked out his chronology with the greatest care, and succeeded in producing a clear narrative of events for the whole Mediterranean area during a time of bewildering political changes. In this, perhaps, he may occasionally remind one of Macaulay. But although his powers of visualization were great, the same cannot be said for his critical ability. Narrow, opinionated, honest, and rather complacent, Polybius is not altogether an amiable figure; but amiability has never been a prerequisite for the historian. Nor should we allow ourselves to be prejudiced by his inability to write the graceful prose of Xenophon, for who outside of Athens could do that? The lack of critical judgment—in which he resembles Xenophon—is a much more serious defect and one of which he is quite unaware. Therefore, since he writes with force and with obvious sincerity, and since also he professes to be well informed and conscientious, his remarks about other writers have a way of imposing themselves even against our better judgment.

A glance for a moment at what he has to say about another Greek historian, Phylarchus, presents further perspective on Polybius. He interrupts his account of the Cleomenian War for an eight-chapter digression on Phylarchus (II, 56–63). Since this part of Polybius has reached us unabridged, we are able to follow his whole argument without feeling, as we do with Timaeus, that something may have been left out. He begins by stating his reasons for digressing. Phylarchus, who lived through the events he describes, wrote an account of the period which differs materially from that of Aratus, whom Polybius has taken as his own source. Because Phylarchus has sometimes been regarded with favor, it becomes imperative to examine his account "lest we permit falsehood to carry the same weight as truth in historical works" (II, 56, 2). Whereas Phylar-

chus' whole history is written in a slovenly fashion, Polybius feels that
it will be sufficient to consider only his account of the Cleomenian War
in order to demonstrate his untrustworthiness. His first specific charge
against Phylarchus is that he gives a lurid description of the horrors of
the sack of Mantineia in order to create an impression of the barbarity
of Antigonus, of Aratus, and of his fellow Achaeans. This account he
attacks on several grounds. The first is really a criticism of style. The
historian, unlike the tragedy writer, should not try to stir the emotions.
In tragedy the object is plausibility for the moment, but in history it is
enlightenment for all time. The historian ought not to be on the lookout
for the sensational, but rather he ought to "record truthfully what was
done and what was said, even though it happens to have been quite
ordinary" (II, 56, 10). His second criticism is of a different kind. The
historian has no right to appeal to our sympathy merely because he describes frightful things, for we cannot feel pity unless we know the reasons
behind the events. Polybius gives a number of examples of acts of vio-
lence that are not censured, such as killing a thief or an adulterer, and of
others which are warmly praised, such as killing a tyrant or a traitor.
After raising these general objections to Phylarchus' methods as shown
in his description of Mantineian sufferings, Polybius tries to show that
the Mantineians did in fact deserve the treatment Phylarchus describes.
He recounts their perfidy. Having deserted the Achaean alliance, first
for the Aetolians, then for Sparta, they were captured by treachery, and
fell into the hands of Aratus. Instead of wreaking vengeance he brought
them back into the Achaean League, and they fraternized with their
erstwhile deadly enemies. Later, fearing internal disturbances as well as
outside plots, the Mantineians asked the Achaeans for help. This help
was forthcoming, in the form of a force of 300 citizen militia and 200
mercenaries. Later the Spartans were admitted into Mantineia, and the
Achaean soldiers were put to the sword. For this, according to Polybius,
it would have been an inadequate punishment if all the Mantineians had
been sold into slavery, because such treatment was approved by the
rules of war even when no special act of impiety had been committed
(II, 58, 9–10). What did happen to the Mantineians was merely that the
men were sold into slavery and their property confiscated. Phylarchus
had described a slaughter. Polybius' final criticism concerns a point of
logic. If the Mantineians were treated harshly because Antigonus and
Aratus were brutes, then why, when Tegea was captured, were the inhabitants not treated in the same way? Since in fact they were not so

treated, the explanation must lie in the different background of the two events—that is, the Tegeans had not been guilty of perfidy.

For a historian of Polybius' reputation this is an extraordinary performance. The only fact he introduces against Phylarchus is implied, not stated outright. He implies that Phylarchus made a misstatement in describing a slaughter of the Mantineians, though he does not say that such a slaughter did not occur in the first flush of victory; there would still be men left, perhaps in the temples, who could later be sold into slavery. His assumption that it would have been justifiable to kill everyone is so callous that one wonders whether his long sojourn in Rome had not coarsened him. But the worst part of his argument, historically, is its superficiality. Clearly the Achaeans were not actuated primarily by philanthropic motives when they spared the Mantineians the first time, as he says they were,[21] any more than the Athenians were in their treatment of Mitylene. And the very fact that immediately thereafter the Achaeans have to put in a garrison because of dissension in Mantineia is proof enough that matters were very much less clear than Polybius tells us. He throws no light on the internal situation and on the various factions, which alone could bring any sort of understanding to the narrative.

The next example chosen by Polybius concerns the death of Aristomachus of Argos. Phylarchus had spoken of his death by torture, after being captured by Antigonus and the Achaeans, as an outrage; and he evidently painted a pathetic picture. Aristomachus' shrieks pierced the night air in the neighborhood of Cenchreae, and everyone who heard them was shocked at such an exhibition of brutality. Some even tried to rush the building. Polybius' procedure is much the same as before; he builds up his case against Aristomachus, then states that even though he had died in the way described by Phylarchus, he richly deserved it (II, 59, 7; 60, 7). The indictment is made both on general and on particular grounds. That he was a tyrant and descended from tyrants is enough by itself to condemn him, for every lawless act known to man is comprised in that one word "tyrant" (II, 59, 6). The particular charges against him are two. While he ruled in Argos the Achaeans, led by Aratus, succeeded in breaking into the city. But the citizens failed to rise in rebellion "out of fear of the tyrant," so the Achaeans were driven out again. Subsequently, Aristomachus put eighty leading men to death under torture in the presence of their relatives for alleged sympathy with the Achaean plot. The other charge is that later on, when he found his position threatened by events following the death of Demetrius, the

Macedonian king, Aristomachus gave up his tyranny. However, thanks to the "mildness and gentlemanliness of the Achaeans," he was unexpectedly saved. Not only he but also his city joined the Achaean League, and his impious acts as a tyrant were forgiven. Nor was this all, for he was actually elected to the highest office in the league (II, 60, 5). Forgetting his obligations to his benefactors, he listened to the blandishments of Cleomenes and withdrew his city from the league at a critical time. When he fell into Achaean hands again, Polybius said that he deserved to be carried around the Peloponnese and tortured at every stop, as a public example. Instead, he was merely drowned quietly off Cenchreae, not tortured in the night as Phylarchus said (II, 60, 8).

But who is illogical this time? Polybius has yielded to an obvious temptation. The case against Aristomachus is built up to a climax with all the flourishes of rhetoric. Crime is added to crime, until mere drowning seems an act of Christian charity. There are no bright spots in his character. He might well reply like Aristophanes' Sausage-Seller when asked if he were descended from men of breeding: "Not I, by the Gods, but only from rascals!" Twice Polybius tells us Aristomachus was a tyrant and the descendant of tyrants (II, 59, 1; 5); then he is found guilty of murdering eighty innocent citizens under torture. But what follows? All is forgiven, and he is admitted to the Achaean fellowship, even honored by the office of general. The only crime that arouses Polybius' indignation, really, is his crime in removing Argos from the league to join Cleomenes. It is for that that he should have been taken around the Peloponnese and tortured. What is left of the indictment against Phylarchus? One fact. Phylarchus said Aristomachus died under torture, while Polybius, and no doubt Aratus, said he was drowned. And we have no basis for deciding between them.

But Polybius attacked Phylarchus for what he did not say as well as for what he said. All the remainder of his criticism is connected with Megalopolis (II, 62–63) and, as in writing about Mantineia, Polybius proceeds from the general to the particular. In this section are presented the distinguishing features between the functions of poet and historian; we are told that it is the positive duty of the historian to influence the future by praising good deeds in the past. This view is presented negatively in that Phylarchus is said to have written as if he thought it were incumbent on the historian to describe horrors rather than to record noble actions. Phylarchus writes as though "the readers of histories were less improved by the recital of splendid and enviable deeds than they are by lawless and despicable ones" (II, 61, 3). Polybius then summarizes

Phylarchus' account of Cleomones' capture of Megalopolis. The citizens
had fled to Messene, and they refused his offer to spare the city if they
returned and changed sides. This act of the exiles should have been
praised as an act of self-renunciation by men who refused to betray their
allies for any price. But Phylarchus fails to do so because he is blind to
the historian's duty of emphasizing noble actions (II, 61, 12). This is an
incredibly naive criticism, and one which is twice contradicted by the
facts as Polybius himself gives them. He accuses Phylarchus of describing Cleomenes' liberal offer to the exiles only because he wanted to emphasize Cleomenes' magnanimity (II, 61, 4). Yet surely this offer of
clemency by a victorious general should qualify, on Polybius' own terms,
as one of those fine actions it was the historian's duty to emphasize? The
second fact is that Cleomenes' offer, in the form of a letter, was not read
through to the Megalopolitans to the end, because the reader was
drowned out by shouts (II, 61, 5). If they did not know how generous the
offer was, can we be sure that the exiles were so self-sacrificing?

What follows is so different in quality from all the preceding that it is
hard to realize the same man wrote it. Polybius takes note of Phylarchus'
statement that the Spartans obtained 6,000 talents in booty from Megalopolis, 2,000 of which were turned over to Cleomenes (II, 62, 1). And
Polybius goes on to demolish this assertion with relentless thoroughness.
He begins by saying that figures of this kind show the writer to be ignorant of the most elementary facts about the wealth of the Greek states.
In his own day, when everyone admitted the Peloponnese had attained
a high level of prosperity, not all the cities together could furnish 6,000
talents from their movable property exclusive of slaves. Yet when
Cleomenes ruled, the area had been impoverished by civil war and by
successive Macedonian invasions. Further, he demonstrates that when
Athens was a great power, on the eve of a war with Thebes as her ally, an
assessment of the property of Attica, including the houses themselves,
fell short of this figure by 250 talents. The clinching argument is that
Mantineia, which by Phylarchus' own admission was second to none in
Arcadia, yielded booty worth only 300 talents (II, 62, 11–12). He then
shows that Phylarchus' statement is inconsistent with his own narrative
of subsequent events. Phylarchus says that Cleomenes was forced to
gamble on an immediate battle against Antigonus, because he had just
heard from Ptolemy of Egypt that there would be no further subsidies.
Yet if there had really been 6,000 talents booty from Megalopolis, "he
would have been able to surpass Ptolemy himself in his expenditures"
(II, 63, 3)! Even Thucydides would not have been ashamed of this
exposition.[22]

Our examination of the criticism of Phylarchus suggests that, far from being an impartial judge of the works of others, Polybius is at the mercy of his own prejudices. This applies particularly to the period before his own day, because he was not trained sufficiently in the evaluation of literary sources. Growing up in Megalopolis, he was fired with enthusiasm for the Achaean League and for its leading figure, Aratus, and he saw only confirmation of this view in the memoirs Aratus had written. Obviously, it did not occur to him to make any allowance for Aratus' motives. The apologia is accepted at face value, but the motives of his adversaries are carefully weighed and discredited. He is no less prejudiced here than he accuses Timaeus of being in his account of Timoleon. But entirely aside from the matter of bias, Polybius shows an astonishing lack of sophistication in handling his sources. He seems to have been content to follow one writer at a time, in this instance Aratus, without making any effort to compare statements from different authors in order to produce a better rounded account than any one contemporary narrative could possibly be. Just as we have seen him earlier backing Aristotle to the hilt against Timaeus on the colonization of Locri,[23] so here he identifies Aratus with Clio herself, while he regards Phylarchus, who was also an eyewitness, as completely without value. Yet today it is recognized that any contemporary account, however slanted, can be made to yield valuable information, just as a deliberate falsehood will often point the way to the truth it is intended to conceal. Whereas he seems to have been incapable of this kind of analysis, Polybius is not to be denied when he fastens on to a particular misstatement within the realm of his own experience. All his general arguments fail to achieve their purpose, but his examination of the figure of 6,000 talents is so effective that no rebuttal is possible. It remains to be seen whether his criticism of Timaeus is equally unanswerable.

Most of what Polybius has to say on this subject has already been discussed piecemeal in earlier chapters. Here it will be convenient to arrange his arguments in the order in which they seem to have been given originally in Book XII, referring back to previous discussion where possible, supplementing where necessary. It will be remembered that Book XII now consists of a series of excerpts, some quite long, some short, whose preservation is owed to later writers. They have been arranged in chapters for the convenience of the modern reader, but no arrangement can disguise the fact that the text is uneven. Sometimes it is full, at other times woefully abridged. The first chapter is merely a series of bald statements on Libyan geography picked up by Stephanus of Byzantium;

the second, found in Athenaeus, gives an account of the Libyan lotus and its uses. These explain the position of chapters three and four, which have been given the special heading by the German editor, *Timaei de Africa et Corsica Errores*, and comprise a single excerpt.[24] The part on Africa is very brief and, as noticed earlier, Polybius contradicts himself in criticizing Timaeus.[25] The Corsican section is longer, serving double duty as a fragment of Polybius and one of Timaeus.[26] Polybius here brings his personal experience to bear. He has seen swineherds in Italy whose charges respond to the horn. Each recognizes the sound of his own master's instrument, and this serves as a means to unscramble the herds when they have gone off together grubbing for nuts. But we are not quite clear what Polybius is criticizing. Is it merely that Timaeus had spoken of herds responding to the shepherd's flute, and that Polybius believes this is too commonplace to be worth recording in a history? Or is it because Timaeus mistakenly spoke of wild animals in Corsica which really were not wild at all, but only appeared to be so because they wandered off by themselves? If Diodorus is following our historian in his description of Corsica, then Timaeus spoke of herds as being distinguished by special marks (brands?),[27] rather than separated by the flute. Polybius would not have argued from the behavior of Italian herdsmen, had he ever visited Corcyra.[28]

The next section is more general and conveniently labeled *De aliis Timaei Erroribus*.[29] The first chapter (4a) attacks him for quibbling with Theopompus over the type of ship on which Dionysius the Younger left Sicily for Corinth,[30] and also for attributing a simple mistake in arithmetic to Ephorus in computing the length of the reign of the elder Dionysius. Here, as we have seen, Polybius completely missed the point of Timaeus' criticism.[31] Next comes the well-known bit about a Roman sacrifice said to derive from memories of the Trojan Horse (XII, 4b–4c, 1).[32] There follows the accusation that Timaeus is inaccurate when he writes about Libya, Sardinia, and Italy. Although the historian cannot be expected to visit every part of the world, he should make as many inquiries as possible and follow the best sources. Also, he should be a good judge of "reports" ($\tau \hat{\omega} \nu \ \pi \rho o \sigma \pi \iota \pi \tau \acute{o} \nu \tau \omega \nu$—XII, 4c, 2–5). Timaeus is not only unable to judge accurately what he hears from others, but he cannot even be trusted to tell the truth about Sicily, which he knew at first hand; this is shown by his account of the Fountain of Arethusa.[33]

The next section, on Locri, *De Timaei Erroribus Commissis de Rebus Locrensium* (XII, 5–22) is a long one, and Polybius' chief criticisms have already been discussed in some detail.[34] Here the interest lies in the way

Polybius develops his attack. He begins by stating his own position very clearly. He has often visited Locri. He likes the Locrians and they like him; they have even bestowed honors on him for his influence in obtaining favors for them from Rome. But despite his natural inclination to speak well of them, he finds it necessary to admit that Aristotle was right and Timaeus wrong about the history of the colony (XII, 5, 1–4). Then he offers on-the-spot evidence for Aristotle's statement that the colony was founded by former slaves. This includes their tracing their ancestry through the female line back to the One Hundred Houses and their adoption of Sicel institutions because they lacked ancestral ones of their own (XII, 5, 5–11). Next comes the story of how they got around their treaty with the Sicels by equivocating.[35] Then, for the first time, Polybius alludes to one of Timaeus' arguments—that the old Greeks did not have slaves at all—which he tries to refute by quoting Timaeus against himself (XII, 6, 7).[36] After suggesting that Aristotle's version has already been shown to be superior, Polybius mentions another ridiculous statement by Timaeus—that former slaves of Sparta would not have been on good terms with Sparta's allies. Polybius' argument is tedious, based on generalities. Slaves would naturally try to conceal their origin and pretend to be their masters' descendants rather than their freedmen (XII, 6a, 1–3). Especially would this apply to the Locrians after years had passed, years spent in a remote area where their antecedents were unknown (XII, 6b, 1–2). Nothing disproves Aristotle's statement that the Athenians ravaged Locrian territory (XII, 6b, 3–4). Then he takes the matter up from the Spartan point of view. Their own history and institutions would preclude them from holding any grudge against the Locrians; therefore the close relations between them are perfectly reasonable (XII, 6b, 5–10). From there Polybius returns to the attack. He accuses Timaeus of telling lies out of a desire to defame some persons and to extol others. Aristotle's motives, he implies, were more respectable. Therefore he is able to reason more accurately from the same data. Timaeus cannot be excused on the ground of ignorance of the facts (XII, 7 entire). Next he criticizes him for his vilification of Aristotle. The proper procedure would have been to show that Aristotle wrote from interested motives. Since that was impossible, he has resorted to a kind of personal abuse which no true historian would even entertain in his inmost thoughts, let alone put on paper (XII, 8 entire).[37] Polybius now shifts from the general to the specific. He proposes to examine Timaeus' account in comparison to that of Aristotle and tells how Timaeus claims documentary support for his views. He professes to have seen documents among the Greek Locrians, including a treaty they had made with the Italian Locrians. He also urges that the laws of Italian Locri prove that the colony was founded by free men (XII, 9 entire). Polybius' clumsy effort to prove that Timaeus faked this evidence has already been discussed,[38] and need only be referred to here. The chief argument is that Timaeus was suspiciously vague as to where he had seen the documents of the Greek Locrians, particularly in view of the pains he takes to authenticate his information about Italian Locri (XII, 10 entire).[39] Other examples of Timaeus' expertness in documentation and chronology are given (XII, 11, 1–3)[40] to show that he was not the man to be reticent about a document unless he had invented it. But such a savage critic of others need expect no mercy for his own lapses. Timaeus has lied, and he has accused Aristotle and Theophrastus of slandering Locri (XII, 11, 4–5). Excusing himself for this long digression on the ground that by speaking out now he will not have to interrupt the narrative later on, he turns next to Timaeus' pronouncement on the subject of truth in history. This passage has not been discussed and is worth quoting in full as the most reliable statement we have of Timaeus' views on the matter of professional ethics (XII, 11, 8–12, 2 = Tim. F 151):

Now Timaeus says that the greatest fault in a history is to lie. Therefore, he advises those whom he convicts of falsehood to find some other name for their books, and to label them anything rather than *history*. *12.* For just as in the case of a carpenter's square, even though it is less in length and also inferior in width, and yet it still possesses the character of a carpenter's square, he says it should also be given that name. But when it is not straight and does not even approximate this quality, then it should be called anything rather than a square. (2) In the same way, he says, when writings are deficient in style or treatment, or in any other particular aspect, yet still cling to the truth, the name of *history* still belongs to such works, but when they depart from this, one should no longer speak of them as *histories*.

Polybius professes to agree wholeheartedly with this statement. But he uses it as a further justification for a favorite pronouncement of his own, that those who err out of ignorance deserve good-tempered correction, but the deliberate liars should be eternally damned. We are not surprised to hear that Timaeus belongs in the latter category (XII, 12, 3–7). There follows another instance of treaty-breaking by Locrians, this time the Greek ones (XII, 12a, 1–3).[41] The relevance to the attack on Timaeus is not clear, but one does begin to wonder whether Polybius is quite so devoted to the Locrians, either in Greece or in Italy, as he professes to be.

The text of what follows is corrupt, though the gist of it seems to be that Timaeus ought not to criticize others for including dreams and other fancies in their histories, when he does the same thing himself (XII, 12b,

1).[42] Then Polybius takes up Timaeus' abusive language about Callisthenes (XII, 12b, 2–3),[43] Demochares (XII, 13 and 14 entire),[44] and Agathocles (XII, 15 entire).[45] It is astonishing that Polybius should have devoted so much space and energy to the defense of these three men, especially when we know that he himself was nothing if not critical of Callisthenes.[46] Then, too, Polybius was much annoyed with Phylarchus for writing favorably of Aristomachus because he was a tyrant—the word "tyrant" sums up all possible evil (II, 59–60, especially 59, 5–6); yet what else was Agathocles? His defense of Demochares is based on the principle of innocence by association. He was gently born and a nephew of Demosthenes. To attack Demochares was to impugn the character of the Athenians, who elected him to the highest office (what of the Achaeans who elected Aristomachus?). Then there is the negative evidence. Demochares had enemies, influential men like Demetrius of Phalerum, who would certainly have called attention to Demochares' scandalous behavior had the charges been true. Therefore Polybius chooses to believe Demochares' fellow citizens, who knew him, rather than to accept the malicious reports of Timaeus.[47] But a different method is needed to defend Agathocles. Here Polybius appeals to the inconsistencies in Timaeus' account. No ordinary man could do what Agathocles had done, and Timaeus is unfair in ignoring his successes and in emphasizing his failures.

The next chapter (16) contains an anecdote about a legal dispute, presumably in Locri, and refers to the Code of Zaleucus. Whether this is still a part of the attack on Timaeus is hard to tell, for his name is not mentioned in the excerpt. But it will be remembered that Timaeus denied the historicity of Zaleucus.[48]

The next section of Book XII (*De Callisthenis Imperita in Narrandis Rebus Militaribus*) need not be discussed, since it is a digression within a digression and contains nothing about Timaeus (XII, 17–22).[49] However, he soon returns to the main theme, which continues for the rest of the book (*De Timaeo Historico*—XII, 23–28a). Polybius resumes by reiterating one of his favorite charges against Timaeus: that he accuses others of the very faults he exhibits himself; and that he shows his own corrupt nature by parading his opinions of others. As an example of this, Polybius alludes to his abuse of Ephorus (XII, 23, 1) and elaborates with reference to Callisthenes. Whereas Callisthenes tried to make Alexander a god, Timaeus treats Timoleon as even greater than the gods. Yet Callisthenes' hero was admittedly more than a man, but Timoleon was an ordinary person. Polybius suggests, with heavy irony, that from Timaeus' viewpoint anything that happened in Sicily was more important than what happened in all the rest of the world put toegther, although in actuality events there were of only minor significance. Just as Timaeus over-valued his own Sicilian heroes, so, according to his critic he also over-valued his own *History*, which was not worthy of comparison with a general world history (XII, 23, 3–7).[50] With chapter twenty-four Polybius mentions a favorite dogma of Timaeus', that poets and also historians reveal their characters by frequent repetition of certain subjects in their works. This was true of Homer as it was of Aristotle. Also, the tyrant Dionysius showed what he was by the kind of things he talked about (XII, 24, 1–3). The rest of the chapter, corrupt in part, is clear in its general meaning. Timaeus' work is full of the extravagances he criticizes in others. Also, even an eyewitness can sometimes be said not to be present at all if he lacks experience and judgment. Such a one was Timaeus (XII, 24, 3–6). Then comes the argument about the Bull of Phalaris, already discussed (XII, 25, 1–5).[51]

The remainder of Book XII survives in such a mutilated form as to make any attempt to restore the original context a matter of pure guesswork. Therefore, the conventional order of the fragments will be disregarded and, instead, the subjects treated will be alluded to briefly. Three topics may be singled out for comment: (1) The use of speeches in histories; (2) Timaeus' lack of training for his task; (3) Timaeus' reputation. Most of the rest consists of abusive remarks that may be omitted since they add nothing to Polybius' argument. Polybius maintains that historians should be sparing in their use of speeches. Such speeches as they include ought to be short and pointed, and as close as possible to what was actually said on a particular occasion (XII, 25i, 4; 25f, 6–8). However, he does not minimize their importance, for he admits that they serve to sum up the action and bind the history together (XII, 25a, 3). By giving what was said and also explaining the motivation of the speakers, the historian allows his readers to see just why a certain policy succeeded or why it failed. This true understanding of the past can then be applied to the present, and when an analogous situation presents itself the student of history can profit by his knowledge (XII, 25i, 8; 25b, 1–4). Timaeus makes the mistake of writing his speeches out of thin air in order to display his own cleverness (XII, 25a, 5). This cavalier disregard for what was really said and the substitution of long, irrelevant speeches destroy the very essence of history (XII, 25b, 4). Polybius gives examples of what he means, notably the speeches attributed to Hermocrates (XII, 25k, 2–26, 8)[52] and Timoleon (XII, 26a, 1–4).[53]

In the effort to show that Timaeus was not properly trained for writing a history, Polybius sets up a canon of his own. Like medicine, history contains three essential parts: (1) A synthesis of what has previously been written on the subject; (2) Geography—knowledge of topography, distances, rivers, cities, and so forth; (3) Description of political and military events (XII, 25e, 1–2). The historian who tries to write from books alone resembles the physician who studies medicine in libraries without actually practicing his calling (XII, 25e, 4). The historian, ideally, should have first-hand experience in all the types of activities he describes. Since this is impossible, he should know about the most important of them, war and politics (XII, 25h, 5–6), for no one should write about either unless he has taken an active part in them (XII, 25g, 1). Of the three parts of history, the least important is that connected with books (XII, 26, 2). Timaeus lacks political and military experience (XII, 25g, 3; 25h, 1–4), and he chooses to rely on the accounts of others rather than on his own observation (XII, 27, 2–6). Polybius sums up his view in what is surely a conscious imitation of Plato's famous pronouncement about the philosopher king. For Polybius says that there will be no end to bad histories until men experienced in politics and war undertake to devote the rest of their lives to history, or until the would-be historians first acquire the necessary training in public life (XII, 28, 3–5). It is easy to see that at least one second-century historian had fulfilled these requirements.

Finally, we come to the question that apparently disturbed Polybius most of all. Why was Timaeus so highly regarded? That he was in fact highly regarded is tacitly admitted by Polybius himself by beginning his own introductory books where Timaeus left off; and the detailed treatment in Book XII is alone sufficient to prove Timaeus' popularity. Polybius has set out deliberately to smash his reputation, whether out of a zeal for historic truth or for some less creditable reason we cannot say. But it is evident that Polybius' emotions are involved even when he tries hardest to be fair. He tells us that Timaeus had been highly regarded because he is so critical of earlier writers, and that he is judged more for what he wrote about them than for any very positive contribution of his own (XII, 25c, 1–2). He has the *appearance* of telling the truth, and his arguments, though really illogical, have taken people by surprise and bullied them into acquiescence (XII, 26d, 1). But he is specially famous for his statements about colonization and the relations between one colony and another, where he makes a great show of accuracy. So biting are his criticisms of other writers on these matters that they seem by comparison like men writing in their sleep (XII, 26d, 2–3). But when it is shown that Timaeus was guilty of the very faults he attacks bitterly in others—as in his account of Locri—then his readers become opinionated and stubborn, and this may be regarded as the chief benefit they have gained from studying his work (XII, 26d, 4–5). We may close with Polybius' exasperated comment, made after noting that Timaeus fulfilled none of the essential requirements for a historian (XII, 28, 6):

... and I do not understand how he has gained his reputation, arrogating to himself the dignity of a historian!

Of Polybius' criticism, a good deal is relevant. Surely he is right in refusing to accept Timaeus' popularity as any proof of his merit as a historian. He is probably right, also, in finding Timaeus waspish in his comments on other writers, though here he and his critic stand on the same level. Polybius insists, and quite properly, that the historian must be a man who has lived a full life outside the covers of the books in his library. But few historians now would accept Polybius' narrow definition of a full life as one devoted to politics and the command of armies. At the root of his distrust of Timaeus is the dangerous assumption that history should be written to serve a utilitarian purpose in training future statesmen and generals. Polybius betrays the fact that he is not really interested in the past except as a guide for the present and the future. Such a man could only feel exasperated when he thumbed through long passages dealing with the past glories of Acragas or anecdotes about Pythagoras or Empedocles. And here Polybius' viewpoint is not outmoded; the "practical" man is always with us. But anyone who still possesses a Herodotean curiosity about anything and everything that has happened to people in the past will find Timaeus more to his liking.

NOTES

NOTES

The abbreviations will be understood easily by those familiar with the subject. References to the fragments, in the text as well as in the notes, are to Felix Jacoby's *Die Fragmente der griechischen Historiker* (1923–) unless otherwise stated. Jacoby's numbers are used (e.g., Philistus 556 T 2) without giving the volume in which a fragment (F) or *testimonium* (T) appears. For Timaeus the number (566) is not usually given. Carolus Müller's *Fragmenta Historicorum Graecorum* (1841–1870) is cited by volume and page (e.g., *FHG* II, p. 182 F 261).

NOTES TO CHAPTER I
Timaeus' Life and Writings
(pages 1–20)

[1] See Laqueur's "Timaios," No. 3, *R.-E.*[2], 11 (1936), col. 1082. Laqueur also cites Polyb. III, 32, 2 (where Polybius is speaking in general about the advantages of his own kind of history, which contains a clear account of events in Italy, Sicily, and Libya from the time of Pyrrhus to the Fall of Carthage). But Polybius is speaking very loosely, and even here he does *not* say Timaeus ended with Pyrrhus. In his own account he does touch briefly on Pyrrhus (I, 6, 5).

[2] *Ibid.*, col. 1081.

[3] See *F.Gr.H.* II D, p. 544, ll. 26 ff. That Hieronymus did go down at least to Pyrrhus' death is shown by two fragments (Hieronymus 154 FF 14 and 15).

[4] Polybius writes his first two books as an introduction to the beginning of his own detailed account of events. In these books he bridges the gap between the 129th Olympiad, where Timaeus ended, and the 140th Olympiad, which marks his own true beginning (*cf.* Polyb. I, 5, 1 with I, 3, 1). For Greece he continues Aratus' narrative (I, 3, 2).

[5] On Philistus, *cf.* Plut. *Dion* 35, 6; D.S. XVI, 16, 4. On Timaeus' love of synchronisms, see H. J. W. Tillyard, *Agathocles* (London, 1908), p. 14.

[6] [Lucian] *Macrob.* 22. Also in Phlegon (257 F 37, 81). See T. S. Brown, "Hieronymus of Cardia," *A.H.R.*, 52 (1947), 685–686.

[7] Pietro Rizzo, *Tauromenion, Storia, Topografia, Monumenti, Monete* (Riposto Stab. Tip. Santo Garufi: 1928), p. 56. Beloch believed Timaeus could not have died before 255 B.C. *because* he lived to be ninety-six (*Griechische Geschichte*, IV, 1, p. 484 n. 1). Tillyard seems to have held the same view, however (*op. cit.*, p. 12).

[8] See T. S. Brown, "Herodotus and his Profession," *A.H.R.*, 59 (1954), 841–843.

[9] See Laqueur, "Timaios," cols. 1077–1078. See also the D.S. passages: XIX, 8, 1 (317 B.C.)—Agathocles secures control of Syracuse and some of his old enemies throw themselves down from the walls and escape to nearby towns; XIX, 72, 1 (314)—Agathocles gains control of other Sicilian cities; XIX, 102, 6 (312)—Agathocles kills his enemies in Tauromenium and Messina; XX, 4 (310)—Agathocles' persecutions preliminary to the Carthaginian war.

[10] See Müller, *FHG* I, p. L.

[11] Rizzo, *Tauromenion*, p. 56.

[12] Beloch argued that Polybius used Timaeus rather than Philinus as his source on Hieron (I, 8, 2–10, 1), because his account is favorable and also because it closely resembles that in Justin (XXIII, 4, 1), who followed Timaeus (J. Beloch, "Zur Ge-

schichte Siciliens vom Pyrrhischen bis zum ersten Punischen Kriege," *Hermes* [1893], pp. 487–488). He remarks incidentally that Timaeus owed his return to Sicily to the good offices of Hieron (p. 488), a judgment he reiterates later (*Griech. Gesch.* IV, 2, p. 11). This would mean Timaeus could not have returned before 275, when Hieron first became general, and probably not until 265, when his success against the Mamertines led to his being proclaimed king. It may be admitted that Timaeus wrote approvingly of Hieron without assuming that he was returning a personal favor. We would expect Timaeus to have praised the man who defeated Agathocles' mercenaries, favor or not.

13 Diodorus once calls him a Syracusan (XXI, 16, 5).

14 At least we are not certain that Andromachus' government was secure until 358. See Rizzo, *Tauromenion*, pp. 21, 40.

15 See *ibid.*, p. 22 n. 2.

16 D.S. XVI, 7, 1. N. G. L. Hammond ("The Sources of Diodorus Siculus," II, *C.Q.*, 32 [1938], 148) is uncertain whether this comes from Timaeus. It may, he believes, come from Diodorus' general knowledge. He thinks Diodorus obtained material on the period not covered by Ephorus, "from a short text-book giving the bare bones of the period." (I, *C.Q.*, 31 [1937], 91.) He then cites an Oxyrhynchus fragment proving the existence of such "text-books." One difficulty is that we are not sure when Ephorus ends. Jacoby argues that Ephorus went well beyond 357 B.C. (*F.Gr.H.* II C, p. 100, ll. 32–37).

17 See Edward A. Freeman, *The History of Sicily from the Earliest Times*, Vol. 4 (Oxford, 1894), pp. 503–508, Appendix on the founding of Tauromenium. Freeman attributes D.S. XIV, 59, to Philistus, because it must have been written after the repulse of Dionysius I and before the period of Andromachus.

18 See Rizzo, *Tauromenion*, especially chap. 2.

19 *Ibid.*, p. 22.

20 E.g., Diodorus speaks of Ἀνδρόμαχος ὁ Ταυρομενίτης in the passage just translated (XVI, 7, 1). Since Timaeus was born after the founding of Tauromenium, and since Diodorus refers to his father as a Tauromenian, he surely intends to imply that Timaeus was a Tauromenian, too.

21 See Laqueur, "Timaios," col. 1077.

22 The death of Dionysius I (in 368/7 or 367/6) must have opened up many possibilities in Sicily. It was not until 357/6 that Philip of Macedon and the Phocians made Greece once more the center of attraction for adventurers. Then, after peace in 346, Sicily was again a magnet. See H. D. Westlake, "Phalaecus and Timoleon," *C.Q.*, 34 (1940), 44–45.

23 See the foregoing passage.

24 See Plut. *Timol.* 10, 6 = Tim. 566 T 3b.

25 *Ibid.*, 8. Also see Rizzo, *Tauromenion*, p. 51. H. D. Westlake has a new and interesting interpretation of Timoleon, which emerged from a reëxamination of the texts of the lives by Nepos and Plutarch and also of the account in Diodorus. See particularly "The Sources of Plutarch's Timoleon," *C.Q.*, 32 (1938), 65 ff. He attempts to show that Timoleon was much less of an idealist than he has usually been painted, and also that he was both clever and unscrupulous as well as a master of propaganda (see his *Timoleon and his Relations with Tyrants* [Manchester, 1952]). Westlake does not regard Andromachus as a tyrant, despite Plutarch's references to him as a

"dynast" (*Tim.* 10, 6–7), because Plutarch also says that he *persuaded* the citizens (τοὺς πολίτας ἔπεισε—*Tim.* 10, 8). See *ibid.*, p. 12 n. 3.

[26] Rizzo, *Tauromenion*, p. 55.

[27] D.S. (XVI, 65) says: ὁ δὲ Τιμολέων ἀλλοτριώτατος ὢν μοναρχίας. Westlake (*Timoleon*, pp. 59–61) argues that Plutarch's *Timoleon* gives a much more credible account of the assassination of Timophanes by his brother than Diodorus does. Particularly, he finds it unlikely that Timoleon would have been tried for this deed, then allowed to go to Sicily with the verdict depending on his success or failure there. He rightly prefers Plutarch's version that Timoleon retired into private life from which he emerged to go to Sicily twenty years later.

[28] Athenaeus (XI, 43, p. 471 F = Tim. F 33) has preserved the following direct quotation from Timaeus' 28th book: Πολύξενός τις τῶν ἐκ Ταυρομενίου μεθεστηκότων ταχθεὶς ἐπὶ τὴν πρεσβείαν ἕτερά τε δῶρα παρὰ τοῦ Νικοδήμου καὶ κύλικα θηρικλείαν λαβὼν ἐπανῆκεν. Jacoby dates this tentatively in 339/8—a dating he will no doubt explain in his commentary, as against the suggested emendation from the 28th to the 22d book. Westlake (*Timoleon*, p. 53) interprets the passage as referring to an embassy sent by a faction in Tauromenium opposed to Andromachus and therefore seeking support from Nicodemus and the tyrannical opposition to Timoleon. The success of Polyxenus' mission he infers from the fact that Nicodemus was later deposed by Timoleon. Rizzo, however (*Tauromenion*, p. 52), thinks that the embassy sought to win further allies for the cause of freedom; and it was sent out by the Tauromenians rather than by Andromachus because Tauromenium was a free city with Andromachus as its leader, not its ruler.

[29] If we are to believe Hesychius of Miletus. See *FHG* IV, p. 177, c. 71.

[30] Cf. the *Suda* s.v. Φιλίσκος; *ibid.* s.v. Νεάνθης. Cf. also *FHG* III, p. 2; Solmsen, "Philiskos," No. 9, *R.-E.* 19, cols. 2384–2387.

[31] See *FHG* III, p. 4, F 7 = Athen. XV, 57, p. 699 D.

[32] *FHG* III, p. 2.

[33] *Ibid.*

[34] See Jacoby, *F.Gr.H.* II C, pp. 144–145. But also see Laqueur, "Neanthes," *R.-E.* 16, col. 2109.

[35] As Diodorus says (XXI, 17, 3).

[36] I.e., if we accept, as Jacoby does, Gutschmid's emendation of the *Suda* article (s.v. Τίμαιος) . . . ἔγραψεν Ἰταλικὰ καὶ Σικελικὰ ἐν βιβλίοις ⟨λ⟩η. Müller, however, keeps the η̄ of the manuscript, and treats the Ἰταλικὰ καὶ Σικελικὰ as a section of the whole work (*FHG* I, p. LI). Jacoby's commentary should have the best discussion of this problem.

[37] See n. 9. Laqueur appears to lean toward 317 B.C.

[38] See *FHG* I, p. L. Müller prefers 310.

[39] See Cicero, *De or.* II, 55/8, especially . . . *Timaeus . . . magnam eloquentiam ad scribendum attulit, sed nullum usum forensem.*

[40] See Arr. *Anab.* II, 7, 2

[41] This led some historians to believe that the Persians had planned to put themselves between Alexander and his bases, thus forcing him to fight a battle of desperation (e.g., see K. J. Beloch, *Griechische Geschichte*, III², 1, p. 632; III², 2, pp. 361 ff.). However, this view has not won general favor.

[42] See *ibid.*, p. 95 (or English trans. [New York: 1932], p. 104).

[43] See Arr. *Anab.* I, 16, 6–7.

⁴⁴ *Ibid.*, 29, 5.

⁴⁵ *Ibid.*, III, 6, 2.

⁴⁶ Ptolemy, Aristobulus, and Chares differ on how Callisthenes died, but they all regard him as justly punished. See T. S. Brown, "Callisthenes and Alexander," *A.J.P.*, 70 (1949), 247–248.

⁴⁷ For a discussion of the Sage and Tyrant type of anecdote, see Kurt von Fritz, "Quellenuntersuchungen zu Leben und Philosophie des Diogenes von Sinope," *Philologus*, Supp. 18, No. 2 (1926), pp. 27–29. For a good example of a Cynic dialogue of this kind from *ca.* 100 B.C., see Ulrich Wilcken, "Alexander der Grosse und die indische Gymnosophisten," *S.B.* Berlin (1923), pp. 150–183.

⁴⁸ See Strabo XVII, 1, 43 = Callisthenes 124 F 14a; see also Plut. *Alex.* 27 = F 14b.

⁴⁹ For Demosthenes' sarcastic indifference to Alexander's deification, see Hypereides, *Contra Demosth.* col. XXXI. For discussion, see A. D. Nock, "Notes on Ruler-Cult I–IV," *J.H.S.*, 47 (1928), 21 ff. It will be remembered how willingly the Athenians later granted divine honors to Antigonus and Demetrius (D.S. XX, 46).

⁵⁰ See Brown, "Callisth.," *A.J.P.* 70, p. 242. For the deification of Greek heroes, see W. S. Ferguson, *C.A.H.*, 7, p. 13.

⁵¹ See Brown, "Callisth.," pp. 244–245.

⁵² In Aristotle's day party terms are much more baldly economic than in the great days. As he says himself: διὸ ταῦτα μέρη μάλιστα εἶναι δοκεῖ πόλεως, οἱ εὔποροι καὶ οἱ ἄποροι (Pol. 1291b, 7). The εὔποροι prefer strong government (Macedonian in this instance) to independence. In Asia, where the Greeks had long lived under Persia, it was the "democrats" who welcomed Alexander, and there Macedonia stood for "democracy." (Not that consistency is necessary. Hermias, the tyrant of Assos and a student of Plato's is also pro-Macedonian because he is *persona non grata* to the Persians. See D. E. W. Wormell, "The Literary Tradition concerning Hermias of Atarneus," *Yale Class. Stud.* [New Haven, 1935], p. 58). Later, after Rome's victories, the Greek "democrats" looked hopefully to Macedonia, the oligarchs remained loyal to Rome.

⁵³ As has been argued on p. 6.

⁵⁴ I.e., if Ps.-Lucian got his information from Demochares, and falsely cited Timaeus as in agreement. Timaeus is reported by Diodorus to have said Agathocles died at the age of seventy-two. *Cf.* Tim. FF 123a and 123b.

⁵⁵ The *History* is usually cited simply as Ἱστορίαι (as in FF 1a; 5; 11a; 16; 17; 23; 26b; 28a; 32; 33; 153). But we also have an Ἰταλικὰ καὶ Σικελικά as well as a Ἑλληνικὰ καὶ Σικελικά in the corrupt *Suda* passage (*s.v.* Τίμαιος = Timaeus T 1), and Σικελικαὶ Ἱστορίαι (F 43a) and Σικελικά (F 83), as well as the strange *Historia de rebus populi Romani* (F 42a). The Ὀλυμπιονῖκαι (ἤτοι Χρονικὰ Πραξιδικά) is cited only once (*Suda s.v.* Τίμαιος = T 1), but the work is described by Polybius (XII, 11, 1 = T 10). Polybius also cites a Τὰ περὶ Πύρρου (XII, 4b = F 36), and Cicero compares Timaeus' work on the *Bellum Pyrrhi* with Callisthenes' *Phocicum Bellum* and with Polybius' *Bellum Numantinum* (*Ad fam.* V, 12, 2 = T 9a).

⁵⁶ It is more likely to have been a preliminary work than *fortasse historiis intextum* as Müller suggests (*FHG* I, p. LIV). Why disregard the testimony of the *Suda*? *Cf.*, Jacoby, *F.Gr.H.* III b (Supp. 1), p. 352, ll. 20–22. For Callisthenes' work on the Phocian War, see Callisth. 124 T 25 = Cic. *Ad fam.* V, 12, 2.

⁵⁷ It is called Πυθιονικῶν ἔλεγχος ά.

⁵⁸ See Plut. *Numa* 1, 6, and Jacoby, *F.Gr.H.* III b (Supp. 1), p. 352, ll. 13 ff.

[59] See D.L. V, 1, 26; also *FHG* II, pp. 182–183, FF 261–264.

[60] There are no fragments. See *F.Gr.H.* III b (Supp. 1), p. 352, ll. 7 ff. Jacoby believes there is a difference between an Ὀλυμπιονῖκαι and an Ὀλυμπιάδες.

[61] *Ibid.*, ll. 9–10; *ibid.*, II D, p. 708, ll. 15 ff.

[62] A similar distinction between ἀκοή and ὄψις was made by Herodotus. For discussion and references, see John L. Myres, *Herodotus, Father of History* (Oxford, 1953), pp. 9 ff.

[63] See Polyb. XII, 28a, 3.

[64] This passage is somewhat corrupt, but the general meaning seems clear.

[65] It is mentioned among his works in the *Suda*, *s.v.* Φιλόχορος. See Jacoby, *F.Gr.H.* III b (Supp. 1), p. 375, ll. 21 ff.

[66] See *ibid.*, III B (No. 342) for *Testimonia* and Fragments. See also Jacoby's "Krateros," No. 1, *R.-E.*, 11 (1921), cols. 1617–1621.

[67] See Plut. *Lycurg.* 1, 1 = *FHG* II, p. 128, F 76.

[68] See Euhemerus 63 F 2 = D.S. (VI, 1) in Euseb. *P.E.* II, 2, p. 60E. Like Euhemerus, the mysterious Xenagoras of the Temple Chronicle of Lindus mentions an inscription in Egyptian hieroglyphics (Xenagoras 240 F 16).

[69] Pausanias speaks of a list of victors inscribed in the gymnasium at Olympia at a date put tentatively as 550/40 by Jacoby. See *F.Gr.H.* III B, No. 416 T 1.

[70] See *ibid.* III b (Supp. 1), pp. 381–383; also *ibid.*, II D (No. 241), p. 708, ll. 11 ff.

[71] See Schmid-Stählin, *Gesch. d. griech. Lit.*7, I, 1, pp. 689 n. 3, 696, n. 2.

[72] It is a commonplace that the Babylonians gave fantastic figures for the reigns of early, i.e., mythological, rulers. The Egyptians attempted to reconcile claims of rival gods, as did Babylonians, by arranging them in a genealogical scheme going back to Ra. They also bridged the gap from God to Man by using the Followers of Horus, etc. See Auguste Moret, *The Nile and Egyptian Civilization* [Eng. trans.] (London, 1927), pp. 60–77.

[73] Hellanicus, for example, finds this a useful way of extending Athenian "history" back before the archon lists began, so he adds a king list of 27 generations or 900 years (*F.Gr.H.* III b [Supp. 1], p. 381, ll. 20 ff.).

[74] Jacoby suggests that Hellanicus' effort to span this *spatium vacuum* makes him, in a sense, "more of a historian than Herodotus" (*ibid.*, p. 9). Herodotus' renunciation of the heroic period is explicit (Hdt. I, 5, quoted by Jacoby).

[75] Herodotus' problem was particularly difficult when it came to Greek dating, because, as Jacoby says: ". . . for the chronographer of the Greek people a uniform or authoritative thread on which to string the single facts was lacking" (*F.Gr.H.* III b [Supp. 1], p. 381). Hellanicus later attempted to synchronize the events of Greek history in terms of the lists of the priestesses of Hera at Argos (*ibid.*, p. 15), but Herodotus did not even try to get hold of the Athenian archon list: "He was content for Greece with a chronology of the heroic age and for the barbarians with lists of kings" (*ibid.* [Supp. 2], p. 11 n. 118).

[76] For a discussion of Thucydides' chronology and why he refused to use the archon list, see *ibid.* (Supp. 1), pp. 456–459.

[77] See *ibid.*, especially p. 458, ll. 12 ff.

[78] See n. 75. Hellanicus undoubtedly used the archon list as a basis for his *Atthis* (*ibid.*, p. 15, ll. 28 ff.).

[79] See *ibid.*, p. 381, ll. 37 ff.; *ibid.* II C, pp. 26 ff.

[80] *Ibid.*, III b (Supp. 1), p. 382, ll. 2 ff.

[81] See *ibid.*, II D, p. 708, ll. 11–17. An amateur historian like the author of the *Marmor Parium*, however, did *not* use Timaeus' chronology (*ibid.*, pp. 668, ll. 28 ff.; *ibid.*, 670, ll. 34 ff.).

[82] See *ibid.*, III b (Supp. 1), p. 236, ll. 3–10.

[83] This information comes from Athenaeus (VI, 103, p. 272 B). For further discussion and references see chap. 5.

[84] His popularity is illustrated by the extensive use made of him by later writers. Diodorus is never so consistently dull as when he is following Ephorus. The fragments of Ephorus (No. 70 in the *F.Gr.H.*) do nothing to destroy this impression. Polybius treats him with unusual respect (see V, 33, 2, and see also the references to Polybius' favorable judgment in Strabo (e.g., IX, 3, 11, and X, 3, 5). Polybius flew to Ephorus' defense against the unkind strictures of Timaeus (Polyb. XII, 23).

[85] For the organization of his history, see Jacoby, *F.Gr.H.* II C, pp. 27–30.

[86] See Laqueur, "Timaios," col. 1192.

[87] Discussed in the following chapter.

[88] There had been separate treatises dealing with εὑρήματα as far back as the late fifth century (*F.Gr.H.* II C, p. 41, ll. 18 ff.), but the Peripatetics were particularly fond of the subject (*ibid.* III b [Supp. 1], p. 228, ll. 23 ff.). This is not to be wondered at, when one remembers how even minor innovations in music were believed to have a great influence on character. Timaeus' congenial contemporary, Philochorus, included a Περὶ εὑρήματων in his impressive bibliography (see the *Suda*, s.v. Φιλόχορος = Philochorus 328 T 1). However, εὑρήματα could also be incorporated in a more general history. Müller feels that because of his double interest in philosophy and history Dicaearchus must have stressed inventions in his Βίος Ἑλλάδος (*FHG* II, p. 228). Timaeus, who had such an interest in the early philosophers, would naturally have included the εὑρήματα too. Closely associated with this topic of inventions is the Hellenistic interest in the history of the arts and their practitioners. Here, again, one thinks of Diaearchus, and also of his fellow student, Aristoxenus of Tarentum. Timaeus would have known the writings of both, and may have owed much to them (see Fritz Wehrli's edition, *Die Schule des Aristoteles, Texte und Kommentar* [Basel, 1944]; Dicaearchus' fragments appeared in 1944, those of Aristoxenus in the year following).

[89] On Hellanicus' undertaking, see Jacoby, *F.Gr.H* III b (Supp. 1), p. 9, ll. 29 ff.

[90] This must be Lycus of Rhegium, of whom we know little, except that he was "plotted against" (ἐπιβουλευθείς) by Demetrius of Phalerum (*Suda s.v.* Λύκος ὁ καὶ Βουθήρας), which led Müller to believe he lived in Egypt (*FHG*, II, p. 370). He wrote a Περὶ Σικελίας and a Ἱστορία Λιβύης. Whether he also wrote a Περὶ Ἀλεξάνδρου or merely dedicated his Sicilian work to Alexander depends partly on the way we read the text of Stephanus of Byzantium (*s.v.* Σκίδρος. The choice lies between ὡς Λύκος ἐν τῷ Πρὸς Ἀλέξανδρον or ἐν τῷ Περὶ Ἀλεξάνδρου). *Cf. FHG*, II, p. 370, F 1, with Lycus 570 F 2. He was probably contemporary with Timaeus, but we know nothing of any influence these historians may have had on one another.

[91] Perhaps Eduard Meyer expressed this as well as anyone (*Kleine Schriften* [Halle, 1910], p. 229): "In crossing over to Sicily and attacking Carthage, Rome made the great step which a nation may make of her own free resolution, but which she can never take back."

[92] See Timaeus F 60. This sense of a fatal association between Rome and Carthage may well have been in Scipio's mind when he watched Carthage burn and quoted

Homer's famous lines to his friend Polybius (App. *Pun.* 132). It also had something to do with the superstitious fears over Caius Gracchus' proposed colony on the site of Carthage (App. *B.C.* I, 24).

⁹³ This will be discussed in the next chapter.

⁹⁴ See Jacoby's general remarks in the *Vorrede* to III B (p. 6) about this anonymous material and the impossibility of doing full justice to it in any collection of fragments.

⁹⁵ See *ibid.*, with special reference to the Chronicle of Lindus. Usually, however, it is a matter of only a column or so.

⁹⁶ No. 554 in Jacoby (III B, p. 540). See Müller's discussion (*FHG* II, pp. 12 ff.).

⁹⁷ Strabo is the source of eight fragments (see Strabo: V, 4, 3; VI, 1, 1; 1, 4; 1, 6; 1, 12; 1, 14; 1, 15; 3, 2) and Dionysius of four (see *A.R.* I; 12, 3; 22, 1; 35, 1; 73, 3). The only other considerable fragment is from Pausanias (X, 11, 3). It is perhaps indicative of Timaeus' popularity that Strabo does not refer to Antiochus once in his special Sicilian section (i.e., VI, 2).

⁹⁸ Joseph. *C. Ap.* I, 17, in Euseb. *P.E.* X, 7, 13 = Antioch. 555 T 5.

⁹⁹ See T. S. Brown, "Timaeus and Diodorus' Eleventh Book," *A.J.P.*, 73 (1952), p. 353 and n. 84.

¹⁰⁰ See No. 556 in Jacoby, and the *Suda* passages there (T 1a and 1b).

¹⁰¹ I.e., the alleged pupil of Isocrates and teacher of Timaeus. See p. 5 and n. 30.

¹⁰² See *FHG*, I, p. XLV.

¹⁰³ *Ibid.*, p. XLVI.

¹⁰⁴ See Plut. *De exil.* 14, p. 605 C = Philistus 556 T 5a; and D.S. XV, 7, 3 = T 5b, for his exile. For his career in general, see *FHG*, I, pp. XLVI–XLVII. According to Diodorus the exile occurred in 386/5, resulting from Dionysius' jealousy over criticisms of his poetry. Diodorus has Philistus return under Dionysius I, while Plutarch does not bring him back until the new reign has begun.

¹⁰⁵ Plutarch says as much in his *Dion* (11, 6): φυγόντα παρὰ ξένους τινὰς εἰς τὸν Ἀδρίαν, ὅπου καὶ δοκεῖ τὰ πλεῖστα συνθεῖναι τῆς ἱστορίας σχολάξων.

¹⁰⁶ See Müller, *FHG*, I, pp. XLVIII–XLIX. Jacoby follows the same scheme.

¹⁰⁷ For Cicero, see *Ad Q. fratrem* II, 11, 4 = Philist. 556 T 17a; *De or.* II, 57 = T 17b; *Brut.* 66 = T 21. For Dionysius, see his *Ad Pomp.* 3, 1; 4 = T 15a and T 16b. Also see Dionys. *De imit.* 3, 2 = T 16a. See Quintillian, *Inst. or.* X, 1, 74 = T 15c.

¹⁰⁸ See Isocrates' *Letters:* to Dionysius (No. 1); to the children of Jason (No. 6); and especially his second letter to Philip, where he urges him to stop the madness of warfare among the Greek states and to make war on Persia. It will be a simple matter to subdue the Great King, and then: οὐδὲν γὰρ ἔσται λοιπὸν ἔτι πλὴν θεὸν γενέσθαι (No. 3, 5). All references are to Hercher's *Epist. Graec.*

¹⁰⁹ See *Pol.* 1313a, 34. αἱ δὲ τυραννίδες σῴζονται κατὰ δύο τρόπους κ.τ.λ.

¹¹⁰ Two examples are sufficient for purposes of illustration (Philistus 556 F 29 = Steph. Byz., *s.v.* Ἀρβέλη· πόλις, Σικελίας · τὸ ἐθνικὸν Ἀρβελαῖος· Φίλιστος Σικελικῶν ῆ. and F 38 = *ibid.* *s.v.* Λογγώνη· Σικελίας πόλις. ὁ πολίτης Λογγωναῖος, Φίλιστος ῑ.).

¹¹¹ F 15 cites Philistus alone; F 49 and F 50 cite both Philistus and Timaeus.

¹¹² Pliny (*N.H.* VIII, 144) says: *memorat et Pyrrhum Gelonis tyranni canem Philistus*. This is interesting, since Tzetzes (*Chil.* IV, 266) relates an anecdote about Gelon's dog, and cites Timaeus (see Timaeus F 95), Dionysius, and Diodorus. However, it is not clear from the passage whether Timaeus is cited for the dog story or for the wolf story that follows. But evidently Timaeus wrote in detail about Gelon, including his

early life, and he may have obtained much of this material from Philistus, who had a similar interest in Gelon. Timaeus' hatred of Syracusan tyrants does not extend to the hero of Himera.

[113] See Theon *Progymn.* II, 63, 25 Spengel = Philistus 556 F 51, for the statement that Philistus copied Thucydides. See Plut. *Nic.* 1 = Timaeus F 18, for the differences between Timaeus and Thucydides; see also *Nic.* 28, 5 = Tim. F 101, for differences between Timaeus and Philistus.

[114] See Cicero *Brut.* 66 = Philistus 556 T 21. It was also Cicero who referred to Philistus as almost a *pusillus Thucydides* (*Ad Q. fratrem* II, 11, 4 = Philist. T 17a).

[115] This will be discussed on pp. 76–77.

[116] See Plut. *Alex.* 8, 3 = Philistus 556 T 22. The other five authors whose works Alexander required were all poets.

[117] Dionysius (No. 557) is referred to as follows in the *Suda* (*s.v.* Διονύσιος, Σικελίας τύραννος): ἔγραψε τραγῳδίας καὶ κωμῳδίας καὶ ἱστορικά.

[118] Diodorus (XV, 37, 3 = Hermias 558 T 1) says that Hermias continued "to this year" and Diodorus was then describing the events of the first year of the 101st Olympiad, i.e., 376/5 B.C.

[119] Polycritus is No. 559 in Jacoby. The three fragments come respectively, from: D.L. II, 63; [Arist.] Θαυμ. ἀκ. 112; and D.S. XIII, 83, 3.

[120] See Timaeus F 26a, especially the part found in D.S. XIII, 83, 2.

[121] The fragments referred to are: Alcimus 560 F 2 = Athen. X, 56, pp. 440E–441B; F 4 = Festus, p. 266 Mü, or p. 326, 35 Li; and F 5 = Schol. Theocrit. 1, 65/66a.

[122] There is only one fragment and it is woven into Diogenes Laertius' life of Plato (III, 9 ff.) in such a way that it is hard to separate out Alcimus from Diogenes' other sources. For a recent discussion of Alcimus see Jacques Perret, *Les Origines de la Légende Troyenne de Rome* (Paris, 1942), especially pp. 386 f. He argues for a much later date for the legend linking Troy with Rome than the view accepted here. He also believes all legends of Trojan colonization in the west derive from the Roman one. However, when he wrote, Jacoby's text of Alcimus and the other Sicilian historians had not yet appeared.

[123] Both Plutarch (*Dion* 35, 4) and Diogenes Laertius (IV, 5) say that Timonides wrote to Speusippus about the deeds of Dion, but the latter speaks of what he wrote as a *history.* Timonides probably left Sicily after taking part in Dion's expedition, perhaps to return to his native Leucas, there to write his adventures with a view to informing Speusippus about the details. The Academy would naturally be interested in having a firsthand report of the activities of Plato's close friend Dion.

[124] All three versions of Philistus' death are to be found in Plutarch's *Dion* (35, 3–6). Diodorus also describes this event (XVI, 16, 3), and his account, like that of Ephorus, has Philistus take his own life. For Jacoby's comments on the source problem, see *F.Gr.H.* II C, p. 100, ll. 32 ff.

[125] *Cf.* Timonides 561 F 1 with Timaeus F 114, both from Plut. *Dion* 31, 2–3.

[126] See H. D. Westlake, "The Sources of Plutarch's Timoleon," *C.Q.*, 32 (1938), 65 ff.

[127] Athanis is No. 562 in Jacoby. The information comes from D.S. XV, 94, 4.

[128] The passages are: Athen. III, 54, p. 98D; Plut. *Timol.* 23, 6; 37, 9.

[129] Still basic for the discussion of Duris on Agathocles is Wilhelm Nitsche, *König Phillips Brief an die Athener und Hieronymos von Kardia* (Berlin, 1876), especially pp. 5–12. For two extreme views on Duris as a historian, *cf.* Rudolf Schubert, *Die*

Quellen zur Geschichte der Diadochenzeit (Leipzig, 1914), p. 60 (". . . unter den Histori-kern seiner Zeit geradezu der elendste gewesen. . . ."), and Karl Julius Beloch, *Griechische Geschichte* IV, 1 (1925), p. 480 ("Dabei hat Duris . . . ein Werk geschaffen das zu den hervorragendsten Leistungen der antiken Historiographie gehört"). Both agree that Diodorus used Duris as a source on Agathocles. For the fragments of Duris' τὰ περὶ 'Αγαθοκλέα, see Duris 76 FF 16–21 and Jacoby's commentary (*F.Gr.H.* II C, pp. 120–121).

¹³⁰ Nitsche suggests that Duris' judgment of Agathocles was affected by his having been a tyrant himself (*op. cit.*, p. 8). H. J. W. Tillyard (*Agathocles*, [London 1908]) is even more specific. He writes (p. 20): "As Duris was himself a prince he was not likely to judge a fellow ruler harshly, so that his account seems to have been favorable to Agathocles." We do not know when, for how long, or under what circumstances Duris became tyrant of Samos. There is only the bald statement in Athenaeus (VIII, 18, p. 337D). See *F.Gr.H.* II A, Duris 76 T 2; T 4, and also II C, p. 116, ll. 17 ff.

¹³¹ Callias is No. 564 and Antander No. 565. The Diodorus statement is in XXI, 16, 5. Schubert contents himself with asserting that Diodorus used only Timaeus and Duris on Agathocles, because Callias' account was too long for his purposes (*op. cit.*, p. 62).

¹³² Timaeus needed information on Libyan geography when he came to describe Agathocles' expedition.

¹³³ We are told that Antander remained in charge of Syracuse during his brother's absence in Libya (D.S. XX, 4, 1). Therefore, he would have been in a position to supplement Callias' account, however voluminous, since Callias evidently accom-panied Agathocles. The assumption that, like Callias, he wrote a Τὰ περὶ 'Αναθοκλέα was made by Müller (*FHG*, II, p. 382), and accepted by Jacoby (*F.Gr.H.* III B, p. 580), who calls it tentatively Περὶ 'Αγαθοκλέους. For the strong possibility that part of Antander's history may now have been found among the Oxyrhynchus papyri, see p. 88.

NOTES TO CHAPTER II

Geography, Myth, and Prehistory

(pages 21–42)

¹ See p. 10.

² See Richard Laqueur, "Timaios," No. 3, *R.-E.*², 11 (1936), coll. 1076–1203. For discussion see T. S. Brown, "Timaeus and Diodorus' Eleventh Book." *A.J.P.*, 73 (1952), 337 ff.

³ See E. Schwartz, "Diodoros," No. 38, *R.-E.*, 5 (1905), especially coll. 684 ff. See also Jacoby, *F.Gr.H.* II D, p. 544; T. S. Brown, "Hireonymus of Cardia," *A.H.R.*, 52 (1947), 692 ff.

⁴ See pp. 15–20 ff.

⁵ Based on *F.Gr.H.* III B, pp. 592 ff.

⁶ This is the distribution: Cicero (FF 40; 130a; 130b; 138; 150a); Pliny (FF 61; 63; 67; 74; 75a; 75b); Censorinus (FF 125; 147); Aulus Gellius (F 42a); Varro (F 42b); Tertullian (F 62); Nepos (F 99).

⁷ Polybius: FF 3; 7; 12; 22; 28b; 31a; 31b; 34; 35b; 36; 41b; 68; 81; 94; 110; 111; 117; 119a; 124a; 124b; 124c; 151; 152; 155; 156.

Athenaeus: FF 1a; 1b; 5; 9; 10; 11a; 11b; 16; 23; 24a; 32; 33; 44; 45; 47; 48; 49; 50; 51; 52; 112; 140; 144; 149; 158a.

⁸ Diodorus: FF 25; 26a; 27; 28a; 38; 85; 89; 90; 103; 104; 106; 107; 108; 120; 121; 123a; 124d.

Plutarch: FF 100a; 100b; 101; 102b; 105, 109; 113; 114; 115; 116; 118; 119b; 127; 128; 154.

⁹ Diogenes Laertius: FF 2; 4; 6; 13b; 14; 17; 26b; 30; 134.

¹⁰ Strabo: FF 41c; 43b; 58; 65; 70; 129; 150b.

¹¹ Scholiasts (Pindar): FF 18; 19a; 19b; 20; 21; 28c; 39b; 92; 93a; 93b; 96; 97; 141; 142a; 142b; 145.

(Ap. Rhod.) FF 37; 79; 80; 84; 86; 87; 88.

(Lycophr.) FF 53; 55; 56a; 66; 98; 146a.

(others) FF 13a; 29; 64; 91; 132; 143a; 143b.

¹² E.g., Steph. Byz. (FF 24b; 39a; 72; 78).

¹³ Antigonus of Carystus (FF 41a; 43a; 46; 57).

¹⁴ Istrus wrote a Πρὸς Τίμαιον 'Αντιγραφαί (Istrus 334 F 59; see *F.Gr.H.* III b [Supp. 1], p. 656). Polemon wrote a Τὰ πρὸς Τίμαιον that is cited as far as Book XII. For his fragments see *FHG* III, pp. 126 ff., FF 39–46.

¹⁵ For discussion see pp. 94 ff.

¹⁶ E.g., Antiochus of Syracuse who, like Diodorus, derives the name *Trinacria* from its triangular shape. He says it was called Trinacria until the Sicans renamed it *Sicania* on their arrival from Spain (see Antiochus 555 F 4 = Dion. H. *A.R.* I, 22, 2). Diodorus certainly was familiar with Timaeus, but there are reasons for believing he also knew Antiochus (see Brown, "Tim. and Diod.," *A.J.P.*, 73, p. 353 and n. 84). Therefore, in V, 2, 2, and in the rest of F 164 we must be on the lookout for sources other than Timaeus.

¹⁷ No doubt the Greek was Σανδαλώδης. Pliny also says (*N.H.* III, 85) that Myrsilus, Timaeus' contemporary (No. 477 F 11), called Sardinia *Ichnusa* because of its resemblance to a footprint. This is so close as to suggest a connection. Perhaps Antiochus is responsible—or Philistus.

¹⁸ They are given in the following order. (1) Pliny *N.H.* IV, 104 = F 74; (2) IV, 94 = F 75a; (3) XXXVII, 35–36 = F 75b.

¹⁹ Hans Joachim Mette, *Pytheas von Massalia* (Berlin, 1952).

²⁰ See Strabo II, 4, 2; Mette, *op. cit.*, p. 1.

²¹ See Strabo II, 4, 2; Mette, *op. cit.*, pp. 4, 37.

²² Strabo II, 4, 2; Mette, *op. cit.*, p. 12 and n. 4 (on Antiphanes of Berge).

²³ See *ibid.*, pp. 13–15.

²⁴ *Ibid.*, p. 13 and n. 2; also pp. 36–39.

⁴⁵ *Ibid.*, pp. 10–12, 37.

²⁶ *Ibid.*, pp. 12, 37.

²⁷ See E. Honigmann, "Strabon," No. 3, *R.-E.*², 4, col. 133.

²⁸ See Mette, *op. cit.*, p. III. Also see F 13a = Pliny *N.H.* II, 186.

²⁹ See Mette, *op. cit.*, F 2 and p. 15.

³⁰ See Strabo II, 4, 1: ταῦτα μὲν τὰ τοῦ Πυθέου, καὶ διότι ἐπανελθὼν ἐνθέν δε πᾶσαν ἐπέλθοι τὴν παρωκεανῖτιν τῆς Εὐρώπης ἀπὸ Γαδείρων ἕως Ταναΐδος.

³¹ See Mette, *op. cit.*, p. 9.

³² See especially *ibid.*, F 7a (= Strabo II, 4, 1), p. III. The sense of "chain" (δεσμόν) here is apparently that because it could not be crossed, it served as a barrier (μήτε πορευτὸν μήτε πλωτὸν ὑπάρχοντα).

³³ See Mette, *op. cit.*, pp. III–IV; F 15 = Schol. Ap. Rhod. IV, 761/65a.

[34] Rather speculative, since we know virtually nothing about Philemon (*FHG* IV, p. 474). But see Mette, *op. cit.*, p. 40 and n. 2.

[35] See *ibid.*, p. 3, and also Strabo III, 3, 7.

[36] *Cf.* Pliny *N.H.* XXXVII, 36 (= Tim. F 75b) with D.S. V, 23, 1.

[37] Mette, *op. cit.*, p. 41 n. 1.

[38] *Ibid.*, p. 1.

[39] Polybius, himself, indulged in some rather speculative conclusions about ocean-ography in his account of the Black Sea (IV, 39, 7 ff.), but it must be granted that in describing he is clear and sensible. That Timaeus accepted Pytheas may have been enough to make Polybius suspicious, but his disregard of Eratosthenes' judgment is less defensible. However, Polybius, like Strabo, was probably in no position to appreciate the mathematical background of Eratosthenes' observations.

[40] See Jacoby, *F.Gr.H.* II D, p. 422; T. S. Brown, "Callisthenes and Alexander," *A.J.P.*, 70 (1949), p. 231.

[41] For the Tyrian histories see Polyb. XII, 28a, 3.

[42] Yet it is by no means certain that Polybius had ever visited Corsica. See C. O. Brink and F. W. Walbank, "The Construction of the Sixth Book of Polybius," *C.Q.*, 4 (1954), 102 (continuation of 101. n. 8).

[43] Strabo says that Polybius upbraided Timaeus for saying there were five mouths when in fact there were only two; Artemidorus had said there were three.

[44] However, Timaeus also worked out the date of the colony, which he said was founded 120 years before the Battle of Salamis (F 71 = Ps. Scymnus, *Perieg.* 209. This yields 600/599 B.C.—as Jacoby has it). Why did he not use an Olympic year? Perhaps he *did* give two figures, and Ps. Scymnus has kept only one.

[45] See Mette, *op. cit.*, Index *s.v.* Μασσαλία. Although reported by more than one writer, only his observation of the latitude in terms of the shadow on the sundial survives.

[46] Timaeus very sarcastically refuted Heracleides Ponticus' account of Empedo-cles' death (Tim. F 6 = D.L. VIII, 71). For discussion see Fritz Wehrli's *Die Schule des Aristoteles*, Part 7, *Herakleides Pontikos* (Basel, 1953), and his comments on F 84; also on the Avernus passage (Herac. F 128).

[47] See Ps. Arist. *Physiog.* 812a, where we read: οἱ ἄγαν μέλανες δειλοί (associated with Egyptians and Ethiopians); οἱ δὲ λευκοὶ ἄγαν δειλοί (associated with women). The shade of courage is in between, and: οἱ ξανθοὶ εὔψυχοι · ἀναφέρεται ἐπὶ τοὺς λέοντας. But a "fiery" color is a bad sign, associated with the fox. These statements continue through 812b.

[48] See F 56a = Schol. Lycophr. *Al.* 1050; F 56b = *Et. Gen.*, p. 320, 1 Rei (*Et. M.*, p. 63, 3).

[49] Jacoby notes that D.S. V, 23 (part of F 164) also has an account of Phaethon's fall into the Po. It is impossible to tell from Polybius' words (F 68) just what Timaeus said, except that he said showed his ignorance of the area. But it may well be that Polybius fails to separate the mythographer from the geographer in Timaeus.

[50] For the others see (Callimach.-)Antigon. *Hist. mir.* 140 (= F 41a); and Polyb. XII, 4d (= F 41b). For modern discussion of Arethusa, see James R. Smith, *Springs and Wells in Greek and Roman Literature, Their Legends and Locations* (New York and London, 1922), No. 486.

[51] Presumably when working on his *Olympionicae*. See p. 12.

[52] Nearchus, on the voyage back from India, heard a story of an island where anyone

who landed disappeared forever from mortal view. Both Nearchus and Onesicritus repeated the tale, but Nearchus also headed a landing party to refute it. Arrian's point of view is that Nearchus is being boorish.

[53] J. Enoch Powell (*The History of Herodotus* [London, 1939], pp. 44–45) speaks of three innovations that characterize Greek historiography in the century from Hecataeus to Thucydides. First came the combination of geographic description and local tradition in the form of a narrative; and this he finds in Charon of Lampsacus, Xanthus, and Herodotus. The second achievement was distinguishing between the ascertainable and the mythical past. This also Herodotus attempted, but as Jacoby says, without a clear realization of what he was doing (F. Jacoby, "Herodotos," No. 7, *R.-E.*, Supp. 2 [1913], col. 474). The third stage in Powell's somewhat dogmatic appraisal came with Thucydides' insistence on rejecting as myth everything that did not come under the direct control of the historian.

[54] See Jacoby, *F.Gr.H.* III b (Supp. 1), p. 9.

[55] Diodorus continues with a different version: the Argonauts sailed up the Danube, then down another river to the Adriatic. He says this has been refuted by later knowledge of geography. This bit, evidently not from Timaeus, Laqueur derives from Posidonius ("Timaios," *R.-E.*², 11, col. 1179).

[56] Strabo is our best source on Patrocles whom, unlike Pytheas, he trusts completely (e.g., II, 1, 6; 1, 9). Yet Patrocles said that one could sail from India to the Caspian, and he wrote, according to Strabo, as: ὁ τῶν τόπων ἡγησάμενος τούτων (II, 1, 17). Eratosthenes, however, does not always believe Patrocles. He preferred to rely on Daimachus and Megasthenes (Strabo II, 1, 7). The seven fragments of Patrocles, all from Strabo, will be found in the *FHG*, II, pp. 442–444. Jacoby believes Patrocles was sent out to explore the Caspian by Seleucus, *ca.* 285/2 (see his "Kleitarchos," No. 2, *R.-E.*, 11 [1922], col. 627; see also T. S. Brown, "Clitarchus," *A.J.P.*, 71 [1950], p. 138).

[57] See p. 26. Hecataeus of Miletus apparently thought of the Argonauts as returning by a southern route, including Ocean and the Nile river. See J. Wells in W. W. How and J. Wells, *A Commentary on Herodotus*, Vol. 1 (Oxford, 1912), commenting on Hdt. IV, 36, 2, and Jacoby, *F.Gr.H.* I, p. 323, ll. 13 ff., commenting on Hecataeus 1 F 18.

[58] F 87 = Schol. Ap. Rhod. IV, 1153/4; F 88 = *ibid.* IV, 1217/9b. It is also natural that for Timaeus the πλαγκταὶ πέτραι are to be found in the Straits of Messina, and not surprising that in this he is followed by his fellow Sicilian Pisistratus of Lipara (Tim. F 86 = Schol. Ap. Rhod. IV, 786/7; see also Pisistratus 574 F 1). These were "Wandering Rocks" indeed, as can be seen by looking up *Planetae Petrae, Cyaneae* and *Symplegades* in the index to the Müller Strabo. They range all the way from the Bosporus to Gibraltar! See also Arrian, *Peripl. M. Eux.* 25, 3. For Timaeus' probable influence on Apollonius Rhodius' *Argonautica*, see Schmid-Stählin, *G. d. Gr. Lit.* II, I⁶, p. 143 n. 1.

[59] See F 133 = Clem. Al. *Strom.* I, 64, 2. For Xenophanes' emigration, see D.L. IX, 18.

[60] There is some indication that Timaeus has a long mythological period preceding the period of historical colonization. The transition seems to have been made by a rapid summary, including the extinction of the heroic ruling families in each area and the progressive barbarization of the colonies founded by them. E.g., see p. 59 (Aeolian islands).

⁶¹ See Polycritus 559 F 2. See p. 18 and n. 119 to chap. 1.

⁶² See p. 18.

⁶³ At least he knows of a fugitive from Rome long before Aeneas (Dion. H. *A.R.*, I, 73, 5 = Antiochus 555 F 6).

⁶⁴ Dion. H. *A.R.* I, 74 = F 60. Here we note his use of the Olympic era as we use B.C. dating.

⁶⁵ His perplexity is shown earlier (Dion. H. *A.R.* I, 73, 3–5), when he notes that Rome was founded twice: τὴν μὲν ὀλίγον ὕστερον τῶν Τρωικῶν γενομένην, τὴν δὲ πεντεκαί-δεκα γενεαῖς ὑστεροῦσαν τῆς προτέρας. He goes on to remark that, if desired, one might infer a third foundation earlier than either of the others: γενομένη πρὶν Αἰνείαν καὶ Τρῶας ἐλθεῖν εἰς Ἰταλίαν. This inference is based on Antiochus of Syracuse who says that when Morges ruled over Italy (an Italy confined in those days to the coast from Tarentum to Posidonia), a fugitive came to Morges, *fleeing from Rome.* He quotes Antiochus' exact words (see also Antiochus 555 F 6): "ἐπεὶ δὲ Ἰταλὸς κατεγήρα, Μόργης ἐβασίλευσεν· ἐπὶ τούτου δὲ ἀνὴρ ἀφίκετο ἐκ Ῥώμης φυγάς · Σίκελος ὄνομα αὐτῷ."

⁶⁶ The volcanic fires of the Aeolian islands "cooked" the sea nearby, according to Pytheas (see Mette, *op. cit.*, F 15 = Schol. Ap. Rhod. IV, 761/65a, and introd. pp. III-IV). Timaeus may have been rationalizing the epic tradition about Aeolus in the light of Pytheas' observations, while also preserving, as he always does, any Greek legend connected with the west. Here he is also adding to the εὑρήματα claimed for the Sicilian area. It was no mean boast that sails were a western discovery. Cf. Strabo VI, 2, 10.

⁶⁸ See Varro *De re rust.* II, 5, 3, where Hercules is said to have pursued a bull named Italus from Sicily over to Italy. Varro clearly distinguishes this story from the version he found in Timaeus. We have already seen that Antiochus (No. 555 F 5; and see n. 65) has still a different account. Evidently Italy was named for the ruler, Italus, while Siculus, the eponym of the Sicels, was an Italian.

⁶⁹ This formed part of the original plan of Timaeus' *History*, since he dealt with it in Book I (see Athen. IV, 38, p. 153D; XII, 14, p. 517D). The origins of the Tyrrheni (Etruscans, in the west) had long interested the Greeks. See W. Brandenstein, "Tyrrhener," *R.-E.²*, 7 (1948), cols. 1915 ff. An entire number of *Historia* has been devoted to summarizing recent scholarship on the Etruscans—*viz.* 6, 1 (1957).

⁷⁰ See F 62 = Tertullian *De spectac.* 5. On Tyrrhenus, see G. Radke, "Tyrrhenos," No. 1, *R.-E.²*, 7 (1948), cols. 1938–1939.

⁷¹ See F 1a = Athen. IV, 38, p. 153D; F 1b = *ibid.* XII, 14, p. 517D. This was evidently a subject made to order for Athenaeus, who was an expert on τρυφή. He also preserves the short but helpful fragment of Alcimus (No. 560 F 3 = Athen. XII, 14, p. 518B), which says the Etruscans did everything to the sound of the flute—fighting, kneading bread, even laying on the whip. But the account that pleased Athenaeus most was that of Theopompus, which he gives in considerable detail, some of it verbatim (Athen. XII, 14, pp. 517D–518B = No. 115 F 204). The Etruscans are said to have held their women in common. The children resulting from such promiscuity are brought up by the Etruscans, no one knowing either his parents or his offspring. Here one suspects that Theopompus the moralist cannot resist a thrust at Plato. The general atmosphere reminds one of the *Ecclesiazusae* of Aristophanes, although genuine ethnographic material probably underlies it. The satirist has adapted this to suit his purposes. Marriage customs had formed a regular τόπος with the old Ionian writers, and also with Herodotus (see Karl Trüdinger, *Studien zur*

Geschichte der griechisch-römischen Ethnographie [Basel, 1918], pp. 31–32), as had matters relating to δίαιτα in general—especially for Herodotus (*ibid.*, p. 21). For examples of promiscuity among primitive peoples *cf.* Hdt. I, 216, 1 (the Massagetae) and IV, 172, 2 (the Nasamones).

Theopompus emphasizes the shamelessness (οὐδὲν δ' αἰσχρόν ἐστι Τυρρηνοῖς οὐ μόνον αὐτοὺς ἐν τῷ μέσῳ τι ποιοῦντας, ἀλλ' οὐδὲ πάσχοντας ⟨φαίνεσθαι⟩). One sign of their shamelessness is that women are not concerned at appearing naked before the men, and here we see some relationship with the Timaeus fragment, though Timaeus seems to have limited this to girls, not full-grown women (see F 1a). Further, and here there may be a remnant of actual practices, Theopompus says the Etruscans employ persons to remove their body hair, "just the way we have barbers." We may read in the pseudo-Aristotelian *Physiognomica* of the character traits associated with hair, or the lack of hair, on various parts of the body (*Physiog.* 812b). E.g., οἱ τὰ στήθη ψιλὰ ἄγαν ἔχοντες ἀναιδεῖς—and that seems to suit Theopompus' Etruscans. It is a pity that Athenaeus was the one to decide for us which account of Etruscan mores should survive. Either Timaeus or Alcimus would probably have been a better choice. Yet behind all three there may well be a lost ethnographer, perhaps one of the old logographers, whose report would be invaluable if we had it. Some such account must have existed to explain the later ones, all three of which have a literary flavor far removed from the freshness of the old ἱστορίη. Timaeus, as we will see in the next chapter, may have had another reason for his interest, because Pythagoras is often connected with the Etruscans (e.g., Porphyry *Vit. Pythag.* 10).

⁷² See Philistus 556 F 45. Antiochus was probably his source (Ant. 555 F 4 = Dion. H. *A.R.* I, 22, 2).

⁷³ See Timaeus F 38 = D.S. V, 6, 1. Timaeus, characteristically, rebukes Philistus for his ignorance.

⁷⁴ Laqueur has carefully analyzed the passages in D.S. IV ("Timaios," *R.-E.²*, 11, cols. 1175 ff.), but it seems unwise to attribute as much to Timaeus as he has done. There are only three references to Timaeus in the whole book, and only two of these to Heracles (*viz.*, IV, 21, and 22, 6). These are too close together to prove extensive use of Timaeus outside this small part. Schubert surely gave sound advice about Diodorus when he urged that in case of doubt it is better to attribute too little rather than too much of the context to a particular source (see Rudolf Schubert, *Die Quellen zur Geschichte der Diadochenzeit* [Leipzig, 1914], p. 2).

⁷⁵ Clem. Al. *Strom.* I, 1, 2 = T 15a. See also T 15b = Philodem. Π ποιημ. 5 col. 5, 22 (Jensen).

⁷⁶ Apparently a whole section of his *Philippica* was called Θαυμάσια. For discussion and references, see T. S. Brown, *Onesicritus, A Study in Hellenistic Historiography* (Berkeley and Los Angeles, 1949), pp. 64–66.

⁷⁷ Corsica offers other points of interest worth noting. One is a εὕρημα, for it is here that wild honey was first discovered (V, 14, 1). Then there is the statement that the livestock are marked in such a way that even when untended they cannot be lost by their owners (*ibid.*). Aside from this curious suggestion of branding, the statement supplements Polyb. XII, 4, 2 (= Tim. F 3). The Timaeus fragment shows *why* the livestock cannot be tended in the usual way, and also shows how the animals can be summoned by trumpet whenever external dangers threaten. The Diodorus passage explains how rights of ownership are maintained, and adds the further touch that the inhabitants are amazingly fond of righteousness. Then reference is made to an

extraordinary Corsican custom: when a child is born, it is the husband who takes to his bed with groans, while no fuss at all is made over the wife (V, 14, 2). This has a special flavor, a bite to it, that suits what we know about Theopompus better than it does Timaeus (see n. 71). Finally, an interesting point is made about the Corsican language—that it is spoken by barbarians and very difficult to learn (V, 14, 4).

In Diodorus' account of the Balearics he mentions a strange marriage custom by which on the wedding night every male guest has intercourse with the bride, the bridegroom last (V, 18, 1). This custom has been observed among primitive peoples in modern times, and is sometimes referred to by students in the field as "expiation for marriage" (see William G. Sumner and Albert G. Keller, *The Science of Society*, Vol. 3 [New Haven, 1927], p. 1550). The contrast in tone between this and the account of childbirth on Corsica serves to remind us of the complexity of the sources used by Diodorus.

⁷⁸ D.S. V, 15. The brackets enclose what Diodorus added.

⁷⁹ It is interesting that Strabo calls the Sardinian mountaineers by a different name (Διαγησβεῖς), but adds that *formerly* they were called Iolaëis from Iolaus, who led a colony there of Heracles' children (Strabo V, 2, 7).

⁸⁰ If we may supplement by Timaeus F 63 (= Pliny *N.H.* III, 85), where it is said to be shaped like a sandal.

⁸¹ Although Diodorus attributes this to the oracle, Strabo is more cynical. After speaking of the banditry of some of the mountaineers (a detail omitted by Diodorus), he says the Romans tended to overlook their depredations—ἐπειδὰν μὴ λυσιτελῆ τρέφειν συνεχῶς ἐν τόποις νοσεροῖς στρατόπεδον (Strabo V, 2, 7).

⁸² On this, see Arthur O. Lovejoy and George Boas, *Primitivism and Related Ideas in Antiquity* (Baltimore, 1935), especially chap. 2 ("Chronological Primitivism") and 7 ("Antiprimitivism in Greek Literature").

⁸³ In D.S. V, 17, 4, it is worth noting that the inhabitants of the Balearics deliberately avoid the acquisition of gold and silver. This is a good example of primitive simplicity explained on sophisticated grounds.

⁸⁴ The passage occurs in Strabo (XV, 1, 64 = Onesicritus 134 F 17a). For translation and discussion see Brown, *Onesic.*, pp. 38 ff.

⁸⁵ A good account of Cynicism is that of Donald R. Dudley (*A History of Cynicism from Diogenes to the Sixth Century A.D.* [London, 1937]). On this particular point see Lovejoy and Boas, *Primitivism and Related Ideas*, p. 121.

⁸⁶ See chap. 1 n. 88. In the fourth century, partly as a result of the influence of the Peripatetic school, there came to be a more intelligent interest in origins—in explaining the growth of a people from barbarism to civilization by means of laws (νόμοι) and also custom (ἔθος). Trüdinger writes: "Die Geschichte dieser Entwicklung zu verfolgen, bedeutete etwas durchaus neue. Kulturgeschichte stellt sich damit neben die politische Geschichte" (*Gesch. d. griech.-röm. Ethn.*, p. 49). In that development Dicaearchus' Βίος Ἑλλάδος admittedly played an important part.

⁸⁷ As he is known to have done for the distance between Sicily and Italy (see F 90 = D.S. IV, 22, 6).

⁸⁸ Strabo says that Iolaus brought the children of Heracles with him and set up a mixed colony *with the barbarians who held the island*, and adds that they were Etruscans (Strabo V, 2, 7). This is not quite consistent with Diodorus, who has Greeks and barbarians coming to Sardinia with Iolaus, and does not mention any previous inhabitants. But the accounts are so much alike that they suggest the use of a common

source. Both are greatly abridged. Strabo, by speaking of the previous inhabitants as participating in the colony, shows why there was no resistance. Diodorus *may* have read that there were Etruscans already on the island who joined Iolaus, and he may have obscured this fact in making a brief summary. Otherwise, we must suppose that Diodorus' source was different from Strabo's. Perhaps the likeliest answer is that they used the same source, but that Strabo left out the coming of the Etruscans, who found an uninhabited island, while Diodorus implies that the island was uninhabited when Iolaus came, and thus collapses two separate colonizing expeditions into one. Because he has to explain the barbarian population, he brings them in with Iolaus.

[89] For example, in the utopian romance of Iambulus, when a man reached the age of one hundred and twenty, he lay down beside a remarkable plant which had the virtue of sending him off into a mortal sleep (see D.S. II, 57).

[90] They were also called the Aeolian islands. Diodorus' account has been discussed briefly (D.S. V, 7–11) on p. 59, also chap. 3, n. 56. Here we may note the successive stages of change on these islands: 1. They were uninhabited; 2. Colonized by Liparus from Italy; 3. Arrival of Aeolus, mixed colonization, and a line of kings stemming from Aeolus; 4. Extinction of this line after many generations; 5. Period of fighting and civil war, ending with the islands once more uninhabited; 6. Arrival of colonists from Cnidus and Rhodes; the historical period began.

[91] Here we find a Greek colony founded by Hyllus, Heracles' son, which gradually became barbarized through the influence of its rude neighbors. This corresponds roughly with steps 1. to 5. as outlined in the preceding note. The historical era perhaps begins with the coming of a Syracusan colony to the island of Issa.

[92] See F 64, translated on p. 40. Jacoby has brought together the texts and discussed the question of *sardonic laughter*. See *F.Gr.H* III b (Supp. 1), pp. 214–217. See also Cicero's use of the expression (*Ad fam.* VI, 25, 1).

[93] See Clitarchus 137 F 9 = Schol. Plat. *Resp.* 337A; and also Jacoby's comments (*F.Gr.H.* II D, p. 489), where Curt. Ruf. IV, 3, 23 and D.S. XX, 14, 6 are also cited.

[94] See Demon 327 F 18a = Schol. V Hom. *Od.* XX, 302; F 18b = Phot. *Sud. s.v.* Σαρδόνιος γέλως.

[95] In my "Clitarchus," *A.J.P.*, 71 (1950), pp. 134 ff.

[96] See Silenus 175 F 5 and the comments in *F.Gr.H.* II D, p. 602. This interpretation depends on inserting σεσηρέναι in the text. The old *FHG* (III, p. 101, F 9) does not do this because Müller apparently never collected all the references to "sardonic laughter" in one place.

NOTES TO CHAPTER III

The Good Old Days

(pages 43–70)

[1] Book XV of Timaeus' *History* is cited. Athenaeus twice cites Book XIII (*Deipnosoph.* VII, 132, p. 327B, and XIII, 55, p. 589A). The references are to a siege of Syracuse, presumably the siege by the Athenians.

[2] Both Books I and II are cited, but there may be an error.

[3] Various corrections for the δ have been suggested. See Jacoby's text.

[4] See F 30 = D.L. VIII, 60. Beloch emended this to ιβ. See Jacoby's text.

[5] See F 100a = Plut. *Nic.* 19, 5; F 100b = *ibid.* 28, 4; F 100c = Plut. *Timol.* 41, 4.

[6] Eratosthenes, like Timaeus, based his chronology on Olympiads (see Jacoby, *F.Gr.H.* III b [Supp. 1], p. 382, ll. 5 ff.); in counting back he arrived at 1184/3 B.C. for the Fall of Troy. Timaeus' date works out as *ca.* 1350. For a comparison on the alleged dates for the Fall of Troy, see Clem. Alex. *Strom.* I, 139, 4, p. 86, 16 Stäh (conveniently accessible in *F.Gr.H.* No. 137 F 7). Here we find Clitarchus and Timaeus in agreement. Duris (76 F 41) is not very different, putting Alexander's crossing over into Asia 1,000 years after the Fall of Troy. On Timaeus' date see p. 58.

[7] For the quotation, see Polyb. XII, 5, 8; for what follows, *ibid.*, 6b, 9–10.

Konrat Ziegler ("Polybios," No. 1, *R.-E.* 21, col. 1470) implies that Polybius, in supporting Aristotle against Timaeus' attack, knew no more of Aristotle's argument than he read in Timaeus. F. W. Walbank (*A Historical Commentary on Polybius*, Vol. 1 [Oxford, 1957], p. 2) contents himself with the general statement that Polybius "shows little evidence of deep study of these writers" (i.e., Aristotle and other philosophers), but that ". . . he had obviously read closely and critically the historians of his own and preceding generations, such as Timaeus, Phylarchus, Theopompus and Ephorus." Ziegler's position is untenable since it rests solely on Polybius' failure to cite Aristotle independently. Yet Ziegler himself admits that one half of Polybius' Book XII has been lost (*op. cit.*, col. 1480). To prove his point he would have to show that Polybius misrepresents Aristotle's argument.

[8] The Locrians were said to have sworn to uphold the treaty as long as "they trod on that soil and carried their heads on their shoulders." They are said to have got around this by filling their shoes with dirt, and secretly wearing σκορόδων κεφαλαί ("heads of garlic") on their shoulders, then removing them. There seems to have been a veritable campaign of hate. The Locrians in Greece are said to have betrayed their Peloponnesian allies by failing to light signal fires to warn them of the return of the Heraclidae (Polyb. XII, 12a). But this passage is corrupt as well as condensed. It is just possible Timaeus introduced the story of the Locrians in Greece to explain the proverb about Locrian treaties without admitting treachery by Italian Locri toward the Sicels.

[9] Aristotle knows and rejects, on chronological grounds, the current attempt to provide Zaleucus with a suitable background. Onomacritus the Locrian was held to have studied in Crete and to have become the first lawgiver. Thales was then said to have been one of his associates, and Lycurgus and Zaleucus to have studied under Thales.

[10] Note especially *Pol.* 1255b 6: . . . συμφέρει τῷ μὲν τὸ δουλεύειν τῷ δὲ τὸ δεσπόζειν καὶ δίκαιον καὶ δεῖ τὸ μὲν ἄρχεσθαι τὸ δ' ἄρχειν κ. τ. λ.

[11] See *ibid.* 1254b 34 ff. Aristotle tries to show that the antislavery position is based entirely on the fact that natural slavery and legal slavery do not always coincide.

[12] The tale of Iambulus reaches us by way of Diodorus Siculus (II, 55–60). Slaves are not mentioned among his People of the Sun, and they would, in fact, have been superfluous. All but the aged perform services for the state, as liturgies, in a system of rotation that promoted good health and prevented boredom. See D.S. II, 59.

[13] Plato's failure to mention slaves in the *Republic* does not mean he was an abolitionist. On this see Glenn R. Morrow, "Plato's Law of Slavery," in *Illinois Studies in Language and Literature*, Vol. 3, No. 3 (Urbana, 1939). Timaeus regards the fantastic number of 460,000 slaves for Corinth as an indication of great prosperity (F 5 = Athen. VI, 103, p. 272B).

[14] Morrow suggests that Diogenes attacked slavery as unnatural (*op. cit.*, p. 131 and n. 8).

[15] For translation, discussion, and references see T. S. Brown, *Onesicritus, A Study in Hellenistic Historiography* (Berkeley and Los Angeles, 1949), chap. 3.

[16] See W. A. Oldfather, "Lokroi," No. 1, in *R.-E.*, 13 (1927), col. 1314.

[17] See *ibid.*, col. 1313.

[18] See p. 46 and Athen. VI, 86, p. 264C.

[19] See F 130a = Cicero *De leg.* II, 15; F 130b = Cic. *Ad Att.* VI, 1, 18. Aristotle did accept Zaleucus as a real person (see *Pol.* 1274a 22; also Clem. Al. *Strom.* I, p. 352; and Schol. Pindar *Ol.* XI, 17). See also Heracleides, who has the story that Zaleucus insisted on the conviction of his own son [*FHG* II, p. 221, F 30, 3). There is reason to doubt that this comes from Heracleides Ponticus (see Fritz Wehrli, *Die Schule des Aristoteles*, No. 7 [Basel, 1953], commenting on F 108), but for our purposes it will not be necessary to separate the two Heracleides; both represent an early Peripatetic tradition.

[20] See Oldfather, "Lokroi," *R.-E.*, 13, cols. 1318–1319. He relates the need for a written code of laws with the assumption that Locri was a mixed colony. Is this not really based on Aristotle's assertion that they borrowed customs from the Sicels "because they had no ancestral customs of their own"? (Quoted on p. 46).

[21] *Ibid.*, col. 1319.

[22] See *ibid.*, cols. 1315; 1320.

[23] *Ibid.* See also E. Wellmann, "Echekrates," No. 3, *R.-E.*, 5 (1905), col. 1910. References are given also to Pausan. II, 3, 2; D.L. VIII, 46; Iambl. *V. Pyth.* 251 and 267. A word of caution is in order. There was an Echecrates of Phlius, one of the last Pythagoreans known to Aristoxenus of Tarentum (*fl.* 336 B.C.). Our Echecrates is not called either a Pythagorean or a Phliasian by Polybius. In fact, Polybius does not say he was an exile or that Timaeus met him in Phlius. Nevertheless, the fact that the nobles got into difficulties for supporting Dionysius II, and Polybius' reference to Echecrates' father as the envoy of Dionysius (which one?) make the hypothesis of Oldfather attractive. Surprisingly, Kurt von Fritz, though he does have something to say about the Pythagorean Echecrates (see index to his *Pythagorean Politics in Southern Italy* (New York, 1940), makes no mention of *any* Echecrates connected with Timaeus. This is all the more striking since his whole third chapter is devoted to Timaeus.

[24] Oldfather, "Lokroi," *R.-E.*, 13, col. 1319.

[25] As reported by Polybius (XII, 5, 8). It was this which motivated Timaeus' outburst against Aristotle, discussed on pp. 7 ff.

[26] That Diodorus gives an account of Zaleucus and his laws (XII, 20–21) shows that he did not always follow Timaeus in writing about the west. From Strabo we learn that Ephorus treated Zaleucus as a veridical lawgiver, whose laws were derived from Crete, Sparta, and the "Areopagitic" laws (Strabo VI, 1, 8). For discussion and references, including the term "Areopagitic laws" see *F.Gr.H.* II C, p. 77, commenting on Ephorus FF 138–139.

[27] Timaeus is naive enough to appeal particularly to the laws in Locri protecting the institution of slavery, and to argue that such laws were inconsistent with a servile origin for the colony. He also argues, against Aristotle, that the Athenians spared their territory because of common hatred of Sparta. Polybius' answers are somewhat more logical, but he argues only on the general grounds of common sense. No new

evidence is presented (see Polyb. XII, 6a–8). Also, it is clear that Theophrastus supported Aristotle and he, too, was denounced by Timaeus (*ibid.* XII, 11, 5).

²⁸ Epimenides was the subject of many marvellous stories, including that of his falling asleep for an even longer period than Rip Van Winkle. (See Theopompus 115 FF 67–69).

²⁹ Xenophanes would have interested him particularly, since he emigrated to the west. Timaeus puts him in the time of Hieron, though Apollodorus says he lived much earlier (see F 133 = Clem. Al. *Strom.* I, 64, 2).

³⁰ Little is left of Timaeus on Croton. But Timaeus did stress its citizens having succumbed to luxury after they destroyed Sybaris (F 44 = Athen. XII, 22, p. 522A), and he also held that it was Croton rather than Sybaris that tried to discredit Olympia by games of its own with large cash prizes (F 45 = Athen. XII, 22, p. 522C). For recent discussion and references on the Pythagoreans, see Kurt von Fritz, *Pyth. Pol. in S. It.* The author devotes chapter three to Timaeus and attempts a reconstruction of his account. Much of this is necessarily speculative, and therefore to discuss it would take us too far away from the attested fragments. He rightly points out that compared with Dicaearchus and Aristoxenus, Timaeus "has the enormous advantage that he deals with the Pythagoreans within the framework of a general history of Southern Italy so that he has to correlate and check in all directions" (p. 66).

³¹ Dicaearchus must have been born before 342/1 B.C. to have studied under Aristotle. Wehrli suggests his *floruit* was about the beginning of Alexander's reign (336 B.C.). (*Die Schule des Aristoteles*, No. 1 [Basel, 1944], p. 43). Included in his Βίοι was a life of Pythagoras. For the texts see Wehrli, FF 33–36; and *FHG* II, pp. 244–245, FF 29–32.

³² Aristoxenus was contemporary with Dicaearchus, and also studied under Aristotle, though he was angry when Theophrastus became head of the school (*Suda s.v.* Ἀριστόξενος). We have fragments of three works about Pythagoras and the Pythagoreans: Περὶ Πυθαγόρου καὶ τῶν γνωρίμων αὐτοῦ; Περὶ τοῦ Πυθαγορικοῦ Βίου; and Πυθαγορικαὶ ἀποφάσεις. For the fragments see Wehrli, *Die Schule d. Aristot.*, No. 2 (1945), FF 11–41; and *FHG* II, pp. 272 ff., FF 1–15; 17–24. Wehrli has an excellent discussion with references to the literature (pp. 49 ff.).

³³ Both Porphyry and Iamblichus wrote lives of Pythagoras. Both contain older material along with later acretions. They are easily accessible in the old Didot edition of Diogenes Laertius (reprinted in 1929).

³⁴ See Arist. *E. Nicom.* 1159b, 31.

³⁵ They were called: Κόραι, Νύμφαι, Μητέρες, Μαῖαι. The last has been added from Iambl. *V. Pyth.* 56. Thus there are four ages marked out for women as well as for men. *Cf.* D.L. VIII, 10 on the men.

³⁶ "Liars" come into it, and Hecataeus is called a braggart.

³⁷ See Athen. IX, 68, p. 404C. This reference is uncertain because the manuscript reading is Ἀνθίππῳ. Valck's emendation to Ἀναξίππῳ may not be correct.

³⁸ On Xanthus see D.L. VIII, 63 = *FHG* I, p. 44, F 30. For Ephorus, see Athen. XII, 11, p. 515D = *F.Gr.H.* No. 70 F 180.

³⁹ This nickname was sometimes given as Ἀλεξάνεμος (Porphyry *V. Pyth.* 29). He is also credited with averting a pestilence from Selinus by purifying the river water (D.L. VIII, 70).

⁴⁰ In addition to Dicaearchus (see n. 31) and Aristoxenus (see n. 32), another Peripatetic interested in biography was Phanias of Eresus (in Lesbos). He is said to have

lived at the time of the 111th Olympiad (336 B.C.) and thereafter, and to have studied under Aristotle (see *Suda s.v.* Φανίας ἢ Φαινίας Ἐρέσιος . . .). Presumably this is not when he was born, since Aristotle died in 322. He wrote a work entitled Περὶ τῶν ἐν Σικελίᾳ τυράννων. For the fragments see *FHG* II, pp. 293–301.

[41] For Parmenides see D.L. VIII, 56; for Archytas see *FHG* II, p. 300, F 23.

[42] See Alcimus 560 F 6 = D.L. III, 9, where Alcimus charges Plato with stealing ideas from Epicharmus. On Alcimus see pp. 18 and 34. However, it was apparently a stock accusation that Plato had stolen from the Pythagoreans. See Wehrli, *Die Schule d. Aristot.*, No. 2 (Aristoxenus), p. 67.

[43] Evidently Eratosthenes did not go to Olympia to write his book, as Timaeus probably had done (see p. 12).

[44] D.L. VIII, 69. Hippobotus lived in the late third or early second century B.C. according to Von Arnim ("Hippobotos," *R.-E.*, 8 (1913), cols. 1722–1723.)

[45] Following the fragment proper, we read: κατασκευάσαι δὲ αὐτόν φασι Περίλαον κ.τ.λ. This may or may not have been found in Timaeus.

[46] Actually, when he visited Phasis, Arrian was shown *two* possible Argo anchors, one of iron, the other of stone. Being of an antiquarian turn of mind he decided the iron one was not old enough for the Argo. See his *Peripl. M. Eux.* 9, 2. For a famous example of statue stealing in antiquity, see Plut. *De Iside et Osiride*, 28. But here the culprit (Ptolemy I) was known.

[47] So Athenaeus (XIII, 78, p. 602B) on the authority of Heracleides Ponticus.

[48] See T. S. Brown, "Euhemerus and the Historians," *Harvard Theol. Rev.*, 39 (1946), 271–274.

[49] See F 93a = Schol. Pindar *Ol.* II inscr., p. 58, 12 Dr, where we learn that Theron was descended from King Oedipus; and F 93b = Schol. Pindar *Ol.* II, 29d, where we read that revolutionary troubles in Rhodes led the family to go west.

[50] Polybius' emphasis, as is well known, lay not on the individual but on the constitution. At the very outset he asks rhetorically whether anyone is so insensible that he would not like to know *how and with what form of government* the Romans obtained the supremacy in a matter of fifty-three years (Polyb. I, 1, 5). For discussion see F. W. Walbank, *A Historical Commentary on Polybius*, Vol. I (Oxford, 1957), p. 40.

[51] See pp. 44–50.

[52] Strabo VI, 2, 4. Perhaps in Timaeus' account of Corcyra the Liburnians helped fill the gap between the visit of Medea and Jason and the arrival of Chersicrates. See p. 32 and particularly n. 60 to chap. 2.

[53] On Corinth see FF 5; 10; 145. Josephus refers to Timaeus' abusive language about Athens, Sparta, and Thebes (F 153 = Joseph. *C. Ap.* I, 221). Corinth, as the mother-city of Syracuse and the birthplace of Timoleon, occupied a very special place.

[54] Timaeus, who denies the buying and selling of slaves among the early Greeks, goes to the opposite extreme in exaggerating the later slave traffic. His figure of 460,000 slaves for Corinth is absurd. See F 5 = Athen. VI, 103, p. 272B. However, the authorities whom Athenaeus cites in this same chapter for equally exaggerated figures include Aristotle and Agatharchides. For the best discussion of slave numbers, see William L. Westermann, *The Slave Systems of Greek and Roman Antiquity* (Philadelphia, 1955), pp. 7–9.

[55] See p. 49.

[56] See p. 36. The passage is D.S. V, 7–10 (a part of F 164). There are good reasons

for attributing the account of the Aeolian islands to Timaeus. We have a fragment on these islands from Pytheas (see Hans Joachim Mette, *Pytheas von Massalia* [Berlin, 1952], p. 35, F 15), and another from Antiochus of Syracuse (*F.Gr.H.* No. 555 F 1). In Diodorus the names of the islands (V, 7, 1) correspond closely with Pytheas, but not so closely with Antiochus. Timaeus made use of Pytheas, and therefore it is probable that Diodorus is following Timaeus here.

⁵⁷ The preceding differs with the Antiochus fragment just cited. In Antiochus the initial disaster is caused by Elymaeans and Phoenicians, not by the forces of Egesta.

⁵⁸ *E.g.*, see p. 38 (Sardinia).

⁵⁹ See Paus. X, 11, 3. He does refer to Antiochus immediately afterward, and there are no references to Timaeus in Pausanias.

⁶⁰ *E.g.* see D.S. II, 56–59 for the description of Iambulus' Islands of the Sun; see *ibid.* V, 45 for the social state described by Euhemerus. See also Brown, *Onesicritus*, chap. 3.

⁶¹ Strabo mentions the hot springs, the mineral, στυητηρία (alum?), and vouches for the great fertility of the soil. Like Pausanias, he alludes to the dedications in Delphi (Strabo VI, 2, 10).

⁶² See Pliny *N.H.* IV, 120 = F 67 and see p. 28.

⁶³ This is a part of F 164. One or two details have been left out about Gadira, and also an obvious addition by Diodorus.

⁶⁴ Discussed on pp. 25–27; 32.

⁶⁵ See Strabo III, 3, 13 *ad fin.*; XVI, 3, 3. The careful avoidance of specific directions on how to reach the island finds its parallel in Euhemerus (D.S. V, 41) and also in Iambulus (*ibid.* II, 55).

⁶⁶ See F 96 = Schol. Pindar *Ol.* VI, 158, where we learn that Hieron, Gelon's brother, inherited the priesthood of Demeter and Corē from his ancestor, Telines; and F 97 = Schol. Pindar *Pyth.* I, 112, dealing with marriage connections. In both these passages Philistus and Timaeus are cited together. See also F 93a = Schol. Pindar *Ol.* II, inscr. p. 58, 12 Dr.

⁶⁷ F 95 = Tzetz. *Chil.* IV, 266. Philistus, too, wrote about Gelon's dog (Philistus 556 F 48 = Pliny *N.H.* VIII, 144), but Tzetzes does not mention Philistus by name. In addition to Timaeus he cites Dionysius, Diodorus, and Dion.

⁶⁸ See also F 21 = Schol. Pindar *Nem.* IX, 95a; F 142a = Schol. Pindar *Nem.* I, inscr.

⁶⁹ See FF 19a and 19b from Schol. Pindar *Ol.* V, 5, 19a and 19b respectively. The text of neither is altogether satisfactory. Both use Olympic dates, but in both the figures are corrupt. Camarina was synoecized after its destruction by Gelon. This was done by Hippocrates, according to Philistus (556 F 15).

⁷⁰ Such subjects were not confined to schoolboys. The well-known historian, Dicaearchus of Messene, is more than critical of Penelope (see Wehrli, *Die Schule d. Arist.*, No. 1, F 92; *FHG* II, p. 246, F 33a); so is Duris of Samos (*F.Gr.H.* No. 76 F 21).

⁷¹ See p. 14.

⁷² On this see T. S. Brown, "Timaeus and Diodorus' Eleventh Book," *A.J.P.*, 73 (1952), 344.

⁷³ For discussion see Jérôme Carcopino, *Autour des Gracques* (Paris, 1928), chap. 3.

⁷⁴ See *F.Gr.H.* II C, p. 88, ll. 34–35.

⁷⁵ See Brown, "Timaeus...," *A.J.P.*, 73, pp. 337–355, for discussion and references.

[76] One slight point may be added. The fact that Diodorus refers to this alliance, in his account both of Xerxes' invasion and of Himera's, suggests that he took it from his chief source, i.e., Ephorus, who described events both in the east and in the west.

[77] Eighteen years altogether, according to Aristotle; seven under Gelon, ten under his brother Hieron, and only ten months under Thrasybulus (*Pol.* 1315b, 34–38).

[78] See Plut. *Timol.* 23, 4; this passage may very well come from Timaeus, though Athanas is cited just before.

[79] See Richard Laqueur, "Timaios," No. 3, *R.-E.*², 11 (1936), col. 1088.

[80] See F 142a = Schol. Pindar *Nem.* I, inscr. Timaeus is cited only for the erroneous statement that this particular ode honoring Chromius was for an Olympic victory.

[81] See F 98 = Schol. Lycophr. *Al.* 732 for the admiral, Diotimus, who may have gone out in 439/8 or 433/2 according to Jacoby (see Thucyd. I, 45). Perhaps this is the same Diotimus who was known as Χώνη ("funnel") for his convivial exploits (see Athen. X, 48, p. 436E).

[82] The reference here to the twenty-first book in Timaeus is suspect because the Syracusan expedition seems to have been described in Book 15.

[83] For Thucydides on Gela see IV, 58–64; all but the first chapter gives Hermocrates' speech—but what a different speech! Yet it is unlikely Thucydides had any real knowledge of what Hermocrates said. What he does, and Timaeus so obviously fails to do, is to use the speech as a device for illuminating Syracusan policy. For detailed discussion of this passage and also Polybius' criticism of Timaeus, see A. W. Gomme, *A Historical Commentary on Thucydides*, Vol. 3 (Oxford, 1956), pp. 513–523.

[84] Ferguson, writing on the Syracusan expedition in the *Cambridge Ancient History*, says there is little to do but to paraphrase Thucydides (vol. 5, p. 282 n.).

[85] For Philistus as a "pusillus Thucydides" see Cicero *Ad Q. fratr.* II, 11, 4.

[86] See *F.Gr.H.* II D, p. 393, ll. 7 ff., for Jacoby's comment on the passage.

[87] FF 100b and 101 from Plut. *Nicias* 28, 3–5. For Philistus see *F.Gr.H.* No. 556 F 55.

[88] This should not be explained as religious superstition. It is rather more in the nature of the Elizabethan conceit and characterizes the period rather than the man.

[89] See FF 100a = Plut. *Nicias* 19, 5 and 100c = Plut. *Timol.* 41, 4. He does, correctly, state that Gylippus tried to save the lives of Nicias and Demosthenes (see F 100b = Plut. *Nic.* 28, 3).

[90] See FF 135 and 136 = Marcellinus *Vit. Thucyd.* 25 and 33. Marcellinus rejects the statement about exile, but does not find the idea of Thucydides' burial in Italy absurd.

[91] See Athen. XIII, 54–55, pp. 588B–589A = F 24a. Aside from Timaeus, he cites Polemo, Nymphodorus, and Strattis the comic poet. There seems to have been more than one famous Lais (*e.g.*, D.L. IV, 7), and it is possible our discussion of her is out of order chronologically.

[92] See D.S. XII, 10. The fragments are: 9; 47; 48; 49; 50.

[93] *E.g.*, see Heracleides Ponticus' Περὶ δικαιοσύνης, preserved in Athen. XII, 21, p. 521E. The significance of τρυφή for historians of this age is ably discussed by A. Passerini ("La τρυφή nella storiografia ellenistica," *Studi Italiani di Filologia Classica*, N.S. 11 [Florence and Rome, 1934], pp. 35–56). He refers particularly to Timaeus (see pp. 48; 50; 51 n. 2). Kurt von Fritz also discusses τρυφή in connection with Timaeus (*Pyth. Pol. S. Italy*, pp. 46–47). He regards Theopompus as having played a leading part in developing the idea of τρυφή. Even Polybius, who prefers to explain

change in terms of the constitution, also was influenced by the idea of τρυφή, of decay brought about by too much prosperity. He was impressed by Roman ἤθη (VI, 53–56), but recognized that Rome, too, would eventually succumb (VI, 57); see Passerini, *op. cit.*, p. 43.

⁹⁴ Passerini comments on this as an example of Timaeus' geographical determinism (*op. cit.*, p. 51 n. 2).

⁹⁵ Two other examples of Timaeus' treatment of the period have been omitted with regret. One of them (FF 43a and 43b from Antigon. *Hist. mir.* 1 and Strabo VI, 1, 9) concerns the strange ways of the cicada (much like our cricket), which sings merrily in Locri but is mute across the line in Rhegium. An anecdote is told about two competitors in a musical contest in Delphi, one from Rhegium, the other from Locri. The Locrian won, but only after the string of his lyre had snapped and a friendly cicada had bravely chirruped out the missing notes—perched on his lyre. The other fragment (F 149 = Athen. II, 5, p. 37BD) explains how it was that a certain house in Acragas came to be called "The Trireme." The story concerns a group of young men who became so intoxicated in that house that they imagined themselves to be on a ship at sea during a storm and began throwing cargo overboard, *i.e.*, out of the windows. It is a lively scene, but not one easily related to the *History* as a whole.

NOTES TO CHAPTER IV
MODERN TIMES
(PAGES 71–90)

¹ As H. D. Westlake remarks: "A detailed reconstruction of the second half of Timaeus' History is impossible, since in few cases do the extant fragments indicate the number of the book from which they are derived, and in some of these the numeral is suspect." (See "The Sources of Plutarch's Timoleon," *C.Q.*, 32 [1938], 67).

² Photius, the celebrated ninth-century Patriarch of Constantinople, summarized some 280 prose works he had read, including a particularly useful abridgment of Ctesias' *Indica*, which would be unknown to us otherwise.

³ *Viz.*, FF 25; 26a; 28a; 103; 104; 106; 107.

⁴ Plutarch (no doubt following the reliable Hieronymus) gives the following figures (*Demet.* 28, 6): For Antigonus and Demetrius—over 70,000 foot, 10,000 horses, 75 elephants; for their opponents—64,000 foot, 10,500 horse, 400 elephants, and 120 chariots. The grand total, ignoring the men who fought in chariots or on elephants, is 154,500, far beyond the possibilities for a Punic invading force.

⁵ *E.g.*, when he speaks of the 460,000 slaves in Corinth (F 5). See chap. 3, n. 13.

⁶ *I.e.*, F 26a = D.S. XIII, 81–85. See pp. 69–70.

⁷ For Dexippus see D.S. XIII, 87, 4; 5; 88, 7. On Gylippus see p. 66.

⁸ This last reference to Dexippus may not be intended as favorable, particularly if Philistus, who eulogized Dionysius, is the source. But it does give a contrasting picture with the Dexippus who is distrusted by the assembly in Acragas. The earlier portrait is that of a venal traitor, the later one that of a potential tyrannicide.

⁹ See pp. 54–57.

¹⁰ It is as though Timaeus wished to provide a substitute for the story of the Bull of Phalaris which he rejected.

¹¹ Sicilian affairs are treated in chapters: 2–35; 43–44; 54–63; 75; 79–96; 108–114.

[12] D.S. XIII, 26: οὗτοι γάρ εἰσι οἱ πρῶτοι τροφῆς ἡμέρου τοῖς Ἕλλησι μεταδόντες κτλ . . .

[13] *Cf.* Timaeus F 100b with D.S. XIII, 32.

[14] There are three references in Book IV, two each in Books XX and XXI, and one each in Books V and XIV. See n. 8 to chap. 2 for the list of fragments from D.S.

[15] The problem is not simplified even when Ephorus breaks off (somewhere in Diodorus' XVI book). For the continuation of Ephorus' history by his son, Demophilus, see D.S. XVI, 14, 3; also Jacoby, *F.Gr.H* II C, pp. 33–34.

[16] See pp. 16–18.

[17] This was not the only supernatural indication of his coming greatness. Later in the same book Cicero (*De div.* I, 73) tells a curious story about Dionysius' horse. The episode occurs just before Dionysius became tyrant, and the horse whinnies. Was Philistus trying to outdo Herodotus with this bit of hippomancy? (*Cf.* Hdt. III, 84–85).

[18] See *FHG* IV, p. 641, F 119a for this passage, and also for accounts of the same dreams in Valerius Maximus (I, 7, 6) in the *Suda* and Photius; also for further references and discussion.

[19] See [Arist.] *Physiog.* 812a, 16: οἱ πυρροὶ ἄγαν πανοῦργοι.

[20] *Ibid.* 813b, 9: οἱ δὲ ἄγαν μεγάλοι βραδεῖς.

[21] I have followed Jacoby's text, which differs slightly both from Büttner-Wobst and also from the earlier Dindorf. Apparently there is a typographical error in Jacoby's text (line 7) of διατύπωμα for διάπτωμα.

[22] This information is all to be found in the *F.Gr.H.* See II C, p. 100, comments on Ephorus 70 F 218; also II B, No. 239, A 62 for the *Parian Marble*, and for comments see II D, p. 695.

[23] See particularly I, 14, 4–5, where Polybius tells us that while the brave man loves his country's friends and hates her enemies, he must put that all aside when he becomes a historian. Frequently he will be forced to bestow the highest praise on an enemy and even to rebuke those nearest to him. For a discussion of this passage recognizing Polybius' inconsistency see F. W. Walbank, *A Historical Commentary on Polybius*, Vol. I (Oxford, 1957), p. 66.

[24] Plutarch's statement can be amplified, thanks to Diodorus (XX, 78, 3), who attributes the remark in question to Dionysius' kinsman, Megacles.

[25] See pp. 13–14 and also n. 84 to chap. 1.

[26] See p. 19.

[27] Or, in the year of the 96th Olympiad, as Diodorus puts it.

[28] See F 82, translated and discussed on p. 35.

[29] Discussed on p. 52.

[30] See F 158a = Athen. X, 49, p. 437B; F 158b = Philod. *Ind. Ac. Herc.* 8, p. 43, Mekleri; Aelian *V.H.* II, 41. Aelian says the prize was for the man who drank the most—evidently misled by a contest held by Alexander, which he has been describing. It makes one wonder about Aelian's accuracy in transcribing other passages.

[31] This would be early in the reign, perhaps in 366 B.C. as Jacoby indicates.

[32] The chapters dealing in whole or in part with the west are: XV, 6–7; 13–17; 24; 27 (Rome); 35 (Rome); 37 (for reference to Hermeias' Sicilian history, see p. 18); 70; 73–74; 94 (for reference to Athanas' history, see pp. 19–20); XVI, 5–7; 9–13; 15; 16 (for reference to Philistus, see pp. 16–18); 17–20; 31; 36; 45; 63; 65–73; 77–83; 90. Book XV ends with 361/0 B.C. and Book XVI begins with the year following.

[33] *Viz.*, the story of the advice given Dionysius by his friends (*cf.* D.S. XIV, 108

with XX, 78, 3). See p. 78. For comments minimizing Diodorus' use of Theopompus, see *F.Gr.H.* II D, on Theopompus 115 FF 184; 334; 341.

³⁴ See H. D. Westlake, "The Sources of Plutarch's Timoleon," *C.Q.*, 32 (1938), 68 and 72.

³⁵ Quoted on p. 4.

³⁶ The chronology presents difficulties. See Stier, "Timoleon," *R.-E.*², 11 (1936), cols. 1277–1278.

³⁷ See Westlake, *C.Q.*, 32 (1938), 65.

³⁸ *Ibid.*, p. 66. He remarks that Nepos' account could well pass muster as a slightly inaccurate summary of Plutarch's *Life*, were this not chronologically impossible.

³⁹ See *ibid.* Specifically, Westlake notes that Nepos said Timoleon could have shared in the tyranny, while Plutarch makes no such statement. He says this is one of Nepos' "inventions."

⁴⁰ See *FHG* IV, p. 488, Pythocles F 2.

⁴¹ Instead of . . . τῶν δὲ φίλων τὸν μάντιν, ὃν Σάτυρον μὲν Θεόπομπος, Ἔφορος δὲ καὶ Τίμαιος Ὀρθαγόραν ὀνομάζουσι.

⁴² He is known to have written about Alcibiades, Philip of Macedon, and Dionysius the Younger. See *FHG* III, p. 159; see also Gudeman, "Satyros," No. 16, *R.-E.*², 2 (1923), cols. 228–235. It should be noted that there was another Satyrus living at the time, a man whom Timaeus described as the flatterer of both Dionysiuses (F 32 *ad fin.*); but he seems an unlikely tyrannicide. A third possibility is suggested by the name and by Theopompus' known fondness for irony. Can it be that he called the soothsayer a "satyr" and has been misunderstood?

⁴³ In 1537 when Lorenzino de Medici murdered his kinsman, Count Alessandro, an attempt was made to justify him by appealing to the example of the patriotic Timoleon (Jacob Burckhardt, *Die Culture der Renaissance in Italien*, 5th ed. [Leipzig, 1896], pp. 60–61).

⁴⁴ See H. D. Westlake, "Phalaecus and Timoleon," *C.Q.*, 34 (1940), 45. For Timoleon in general, see his *Timoleon and his Relations with Tyrants*, Univ. of Manchester Faculty of Arts Pub., No. 5 (Manchester, 1952). He finds Diodorus' account "melodramatic" (p. 61).

⁴⁵ *Cf.* D.S. XVI, 65, 8 with Plut. *Timol.* 7, 2. See Westlake, *Timoleon and . . . Tyrants*, p. 61. He believes Diodorus has followed Theopompus here (*ibid.*, n. 2).

⁴⁶ See Athanis 562 FF 2 and 3. Both fragments are in Plutarch's *Timoleon*—whether Plutarch used him directly or found the references ready-made in some earlier writer like Satyrus or Timaeus, for that matter.

⁴⁷ F 33 may be mentioned, with its mysterious reference to a Tauromenian embassy headed by Polyxenus and sent to the tyrant Nicodemus of Centuripa, who was later deposed by Timoleon. See n. 28 to chap. 1.

⁴⁸ See *Gr. Gesch.* IV, 2, p. 3. He includes the whole period from Alexander to Caesar in his statement, citing Polybius' first five books as the only exception.

⁴⁹ See *ibid.*, p. 8. Beloch argues that Diodorus used a second-century source for his history of the Diadochi, with Agatharchides as a likely possibility (p. 5). Also, see n. 129 to chap. 1.

⁵⁰ This has not yet been published and my information comes through the courtesy of the editor, Professor E. G. Turner, Director of the Institute of Classical Studies, University of London. He kindly provided me with a transcript of the text as well as a photostat of the originals. My references are to the transcript, and of course some

changes in the reading are apt to be made before printing. Nevertheless, the document is too significant to be omitted. Slight changes in the reading should not affect the general argument.

[51] Δι[ο]γνητος ο Φαλαινος επικαλουμενος. See col. ii, ll. 7–9.

[52] See *ibid.*, ll. 13–14. The phrase is: μεταστῆσαι τὴν πόλιν. For "betraying" the city we would expect προδοῦναι.

[53] *Ibid.*, cols. iii–iv.

[54] On Antander, see p. 20.

[55] *Cf.* Timaeus F 15 = Cyrill. c. Julian VI, p. 208, with Duris 76 F 78 = D.L. II, 19.

[56] See F 29, translated and discussed on p. 76.

[57] See p. 18.

[58] This is a bowdlerized version of what Timaeus said, if we are to believe Polybius. See F 124b = Polyb. XII, 15, 2.

[59] A view propounded by H. J. W. Tillyard (*Agathocles*, [London, 1908], p. 20). Wilhelm Nitsche was more cautious ("König Philipps Brief an die Athener und Hieronymos von Kardia" [Berlin, 1876], p. 8). Rudolf Schubert (*Die Quellen zur Geschichte der Diadochenzeit* [Leipzig, 1914]) said Duris put love of abuse above questions of policy (p. 103) and that he was no judge of statesmanship despite having been a tyrant (p. 100).

[60] See Tillyard, *Agathocles*, p. 56.

[61] See pp. 9–10 and n. 54 to chap. 1.

NOTES TO CHAPTER V

TIMAEUS AND HIS CRITICS

(PAGES 91–106)

[1] In comparison with the nine books of Herodotus, which were read aloud, the *Philippica* of Theopompus contained fifty-eight books (see Jacoby's table, *F.Gr.H.* II D, p. 359). Such a work would naturally appear in installments and of course the installments might be read aloud. But once the work was complete no one would dream of reading the whole thing orally. Craterus, who may have been the half-brother of Antigonus Gonatas, wrote a Συναγωγὴ Ψηφισμάτων, evidently intended as a reference work (see *FHG* II, pp. 617 ff.; also B. Keil, "Der Perieget Heliodoros von Athen," *Hermes* [1895], pp. 213 ff.; for the fragments see *F.Gr.H.* III B, No. 342). Craterus gave the documents themselves (see *F.Gr.H.* III b [Supp. 1], p. 138), but perhaps not in chronological order (*ibid.*, p. 199).

[2] On Diodorus see Christ-Schmid, *Gesch. d. griech. Lit.*, II, 1⁶, p. 242; *FHG* II, pp. 353–359. Diodorus wrote a Περὶ τῶν μνημάτων and also a Περὶ τῶν δήμων. He is the earliest periegete known to us. For the fragments see *F.Gr.H.* III B, No. 372. Diodorus was used by Didymus and probably by Istrus (see *F.Gr.H.* III b [Supp. 1], p. 641); he thought he might have found Themistocles' tomb near the great harbor of the Piraeus (see Diod. 372 F 35).

[3] See p. 14.

[4] See *F.Gr.H.* III b [Supp. 1], p. 627, ll. 10–20.

[5] See *ibid.*, p. 625, ll. 26–30.

[6] See *FHG* III, pp. 108–116, for discussion; the fragments of Polemon are on pp. 116–148. Müller simply reprinted the fine edition of Preller. The Πρὸς Τίμαιον survives

only in FF 39–46. We do have one fixed date, thanks to a proxeny decree in his honor from Delphi, in 177/76 B.C. (Syll.³ 589, 114 n.). For discussion of this decree and also his alleged Athenian citizenship see K. Deichgräber ("Polemon," No. 9, in *R.-E.*, 21 [1952], col. 1290).

⁷ On Polemon's ἀντιγραφαί see *ibid.*, col. 1304. The author is uncertain whether, in the Πρὸς Τίμαιον he was attacking Timaeus or merely supplementing him, but suggests he probably did both (*ibid.*, col. 1307). He expresses some doubt whether his criticism of Istrus was a separate treatise (*ibid.*, col. 1308). But see Polemon, FF 54 and 55.

⁸ See Deichgräber's "Polemon," *R.-E.* 21, col. 1304 and FF 47–52 (Eratosthenes); F 53 (Neanthes); FF 56–59 (Adaeus and Antigonus).

⁹ See Deichgräber, *op. cit.*, col. 1291. He believes all attempts to classify his writings have been fruitless.

¹⁰ The old Liddell and Scott (with Drisler's additions [New York, 1860]) rather happily referred to Polemon as "a sort of *Old Mortality*, who used to go about copying the inscriptions on public monuments" (*s.v.* Στηλοκόπης).

¹¹ See *FHG* III, Polemon FF 39–42. The text of F 39 (from Athenaeus) is somewhat corrupt (Kaibel).

¹² See Timaeus F 55 (Daunian women resembling Erinyes); F 96; and F 102b (references to Demeter and Corē). See p. 37 on Diodorus' debt to Timaeus for localizing Demeter and Corē in Sicily.

¹³ See p. 14 and n. 88 to chap. 1; also n. 66 to chap. 2.

¹⁴ See p. 67 and n. 91 to chap. 3.

¹⁵ See *FHG* III, p. 129, comment on F 45.

¹⁶ See *ibid.*, p. 115 b (from Preller).

¹⁷ *E.g.* see FF 18 (Athen. XIII, 34, p. 574C); 20 (XI, 59, p. 479F); 28 (XIII, 84, p. 606AB); 36 (IX, 13, p. 372A); 45 (XV, 55, p. 698A–56, p. 699C).

¹⁸ This epithet is mentioned in the *Suda* (*s.v.* Τίμαιος).

¹⁹ See Polyb. III, 4, 13–5, 6, where Polybius explains his revised plan. For discussion, see F. W. Walbank, *A Historical Commentary on Polybius*, Vol. I (Oxford, 1957), p. 303.

²⁰ *Ibid.* III, 2, 6, where Polybius gives his reasons for the excursus on Roman government in Book VI. For discussion and references see C. O. Brink and F. W. Walbank, "The Construction of the Sixth Book of Polybius," *C.Q.* n.s. 4 (1954), 97–122.

²¹ See especially Polyb. II, 57, 8. A recent analysis of Polybius' long fragment on Boeotian history (XX, 4–7) in the light of the inscriptions of the period indicates that here, too, Polybius allowed himself to be deflected by prejudice (see Michel Feyel, *Polybe et l'Histoire de Béotie au IIIᵉ Siècle avant nôtre Ère*, Bibl. des Écoles Franç. d'Ath. et de Rom., No. 152 [Paris, 1942]).

²² If Polybius' copy of Phylarchus was defective, and "6,000" had crept into the text instead of some more reasonable figure, Phylarchus was wronged. But this need not lessen our admiration for Polybius' arguments, which are necessarily directed against the text that lay before him. One would not have expected him to give Phylarchus the benefit of a doubt—even though he had condemned Timaeus for relying (in Polybius' opinion) on a faulty reading of the text of Ephorus (see p. 77). For discussion and full references to the literature see Walbank, *op. cit.*, pp. 267–270.

²³ See the Polybius passage translated on p. 77.

²⁴ See Polyb. XII, 3–4—from *Exc. ant.* pp. 244–245.

25 Discussed on p. 24.

26 See p. 28 and n. 42 to chap. 2.

27 See D.S. V, 14, 1 (part of Tim. F 164): τά τε πρόβατα σημείοις διειλημμένα, κἂν μηδεὶς φυλάττῃ σώζεται τοῖς κεκτημένοις.

28 See n. 42 to chap. 2.

29 This comprises chapters 4a, 4b, 4c, and 4d.

30 See p. 82.

31 See p. 77.

32 For discussion see p. 34.

33 Discussed on p. 30.

34 See pp. 44–48.

35 See n. 8 to chap. 3.

36 See p. 48.

37 The vindictive remarks about Aristotle have been quoted and discussed. See pp. 7–8.

38 See p. 48.

39 On Polyb. XII, 10, 4, see p. 11 and n. 64 to chap. 1.

40 For translation and discussion see p. 11.

41 *Cf.* Polyb. XII, 6; also see n. 8 to chap. 3.

42 Polybius would apparently exclude this material entirely. Timaeus felt differently, but he made a distinction between what he thought to be genuine tradition and stories made up at a later date simply for entertainment (like the account of the Meropes in Theopompus' *Philippica*—see T. S. Brown, *Onesicritus, A Study in Hellenistic Historiography* [Berkeley and Los Angeles, 1949], pp. 64–66). Polybius did not appreciate such subtleties. He was interested only in "facts."

43 See pp. 8–9.

44 See pp. 9–10.

45 See p. 5.

46 See especially XII, 17–22. However, Polybius did include Callisthenes as a very distinguished writer along with Ephorus, Xenophon, and Plato (VI, 45, 1). For his uncritical procedure in doing so, see Walbank, *op. cit.*, pp. 726–728.

47 Polybius says Timaeus cites Archedicus, the comedy writer, as his authority (XII, 13, 7). The *Suda* article (F 35a) mentions Democleides as cited by Timaeus. It also tells us that Duris made the same accusation against Demochares, and that Pytheas said the same thing about Demosthenes. Accusing an opponent of sexual irregularities was a commonplace—before the law of libel. Nor were the Romans less addicted to this kind of slander. Perhaps Polybius reflects the views of his somewhat austere friend and patron, Scipio Aemilianus.

48 See pp. 49–50.

49 It is worth noting that Jacoby, commenting on this passage (*F.Gr.H.* II D, on No. 124 F 35), quotes Beloch's characterization of Polybius' remarks as "oberflächlich und kleinlich."

50 It is unnecessary to discuss Polyb. XII, 23, 8. Polybius merely indicates he has now finished dealing with Timaeus' abuse of Aristotle, Theophrastus, Callisthenes, Ephorus, and Demochares.

51 See pp. 54–57.

52 See pp. 65–66.

53 See p. 87.

INDEXES

GENERAL INDEX

Abalus (Basilia), island of, 25, 27
Achaeans, Achaean League, 93–97, 99
Acragas (Agrigentum), Acragantines, 43–44, 54, 57–58, 69–70, 73
Aeëtes, legendary king and port named for him, 31
Aegyptiaca, attributed to Philiscus, 16
Aeneas, 34, 36
Aeolian islands. *See* Liparian islands
Aeolus, legendary ruler, 36, 59–60
Aeschylus of Corinth, 84–85
Aethalia (i.e., Elba), 31
Aetna, town of, 64, 77
Agatharchides, historian, 2
Agathocles of Syracuse, 2, 5–6, 10, 20, 87–90, 103
Agrigentum. *See* Acragas
Ajax, Locrian hero, 45
Alba, 34
Alcamenes, 57
Alcander, 57
Alcibiades, 66
Alcimus, historian, 18–19, 34–35, 37
Alexander the Great, 8–9, 18, 41, 103
Alpheius river, 30
Althaenus river, 29
amber, 25
Andromachus, Timaeus' father, 3–5
Antander, brother of Agathocles, 2, 20, 88
Antigonus Gonatas, 1, 95
Antimachus of Colophon, 32
Antiochus of Syracuse, historian, 1, 16, 34–35, 58–61, 64
Antiphanes of Berge, 26
Antisthenes of Acragas, 69–70
Aphrodisias, island of, 28
Apollo: of Branchidae, 9; statue of, 74
Aratus of Sicyon, 2, 95–99
Arcadia, 98
Archias, colonizer, 58
Archytas, Pythagorean, 53
Aresas, Pythagorean, 51
Aretaeus, Dion's son (?), 19, 82
Arethusa. *See* Fountain of Arethusa
Argonauts, the, 31
Argos, 11, 13, 33
Argous, and the Argonauts, 31
Aristobulus, historian, 9
Aristomachus of Argos, 96–97
Aristotle: attacked by Timaeus, 7–8, 44; Macedonian sympathies of, 9; on Pythian

lore, 38; on history and prehistory, 31; on theory of history and the historian, 57–58, 102

—*Opinions of, about other writers:* Aristotle, 7–8, 44; Callisthenes, 8–9, 103; Demochares, 9–10, 103; Ephorus, 14, 77, 103; Heracleides, 29, 54; Heraclitus, 51; Homer, 32–33; Philistus, 17, 66, 72, 75, 78, 82; Pytheas, 25, 27; Theophrastus, 102; Theopompus, 82

—*Opinions about, by other writers:* Cicero, 6, 63; Diodorus Siculus, 5, 55; Istrus, 23, 91–92; Marcellinus, 4, 83; Polemon, 23, 92–93; Plutarch, 17, 66, 77; Polybius, 23–24, 30–31, 44–50, 62–63, 83–84, 99–106; Strabo, 30

Timoleon, 4, 83–87, 103

Timon, 51

Timonides of Leucas, historian, 19, 78

Timophanes, Timoleon's brother, 84–85

Trinacria, 24

Triton, and the Argonauts, 31

Troy and Trojans, 33–34, 45, 58

τρυφή, 40, 44, 47

Tyche, 76

Tyre, 74

Tyrian histories, the, 28, 31, 35

Tyrrhenia, mother of Romulus, 34

Tyrrhenus, Etruscan colonizer, 36

Tzetzes, latest source for Timaeus, 23

Varro, 36

Virgil and Timaeus, 33

Xanthus of Lydia, historian, 52

Xenocrates, 81

Xenophanes, philosopher, 33, 50

Xenophon, 72, 94

Zaleucus, lawgiver, 46, 49–50, 103

INDEX OF LEADING PASSAGES

Numbers in parentheses refer to the pages of this book. Fragments are cited from the *FGrH* unless otherwise indicated, and Jacoby's serial numbers are given in brackets.